D1373091

Force.com Cookbook

By Caroline Roth
Mike Polcari
Ron Hess
Andrew Waite
Greg Campbell
Blake Markham

With contributions by
additional members of the salesforce.com
Technology and Services organizations

Force.com Cookbook

ISBN: 978-0-9789639-2-7

The authors would like to thank additional contributors Dave Carroll, Simon Fell, Steve Fisher, Chris Fry, Richard Greenwald, Andrea Leszek, Marcus Spohn, Nick Tran, Craig Weissman, and Sarah Whitlock. Additional thanks to Andrew Albert, Stefanie Andersen, Steve Anderson, Gavin Austin, Eric Bezar, Manoj Cheenath, Leah Cutter, Michael Dannenfeldt, Carolyn Dismuke, Bill Eidson, Adam Gross, Michelle Jowitt, Paul Kopacki, Loretta Macklem, Sarah Marovich, Reena Mathew, Taggart Matthiesen, Chris McGuire, Yudi Nagata, Kavindra Patel, Igor Pesenson, Vahn Phan, Bhavana Rehani, EJ Rice, Emad Salman, Mary Scotton, Jerry Sherman, Sagar Wanaselja, Jill Wetzler, and Jim Yu for their advice and support.

Table of Contents

Introduction

Congratulations! If you're reading this page, you're part of a growing movement of innovative application developers who are curious about the future of computing, and who no longer want to accept the status quo. Maybe your organization has just purchased Salesforce licenses, or maybe you've been using Salesforce for a while and want to extend its capabilities. Maybe you've got a brilliant business idea and are looking for the best and fastest way to start making money, or maybe you're just curious about this thing called Apex and want to keep your skill set up to date with the latest technology.

No matter what angle you're coming from, this book will help application developers leverage the power of salesforce.com's on-demand platform to build fully-functional, integrated Web applications that free you and your organization from the drudgery of maintaining your own software and hardware stacks. Instead, you can spend your time and money on the ideas and innovations that make your business applications special, whether you're a lone developer looking for your first round of venture funding or part of a multi-billion-dollar company with hundreds of thousands of employees.

Welcome to the Force.com Platform

The technology that makes building on-demand applications so easy is called Force.com—the world's first on-demand platform for building, sharing, and running business applications. Force.com is unique among development platforms for the following reasons:

Delivery

Force.com runs in a hosted, multitenant environment. That means you can access any app you build on the platform from anywhere in the world with just an Internet connection and a Web browser. No servers or databases need to be maintained, and no software needs to be installed or upgraded. Instead, salesforce.com provides a hosted environment in which the latest features and functionality are seamlessly available to all users with every new release. And you'll have the peace of mind of knowing that any app you were using or building before the new release will work just as well after the release too, regardless of whether it was a standard CRM app from salesforce.com or a custom app you developed on your own.

As a developer, the platform's multitenant architecture also means that you never have to worry about scaling your apps from one to one thousand or even to one million users—all of the infrastructure to handle such growth is provided free of charge, automatically behind the scenes. That leaves you more time to focus on your business problems and solutions, rather than spending time trying to anticipate the pressures that increased usage might exert on your apps.

Distribution

Any app written on the platform has access to a built-in community of potential customers on the AppExchange at www.salesforce.com/appexchange/. Unlike traditional software, where you have to create an install wizard and send your code to a manufacturer to cut hundreds of CDs, you can easily share and distribute your app on the AppExchange directory with only a few clicks of the mouse. You can quickly share your apps privately with just the people you want, or you can publish your apps for anyone to download.

If you do publish an app publicly, the community of users on the AppExchange can take your app for a test drive and review comments from other users about how well it worked. Additionally, information about the users who end up downloading your app is sent directly to you in the form of a new lead in any Salesforce organization that you specify. When you're ready to release new versions of your app, the AppExchange also helps you communicate and manage the upgrade process for all of your users. You can track which of your customers is on which version of your app, and you never have to worry that your users have broken or deleted any component your app relies on.

Development

Force.com comes with a wide variety of built-in, point-and-click functionality that can help you build your apps faster. Need a way to store data in your app? Define new database objects, fields, and relationships declaratively with the mouse, rather than by composing SQL CREATE statements. Need to control which users have access to different kinds of data? Again, no coding necessary—just use the security and sharing framework to define permissions at different levels of granularity, from individual fields to entire objects and applications. Force.com includes point-and-click tools for everything from string localization to workflow rules and approval processes, from custom reports and dashboards to page layouts and data import wizards—which means you can spend less time recreating the "plumbing" that makes your applications run and more time on the unique functionality that sets your apps apart from your competitor's.

And what happens when you want to go beyond the capabilities of the point-and-click tools the platform provides? The Force.com Web Services API, Apex, and Visualforce give you the flexibility you need to build the applications you want. Integrate third-party Web services with embedded mashups, change the logic behind every function with Apex classes and triggers, and redesign the user interface the way you want with Visualforce. You're limited only by your imagination!

The Force.com platform includes a number of tools that can help you build apps. These tools allow you to define the data, business logic, and user interface for an application.

Force.com Builder

Force.com Builder consists of the declarative, point-and-click setup tools that allow administrators and developers to quickly build common application components without writing any code. Also known as *native* platform functionality, these setup tools allow you to effortlessly build:

Data Components

Data components are equivalent to the "model" in the Model-View-Controller (MVC) application development paradigm. They include:

- **Custom objects**

  Similar to a database table, a Salesforce object is a structure for storing data about a certain type of entity, such as a person, account, or job application. Salesforce includes over a dozen standard objects that support default apps like Sales and Service & Support, but it also allows you to build custom objects for your own application needs. In Salesforce, each object automatically includes built-in features like a user interface, a security and sharing model, workflow processes, search, and much more.

- **Custom fields**

  Similar to a column in a database table, a Salesforce field is a property of an object, such as the first name of a contact or the status of an opportunity. Salesforce fields support over a dozen different field types, such as auto-number, checkbox, date/time, and multi-select picklists.

- **Custom relationships**

  Similar to the way primary and foreign keys work in a relational database, a Salesforce relationship defines a connection between two objects in which matching values in a specified field in both objects are used to link related data.

- **Field history**

  Salesforce field history allows you to track changes to fields on a particular object just by selecting a checkbox on a custom object and field definition. Users can then review audit logs for changes to sensitive records without any additional development work.

Business Logic Components

Business logic components are equivalent to the "controller" in the Model-View-Controller (MVC) application development paradigm. They include:

- **Security and permission settings**

  Salesforce security and permissions tools, such as user profiles, organization-wide defaults, the role hierarchy, sharing rules, and manual sharing, allow you to control the data that users can view and edit, either with broad generalizations or with a fine level of detail.

- **Formula fields and validation rules**

  Formula fields, default field values, and validation rules allow you to use Excel-like syntax to calculate certain data automatically, maintain data quality, and add custom error messages to your apps.

- **Workflow rules**

  Workflow rules are processes triggered by user activity or according to a schedule. These processes can automatically assign tasks to users, send email alerts to multiple recipients, update field values in records, and even generate SOAP messages to external Web services.

- **Approval processes**

Approvals allow you to set up a chain of users who can approve the creation of sensitive types of records, such as new contracts or vacation requests.

User Interface Components

User interface components are equivalent to the "view" in the Model-View-Controller (MVC) application development paradigm. They include:

- **Tabs**

  Tabs give users a starting point for viewing, editing, and entering information for a particular object. When a user clicks a tab at the top of the page, the corresponding tab home page for that object appears.

- **Page layouts**

  Regardless of whether a particular object has a tab, all objects can be viewed or edited. Page layouts allow you to organize the fields, custom links, related lists, and other components that appear on those pages.

- **Custom views**

  Custom views allow users to filter the records they see for a particular object, based on criteria they specify.

- **Reports and Dashboards**

  Salesforce includes a full-featured report building tool, including custom report types that allow you to view data for any combination of objects, and dynamic dashboards that give users a bird's eye view of their application data.

- **Console**

  Salesforce Console allows you to set up a page that displays multiple objects at a time, streamlining the user experience. It includes a list view of several different objects at the top of the page, a detail view in the main window, customizable sidebar components, and mini-detail views of related information in a dynamic AJAX-based interface.

With this native functionality, app developers can build extensive, full-featured applications that handle many business needs. For a more thorough introduction to the native functionality provided by the platform, read *Creating On-Demand Applications: An Introduction to the Force.com*

Platform, available on the Apex Developer Network (ADN) website at wiki.apexdevnet.com/index.php/Creating_On-Demand_Apps.

S-Controls

S-controls allow you to add custom HTML or JavaScript code to a page or button, or reference content from an external Web page or service. They are best for adding additional business logic to your apps or for modifying the user interface.

There are three types of s-controls:

- **HTML**

    HTML-based s-controls allow you to add any custom HTML or JavaScript to a page or button, allowing you to define:

    - Custom tabs
    - Custom components on a standard Salesforce page
    - Custom links and buttons
    - Custom dashboards

    HTML-based s-controls execute directly within a user's browser, so they are most appropriate for performing simple tasks that access data from only a few records at a time, or for modifying the Salesforce user interface.

- **URL**

    Also known as a *Web control*, a URL-based s-control allows you to display the content of an external website within a Salesforce page. Use a URL-based s-control if you want to perform more intensive logic that isn't suitable for execution in a user's browser, or if you want to extend Salesforce using Java, C#.NET, VB.NET, PHP, or any other Web-services enabled language.

- **Snippet**

    S-control snippets allow you to reuse the same HTML or JavaScript code in several different s-controls. Define the common code in an s-control snippet and then include it in another s-control similar to the way you might include a programming library.

The Force.com Web Services API

The API defines a Web service that enables full, reliable access to all of the data in an organization. With more than 20 different calls, the API allows you to request metadata related to standard and custom objects, maintain passwords, perform searches, create custom objects and fields, and much more. Use the API in any language that supports Web services, or within an s-control by using the AJAX Toolkit library.

Apex

Apex is a hosted scripting language for executing flow and transaction control statements on the Force.com platform server in conjunction with database queries, inserts, updates, and deletes. Using syntax that looks like Java and acts like database stored procedures, Apex allows you to add business logic to your applications in a more efficient, integrated way than is possible with the Force.com API.

 Note: As of August 2007, Apex is available in Unlimited Edition and Developer Edition organizations only.

You can manage and invoke Apex scripts using the following constructs:

- **Classes**

    A *class* is a template or blueprint from which Apex objects are created. Classes consist of other classes, user-defined methods, variables, exception types, and static initialization code.

    Once successfully saved, class methods or variables can be invoked by other Apex scripts, or through the Force.com Web Services API (or AJAX Toolkit) for methods that have been designated with the `webService` keyword.

    In most cases, Apex classes are modeled on their counterparts in Java and can be quickly understood by those who are familiar with them.

- **Triggers**

    A *trigger* is an Apex script that executes before or after specific data manipulation language (DML) events occur, such as before object records are inserted into the database, or after records have been deleted. Other than Apex Web service methods, triggers provide the primary means for instantiating Apex.

- **Anonymous blocks**

An *anonymous block* is an Apex script that does not get stored in the metadata, but that can be compiled and executed through the use of the `executeanonymous()` API call or the equivalent in the AJAX toolkit.

Visualforce

Visualforce is a new, tag-based markup language that allows developers to develop their own custom interfaces using standard Salesforce components. Similar to the way Apex dramatically increases the power of developers to customize business logic, Visualforce dramatically increases the power of developers to customize the user interface.

With this markup language, each tag corresponds to a coarse or fine-grained component, such as a section of a page, a related list, or a field. The components can either be controlled by the same logic that's used in standard Salesforce pages, or developers can associate their own logic with a controller written in Apex. With this architecture, designers and developers can easily split up the work that goes with building a new application—designers can focus on the user interface, while developers can work on the business logic that drives the app.

 Note: As of September 2007, Visualforce is available as a Developer Preview only.

About This Book

This book provides over 100 "recipes" for writing s-controls, using the Force.com API, developing Apex scripts, and creating Visualforce pages.

Written by developers for developers, the *Force.com Cookbook* is meant to help developers become familiar with common Force.com platform programming idioms and best practices.

Intended Audience

This book is intended for advanced administrators and developers who are already familiar with the native capabilities of the Force.com platform, as covered in *Creating On-Demand Applications: An Introduction to the Force.com Platform* (available on the ADN website at wiki.apexdevnet.com/index.php/Creating_On-Demand_Apps).

To get the most out of this book, you should also have experience with at least one of the following:

- HTML and JavaScript
- Java
- C#.NET
- VB.NET
- PHP
- Python
- Ruby
- Perl
- Any other Web-services-enabled programming language

The Sample Recruiting App

Some of the recipes in this book require a custom app for illustration. In these cases, this book uses the custom Recruiting app that was developed as part of *Creating On-Demand Applications: An Introduction to the Force.com Platform*. The schema for this Recruiting app is pictured in the following entity-relationship diagram and can be downloaded from wiki.apexdevnet.com/index.php/Platform_Cookbook.

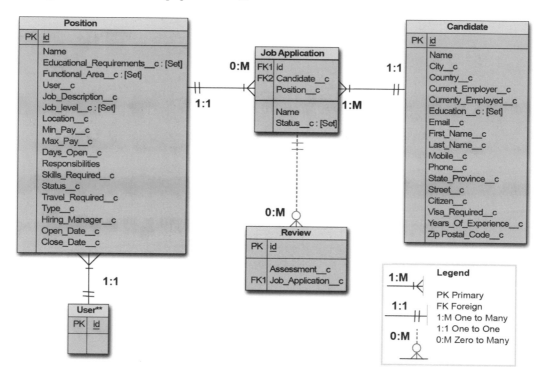

Figure 1: Schema for the Sample Recruiting App

Code Samples

An online version of this book is available on the ADN website at wiki.apexdevnet.com/index.php/Platform_Cookbook. This website also includes links to the code samples found in this book, as well as any errata that are discovered after publication.

Sending Feedback

The authors made every effort to ensure the accuracy of the information contained within this book, but neither they nor salesforce.com assumes any responsibility or liability for any errors or inaccuracies that may appear. If you do find any errors, please send feedback to docfeedback@salesforce.com, or visit the ADN discussion boards at www.salesforce.com/developer/community/index.jsp.

Chapter 1

Getting Started

Like other development platforms you're familiar with, the Force.com platform includes the tools you'll need to make development easier—a free Salesforce organization in which to do your development, salesforce.com-certified documentation and training, an IDE, toolkits, and more. Whether you prefer to develop your on-demand applications on a Windows-based platform or the Mac OS X platform, there are development tools you can use to boost your productivity and make your job a lot easier.

After signing up for a free Developer Edition account from salesforce.com and checking out the documentation and training, you'll want to get set up with the Force.com Toolkit for Eclipse. Use the toolkit to help you manage, author, debug, and eventually deploy s-controls and Apex in the Eclipse development environment. Then, you can explore using other toolkits to develop code, such as the AJAX Toolkit or Adobe® Flex™ Toolkit. The Force.com platform also includes tools to help you view and edit the data in your development organization and test SOSL and SOQL queries on the fly.

Signing Up for a Free Developer Edition Account

Problem

You want to start developing on-demand applications on the platform, but you don't have a login to your own Salesforce organization.

Solution

Visit the Apex Developer Network (ADN) at www.salesforce.com/developer/ and click **Getting Started** to sign up for a free, two-user Developer Edition organization.

Discussion

A Developer Edition organization gives you free access to the entire breadth of platform functionality, including features that are only available in Unlimited Edition and Enterprise Edition organizations. A Developer Edition organization allows you to add one additional user to help you test your applications, and also can be used to deploy your apps to the AppExchange. You can sign up for as many Developer Edition organizations as you need—each one simply requires a unique email address that isn't already associated with an existing Salesforce user.

In addition to the free Developer Edition organization, ADN membership also entitles you to the following benefits:

ADN Newsletter

> The monthly ADN email newsletter brings together top news and announcements for the month, plus the latest on what's happening in the ADN community and with partners on the AppExchange directory.

ADN Discussion Boards

> Members of the Apex Developer Network can log in to the ADN Discussion Boards at community.salesforce.com/sforce ?category.id=developers and join any of the many active conversations underway about platform development. Developers with all levels of experience are welcome to post questions and participate, and are sure to get valuable help from the ADN community.

ADN Premium Content

> The ADN website includes premium, members-only content such as the Force.com Toolkit for Eclipse, the Salesforce Excel Connector, Force.com Explorer, downloadable copies of ADN publications (such as this one!), and more.

ADN Members-Only Events

> ADN members receive invitations to special, members-only events throughout the year such as developer conferences and ADN@Dreamforce.

These events allow you to meet and network with fellow developers and industry thought leaders.

Finding Documentation

Problem

You have a question about native Force.com Builder functionality, s-controls, the API, Apex, or packaging applications for the AppExchange, but you don't know where to look.

Solution

For questions about the following topics, visit the list of resources provided:

Native Force.com Builder Functionality

- Access the Help & Training window by clicking **Help** or **Help & Training** in the upper-right corner of any Salesforce page. Alternatively, access a context-sensitive view of the Help & Training window by clicking **Help for this Page** on the right side of any page title bar, or the help link on the right side of any related list.
- Read *Creating On-Demand Applications: An Introduction to the Force.com Platform*, available on the ADN website at wiki.apexdevnet.com/index.php/Creating_On-Demand_Apps.
- Review whitepapers, multimedia presentations, and other documentation in the Native Framework section of the ADN website at wiki.apexdevnet.com/index.php/Native_Framework.
- Review tips and best practices at success.salesforce.com.

S-Controls

- Access the Help & Training window and search for *s-controls*.
- Review whitepapers, multimedia presentations, and other documentation in the Composite Framework section of the ADN website at wiki.apexdevnet.com/index.php/Composite_Framework.
- Review s-control tips and best practices at success.salesforce.com.

Force.com Web Services API

- Read the *Force.com Web Services API Developer's Guide*, available at www.salesforce.com/apidoc.
- Review whitepapers, multimedia presentations, and other documentation in the API section of the ADN website at wiki.apexdevnet.com/index.php/API.

Apex

- Read the *Apex Language Reference*, available at www.salesforce.com/us/developer/docs/apexcode/ salesforce_apex_language_reference.pdf.
- Review whitepapers, multimedia presentations, and other documentation in the Apex section of the ADN website at wiki.apexdevnet.com/index.php/Apex_Code.

Packaging Applications for the AppExchange

- Access the Help & Training window and search for *packaging*.
- Read through the *Publishing Apps on the AppExchange* website at www.salesforce.com/appexchange/publishing.jsp.
- Review whitepapers, multimedia presentations, and other documentation in the Packaging and Distribution section of the ADN website at wiki.apexdevnet.com/index.php/Packaging_and_ Distribution.

Finding Training Courses

Problem

You want to learn more about the platform in a live or virtual classroom setting, but you don't know where to go.

Solution

Attend one of the classes offered by salesforce.com's Education Services department. You can find a complete list of courses at www.salesforce.com/services-training/education-services. Those targeted specifically for developers include:

Migrating Data (APX-210)

Learn how to import, export, update, and delete data effectively, understand the Salesforce object model, and find out about data cleansing best practices. (One day)

Deploying Force.com Mobile (APX-212)

Increase the productivity of your mobile users by learning how to build a mobile version of any AppExchange application. (Two days)

Extending Applications Using S-Controls (APX-261)

Learn through lecture and hands-on exercises how to extend core platform functionality by building and integrating custom buttons and s-controls. (One day)

Application Laboratory (APX-320)
> Learn everything you need to know about platform development, including the native point-and-click tools provided by Force.com Builder, the API, and the AppExchange directory. (Five days)

Developing with Apex (APX-340)
> Learn through lecture and hands-on exercises how to extend core platform functionality by developing with Apex. (One day)

Deciding What to Build

Problem

You're excited about building applications on the Force.com platform, but you don't know what kinds of functionality your users are looking for.

Solution

Visit Successforce Ideas at ideas.salesforce.com and see what users are asking for. Successforce Ideas is a forum where salesforce.com customers can suggest new product concepts, promote favorite enhancements, interact with product managers and other customers, and preview what salesforce.com is planning to deliver in future releases. You can useSuccessforce Ideas both to find ideas for new applications, and to post your pet peeves about how the platform works for you.

Installing the Force.com Toolkit for Eclipse

Problem

You want to write s-controls and Apex in a development environment that's tightly integrated with the platform.

Solution

Download and install the Eclipse Toolkit:

 Note: The Eclipse Toolkit is one of two unsupported IDE options for platform development. The other is an AppExchange package called *AJAX Tools*.

1. Before installing:

- Verify that you're running Version 5 (also known as Version 1.5) or later of a Java SDK or the Java Runtime Environment. You can download Java from java.sun.com/javase/downloads/index.jsp.
- Download and extract the Eclipse SDK 3.2.2 from www.eclipse.org/downloads.

2. Launch Eclipse and click **Help ➤ Software Updates ➤ Find and Install**.
3. Select `Search for new features to install`, and click **Next**.
4. In the Update Sites to Visit screen:

   a. Select the `Automatically select mirrors` option.
   b. Define a new remote site by clicking **New Remote Site** and entering the following values:

      - `Name`: Force.com
      - `URL`: http://adnsandbox.com/appexchange/e3.2s

   c. Select the `Force.com` and `Callisto Discovery Site` options to include in your search, and click **Finish**.

5. In the Search Results screen, select **Force.com ➤ Force.com Toolkit** and then click **Select Required**. If not already installed, the following components are selected within the Callisto branch:

   - Visual Editor
   - Graphical Editing Framework
   - Eclipse Modeling Framework
   - XSD Schema
   - Web Standard Tools (WST)

6. Click **Next**, accept the terms of the license agreement, click **Next**, and then **Finish**.

Discussion

The Eclipse Toolkit is a plug-in that allows developers to manage, author, and debug s-controls and Apex classes and triggers in the Eclipse development environment. The toolkit leverages Eclipse's native syntax highlighting and file management to accelerate the creation of these components and allows developers to use source control while developing on the platform.

See Also

Creating a Project in Eclipse

Problem

You want to create an Eclipse project that's linked to your Salesforce account.

Solution

Once you've installed the Eclipse Toolkit, create a new project:

1. In Eclipse, click **File ➤ New ➤ Project**.
2. In the `Wizards` text box, type Force.com. As you type, the list of project types filters to include only the Force.com Project type. Once this type is selected, click **Next**.
3. In the Force.com Project screen:

    a. Enter a name for your project in the `Project Name` text box.

     Tip: If you're working in more than one Salesforce organization at a time, use your username as the project name to help distinguish between them.

    b. Specify the same username and password that you use to log in to your organization through the Salesforce user interface.

    c. Click **Finish**.

Discussion

When you define a project in Eclipse, several folders and files are automatically created within your project by default:

Packages

If your organization has Apex enabled, this folder contains all of the Apex classes that have been defined in your organization. Any new Apex classes that you create in Eclipse are also saved to this folder.

S-Controls

This folder contains all of the s-controls that have been defined in your organization. Any new s-controls that you create in Eclipse are also saved to this folder.

Triggers

If your organization has Apex enabled, this folder contains all of the Apex triggers that have been defined in your organization. Any new Apex triggers that you create in Eclipse are also saved to this folder.

appexchange.schema

> This file launches the Eclipse version of the Force.com Explorer. You can use this file to examine the metadata for the objects in your organization and construct and test SOQL (Salesforce Object Query Language) statements.

See Also

- *Signing Up for a Free Developer Edition Account* on page 12
- *Installing the Force.com Toolkit for Eclipse* on page 15
- *Writing Apex in Eclipse* on page 60
- *Writing S-Controls in Eclipse* on page 44
- *Using the Force.com Explorer to Examine Your Data Model* on page 94

Installing AJAX Tools

Problem

You want to write s-controls in a development environment that you can access on the Web directly from your Salesforce organization, and that includes syntax-highlighting, a lightweight version of Apex Explorer, and code samples.

Solution

Get the latest version of AJAX Tools from the AppExchange at www.salesforce.com/appexchange/detail_overview.jsp?id=a0330000002foeKAAQ.

 Note:

- AJAX Tools is one of two IDE options for platform development. The other is an Eclipse plug-in called the Force.com Toolkit for Eclipse.
- AJAX Tools is different from the AJAX Toolkit. AJAX Tools is an IDE while the AJAX Toolkit is a JavaScript wrapper for the API that doesn't require a download.

Discussion

AJAX Tools is an unsupported toolkit that includes a collection of Web-based utilities for developers working with the AJAX toolkit, s-controls, or Apex. The following tools are included in this package:

- A syntax-highlighting editor that can load and save s-controls and Apex classes directly from your Salesforce organization

> **Note:** While AJAX Tools does allow you to display and edit Apex classes, at the time of publication it uses deprecated syntax and does not provide support for triggers. As a result, if you're looking for a separate development environment for Apex, consider using the Eclipse Toolkit instead.

- Extensive code samples that feature the AJAX toolkit, Dojo, Apex, and the Salesforce user interface
- A JavaScript shell with completion and input history—a handy tool for testing commands against the API
- A lightweight version of the Force.com Explorer that allows you to browse your data schema, build SOQL queries, and access documents in your organization

See Also

- *Writing S-Controls in AJAX Tools* on page 45
- *Using the Force.com Explorer to Examine Your Data Model* on page 94

Installing the Force.com Explorer (for Windows)

Problem

You want an easy way to view and edit data in your organization and to test SOQL and SOSL statements on the fly. You develop on a Windows-based platform.

Solution

Download and install the Force.com Explorer:

1. Download the Force.com Explorer zip file from wiki.apexdevnet.com/index.php/Members:Apex_Explorer.

   > **Note:** You must be a member of the Apex Developer Network to access the Force.com Explorer. If you've already signed up, use your Developer Edition login and password.

2. Extract the contents of the zip file to a temporary directory on your local machine.
3. Execute `ApexExplorer.msi` and walk through the simple installation wizard.

After installation is complete, you can find the Force.com Explorer in your Windows **Start** menu by clicking **Programs ➤ salesforce.com ➤ Force.com Explorer 8 ➤ Force.com Explorer 8**.

Discussion

The Force.com Explorer is a lightweight, .NET-based tool that lets you browse the schema within your organization, edit data values, and build and test SOQL and SOSL queries. While the Force.com Toolkit for Eclipse and AJAX Tools include a lightweight version of this handy application, the stand-alone .NET version of the Force.com Explorer includes more functionality, including the ability to test SOSL statements, view documents, and update database values.

See Also

- *Using the Force.com Explorer to Examine Your Data Model* on page 94
- *Constructing SOQL and SOSL Queries in the Force.com Explorer* on page 100

Installing SoqlXplorer (for Mac OS X)

Problem

You want an easy way to view and edit data in your organization and to test SOQL statements on the fly. You develop on the Mac OS X platform.

Solution

Download SoqlXplorer from Simon Fell's PocketSOAP website at www.pocketsoap.com/osx/soqlx. After the download automatically extracts itself, drag the SoqlXplorer icon to your Applications folder to complete the installation.

Discussion

For Mac users, the SoqlXplorer is a great counterpart to the Force.com Explorer for Windows, providing metadata exploration, a SOQL query tester, and a graphical schema view for examining object relationships (a piece of functionality that's only available on the Mac OS X platform!).

 Tip: For other great Salesforce tools and utilities built exclusively for Mac OS X, see www.pocketsoap.com/osx.

See Also

- *Using SoqlXplorer to Examine Your Data Model* on page 96

Installing the Flex Toolkit for Force.com

Problem

You want to build s-controls that leverage Adobe® Flex™ to create rich application interfaces.

Solution

Download and install the Flex Toolkit:

1. Before installing, download and install Flex Builder 2 or the free Adobe Flex 2 Software Development Kit from www.flex.org.

     Note: It is not necessary to install both applications. The Flex 2 Software Development Kit is automatically included with Flex Builder 2.

2. Install the Flex Toolkit by visiting the ADN website at wiki.apexdevnet.com/index.php/Members:Flex_Toolkit_download and downloading the zip file. Extract the contents to a directory on your local machine.

Discussion

The Flex Toolkit is a Flex library named `as3Salesforce.swc` that allows you to access Salesforce data from within a Flex 2 application. It's located in the `bin` directory of the extracted Flex Toolkit directory, and comes with a simple piece of sample code that demonstrates all of the available library functions.

To run this piece of sample code using Flex Builder 2:

1. Create a new Flex project:

    *   Click **File ➤ New ➤ Flex Project**.
    *   Select `Basic`, and click **Next**.
    *   Name the project, and click **Next**.
    *   In the Library Path tab, click **Add SWC**, browse to `<Flex_Toolkit_Install_Dir>\bin\as3Salesforce.swc`, click **OK**, and then click **Finish**.

2. Drag and drop `<Flex_Toolkit_Install_Dir>\salesforce.mxml` into your new project.
3. Edit `salesforce.mxml` so that all instances of `sforce@yourdomain.com` are replaced by your own Salesforce username, and all instances of `123456` are replaced by your Salesforce password.
4. Right-click `salesforce.mxml` and select **Run Application**.

See Also

- *Adding a Flex Application to an S-Control* on page 49
- The ADN's Flex Toolkit information page at wiki.apexdevnet.com/index.php/Flex_Toolkit
- The Flex Toolkit class documentation at www.adnsandbox.com/media/flexsdk/docs/index.html
- Adobe's Flex website at www.flex.org

Chapter 2

Developing On-Demand Apps

In this chapter ...

- Targeting a Salesforce Edition
- Deciding When to Use S-Controls, Client Apps, Apex, or Visualforce
- Building and Deploying an App
- Creating a Sandbox Organization
- Migrating Metadata Between Two Organizations
- Migrating Apex Between Two Salesforce Organizations

Now that you've got your development tools all set up, you're ready to start developing. But wait! What's the best way to develop the different components of your app? What's the difference between s-controls, Web controls, Apex, and Visualforce? And how do you know which Salesforce edition is right for your app?

These are all important questions to ask yourself before you start to develop your on-demand app. Before your start, you'll want to make sure the components you develop will work with the Salesforce edition you're targeting with your app. We'll explore that in this chapter, and we'll also talk about the differences between s-controls, Web controls, Apex, and Visualforce so you'll understand which is the best choice for your app. Finally, this chapter gives you some best practices on how to build and deploy your app once you've developed it. After all, what's the point in developing an app if you can't roll it out to any users?

Targeting a Salesforce Edition

Problem

Your customers use different editions of Salesforce, and you're not sure how that impacts you as a developer.

Solution

Review the Salesforce online help to understand which features are available in each edition, and what limits apply.

For example, if you're not sure whether you can use an approval process for an app that's targeted towards Professional Edition organizations, look up approval processes in the online help and look just under the title of any associated help topic. Every approval process help topic shows that the feature is only available in Enterprise, Unlimited, and Developer Editions.

Discussion

Salesforce.com offers six editions, each with varying limits for the number of custom fields, objects, tabs, and apps that can be created, and different sets of enabled features. As a developer, it's critical that you understand the limitations of each edition you want to target so your users can successfully install and operate your apps:

Personal Edition

Personal Edition is a free CRM solution designed for an individual sales representative or other single user. Personal Edition provides access to key contact management features such as accounts, contacts, and synchronization with Outlook. It also provides sales representatives with critical sales tools such as opportunities.

 Important: Personal Edition organizations are the only ones that cannot download apps from the AppExchange.

Group Edition

Group Edition is designed for small businesses and workgroups with a limited number of users. Group Edition users can manage their customers from the start of the sales cycle through closing the deal to providing customer support and service. Group Edition offers access to accounts, contacts, opportunities, leads, cases, dashboards, and reports.

Professional Edition

Professional Edition is designed for businesses who need full-featured CRM functionality. Professional Edition includes straightforward and easy-to-use customization, integration, and administration tools to facilitate any small- to mid-sized deployment.

Enterprise Edition

Enterprise Edition is designed to meet the needs of larger, more complex businesses. In addition to all of the functionality available in Professional Edition, Enterprise Edition organizations get advanced customization and administration tools that can support large-scale deployments.

Enterprise Edition includes all Professional Edition functionality plus the ability to do the following:

- Access the API
- Create multiple user profiles
- Create multiple page layouts for a single object
- Set field-level security to control which users can view and edit specific fields
- Use the Price Book and Product objects
- Specify sales teams for opportunities
- Restrict users' login hours and IP addresses
- Receive weekly exports of data for backup
- Define workflow and approval processes
- Define record types
- Assign limited administrative privileges to non-administrator users
- Categorize accounts and users into territories
- Use person accounts
- Use the offline client to access Salesforce data

Developer Edition

Developer Edition provides access to the platform, API, Apex, and Visualforce. It allows developers to extend the Salesforce system, integrate with other applications, and develop new tools and applications. Developer Edition provides access to the exclusive features available with Enterprise Edition, but with only two user licenses.

 Note: As of September 2007, Visualforce is available as a Developer Preview only.

Unlimited Edition

Unlimited Edition is salesforce.com's flagship solution for maximizing CRM success and extending that success across the entire enterprise through the platform. Unlimited Edition customers benefit from new levels of platform flexibility for managing and sharing all of their information on demand.

Unlimited Edition includes all Enterprise Edition functionality plus the ability to do the following:

- Author Apex
- Download unlimited custom apps
- Create more custom tabs
- Access Premium Support and administration
- Use Force.com Sandbox
- Use Force.com Mobile
- Use additional storage capacity

Additionally, Salesforce offers a Platform Edition that's based on either Enterprise Edition or Unlimited Edition, but without any of the standard Salesforce CRM apps, such as Sales or Service & Support.

Any organization, except for those that use Personal Edition, can download AppExchange apps. However, an organization can only download a particular app if it uses features that are included in the organization's edition, and if there's space for the custom components that come with the app.

Review the following limitation tables to understand additional details about what each Salesforce edition can accommodate.

Table 1: Custom Object, App, Tab, and Field Limits by Salesforce Edition

Maximum Limit	Custom Objects	Custom Apps	Custom Tabs	Custom Fields
Personal Edition	0	0	0	5 per object, including users, but no more than 1 long text area field per object
Group Edition	50	1	5	100 per object, but no more than: • 20 for users • 5 long text area fields per object • 25 relationship fields per object • 10 roll-up summary fields per object
Professional Edition	50	5	10	100 per object, but no more than: • 20 for activities • 20 for users • 5 long text area fields per object • 25 relationship fields per object • 10 roll-up summary fields per object

Maximum Limit	Custom Objects	Custom Apps	Custom Tabs	Custom Fields
Enterprise Edition **Platform Enterprise Edition**	200	10	25	500 per object, but no more than: • 100 for activities • 20 for users • 25 long text area fields per object • 25 relationship fields per object • 10 roll-up summary fields per object
Developer Edition	200	10	25	500 per object, but no more than: • 100 for activities • 20 for users • 25 long text area fields per object • 25 relationship fields per object • 10 roll-up summary fields per object
Unlimited Edition **Platform Unlimited Edition**	2000	Unlimited	Unlimited	500 per object, but no more than: • 100 for activities • 20 for users • 25 long text area fields per object • 25 relationship fields per object • 10 roll-up summary fields per object

Table 2: Other Setup Limits by Salesforce Edition

Maximum Limit	Custom Report Types[1]	Active Validation Rules	Workflow, Assignment, Auto-Response, and Escalation Rules[2]	API Requests[3]
Personal Edition	0	0	0	0
Group Edition	0	20 per object	0	0
Professional Edition	1	20 per object	50 Workflow rules are not available in Professional Edition.	1,000 calls per license per 24-hour period, or 1,000,000 calls per organization per 24-hour

Maximum Limit	Custom Report Types[1]	Active Validation Rules	Workflow, Assignment, Auto-Response, and Escalation Rules[2]	API Requests[3]
				period, whichever is lowest. API access must be enabled separately for Professional Edition users
Enterprise Edition	5	100 per object	50 Each workflow rule can have: • 40 time triggers • 40 immediate actions, but no more than 10 workflow email alerts, 10 workflow tasks, 10 field updates, and 10 outbound messages • 40 time-dependent actions per time trigger, but no more than 10 workflow email alerts, 10 workflow tasks, 10 field updates, and 10 outbound messages Enterprise Edition organizations can process up to 1,000 time triggers per hour and 20,000 time triggers per day.	1,000 calls per license per 24-hour period, or 1,000,000 calls per organization per 24-hour period, whichever is lowest
Developer Edition	10	100 per object	50 Each workflow rule can have: • 40 time triggers • 40 immediate actions, but no more than 10	5,000 calls per organization per 24-hour period, or 5 concurrent calls at any one time

Maximum Limit	Custom Report Types[1]	Active Validation Rules	Workflow, Assignment, Auto-Response, and Escalation Rules[2]	API Requests[3]
			workflow email alerts, 10 workflow tasks, 10 field updates, and 10 outbound messages • 40 time-dependent actions per time trigger, but no more than 10 workflow email alerts, 10 workflow tasks, 10 field updates, and 10 outbound messages Developer Edition organizations can process up to 1,000 time triggers per hour and 20,000 time triggers per day.	
Unlimited Edition	50	500 per object	50 Each workflow rule can have: • 40 time triggers • 40 immediate actions, but no more than 10 workflow email alerts, 10 workflow tasks, 10 field updates, and 10 outbound messages • 40 time-dependent actions per time trigger, but no more than 10 workflow email alerts, 10 workflow tasks, 10 field updates, and 10 outbound messages	5,000 calls per license per 24-hour period, or 5,000,000 calls per organization per 24-hour period, whichever is lowest

Maximum Limit	Custom Report Types[1]	Active Validation Rules	Workflow, Assignment, Auto-Response, and Escalation Rules[2]	API Requests[3]
			Unlimited Edition organizations can process up to 5,000 time triggers per hour and 100,000 time triggers per day	

[1]Limits apply to custom report types in any combination of deployed and development status

[2]Limits apply to any combination of these rules

[3]When an organization exceeds any limit, the organization may be temporarily blocked from making additional calls until usage for the preceding 24 hours drops below the limit. Administrators can view how many API requests have been issued in the last 24 hours on the Company Information page at **Setup ➤ Company Profile ➤ Company Information**.

Deciding When to Use S-Controls, Client Apps, Apex, or Visualforce

Problem

You have a problem that you can't solve using the native, point-and-click functionality the platform provides, but you don't know whether it's better to solve your problem with an s-control, a client application, Apex, or Visualforce.

Solution

First determine which of those options is available to you, based on the Salesforce edition you're targeting, and whether you have access to the API, Apex, or the Visualforce Developer Preview:

Table 3: Options for Extending Salesforce

Targeted Edition	API Access?	Apex?	Visualforce Developer Preview?	Options
Personal Edition	No	No	No	None

Targeted Edition	API Access?	Apex?	Visualforce Developer Preview?	Options
Group Edition	No	No	No	S-controls
Professional Edition	Yes, for an additional fee	No	No	S-controls + AJAX Toolkit Client applications
Enterprise Edition	Yes	No	No	S-controls + AJAX Toolkit Client applications
Developer Edition	Yes	Yes	Yes	S-controls + AJAX Toolkit Client applications Apex Visualforce
Unlimited Edition	Yes	Yes	No	S-controls + AJAX Toolkit Client applications Apex

Then make your decision based on whether you're primarily updating the user interface, or whether you want to change underlying business logic:

For updates to the user interface:

- **Visualforce**

  The best, easiest, and most powerful way to make changes to the user interface is by creating Visualforce pages. Visualforce pages provide the same features and functionality as s-controls do, but make it far easier to display components with the Salesforce look-and-feel. Visualforce pages are generated on the platform like any standard Salesforce page and can also be backed by logic written in Apex.

  Pros: Easy to write; run directly on the platform; can be backed by logic written in Apex; easy to give components the Salesforce look-and-feel

Cons: As of September 2007, only available as a Developer Edition preview; currently can't be shared on the AppExchange

- **HTML-Based S-Controls**

  If you don't need to display fields from more than a few records at a time, an HTML-based s-control is the next best choice. Because you can leverage the AJAX Toolkit, it's easier to access and update your data than if you used a client application or Web control that runs on a third-party server.

  Pros: Written in HTML and JavaScript; straightforward access to the API with the AJAX Toolkit; can be shared on the AppExchange

  Cons: Runs within a browser; displays poor performance if tasked with processing too many records; harder to give components the Salesforce look-and-feel; JavaScript sometimes hard to debug

- **Client Applications or Web Controls**

  If you need to display or process more than a few records at a time, use a client application or URL-based s-control to link to code that runs on an external server. You can either access this code directly on the external server as a client application or embed it into Salesforce with a URL-based s-control (also called a Web control).

  Pros: Written in languages such as Java, VB.Net, PHP, and C#.Net; can handle tasks that require lots of processing

  Cons: Requires more time to create; harder to give components the Salesforce look-and-feel; must handle batch processing and session management; risk of data corruption if multiple records manipulated within a single transaction; requires you to maintain an external server

For changes to underlying business logic:

- **Apex**

  The best way to make changes to underlying business logic is by writing an Apex class or trigger. Triggers execute before or after records are inserted, updated, or deleted from the database, while class methods can be executed as custom Web services if tagged with the `webService` keyword.

  Pros: Easy to learn for those familiar with Java; runs directly on the platform; locking syntax prevents data corruption when manipulating multiple records in a single transaction; easy to define and execute unit tests; automatically upgraded with every new Salesforce release

Cons: Only available in Unlimited and Developer Editions; currently can't be shared on the AppExchange (as of the Summer '07 release); must learn to process records in bulk to avoid execution governor limits

- **HTML-Based S-Controls**

  If you don't need to query or update more than a few records at a time, an HTML-based s-control is the next best choice. Because you can leverage the AJAX Toolkit, it's easier to access and update your data than if you used a client application or Web control that runs on a third-party server.

  Pros: Written in HTML and JavaScript; straightforward access to the API with the AJAX Toolkit; can be shared on the AppExchange

  Cons: Runs within a browser; displays poor performance if processing too many records; JavaScript sometimes hard to debug

- **Client Applications or Web Controls**

  If you need to process more than a few records at a time or set up an integration between Salesforce and another data source, use a client application or URL-based s-control to link to code that runs on an external server. You can either access this code directly on the external server as a client application, or embed it into Salesforce with a URL-based s-control (also called a Web control).

  Pros: Written in languages such as Java, VB.Net, PHP, and C#.Net; can handle tasks that require lots of processing

  Cons: Requires more time to create; must handle batch processing and session management; risk of data corruption if multiple records manipulated within a single transaction; requires you to maintain an external server

Building and Deploying an App

Problem

You're familiar with the traditional application development process in which a developer writes and tests an application on a local machine, then uploads it to a staging environment

33

where it goes through additional testing, and then rolls it out to the public. You're not sure how to translate that process for creating an on-demand app on the platform.

Solution

Developing an on-demand app poses unique challenges that don't arise during the traditional application development process. For the same reasons that on-demand apps are easy to roll out to users, it's also easy to inadvertently share an on-demand app with users before it's ready if you aren't careful. To avoid confused users and bad data, salesforce.com recommends that developers use the following process for building new on-demand apps:

1. Start building and testing your app in a Developer Edition organization.

   Similar to coding and testing an application on a local machine, a Developer Edition organization gives you a private workspace for building and testing new apps. Each Developer Edition organization comes with access to the API, full Enterprise Edition functionality, and two user licenses to help with testing. Although its limited storage and user accounts prevent it from being good for performance tests or end-user training, Developer Edition organizations are free and have a license that never expires.

2. Migrate your app to a sandbox organization where you can perform integration tests with large sets of data, security checks for multiple users and profiles, and end user training.

   Similar to a staging environment, a *sandbox* is a nearly identical copy of a Salesforce production organization. You can create multiple sandboxes in separate environments for a variety of purposes, such as testing and training, without compromising the data and applications in your production environment.

3. Migrate your app to your production environment during a user-profile-controlled maintenance window.

   Use profiles in the following ways to help you roll an app out to your production organization:

   • Create and announce a maintenance window during which your organization won't be available to most users:

     • Click **Setup ➤ Manage Users ➤ Mass Email Users** to access an email wizard that allows you to alert all active users about the maintenance window.
     • Use the Login Hours related list on user profiles to lock users out during the maintenance window.

   • If you're developing a custom object and don't want users to have access, set the custom object's `Deployment Status` to In Development. Only users with the "Customize Application" profile permission can view or edit a custom object in development.

- Use the deployment control setting to hide related lists, tabs, and links until you're ready to launch them.
- Roll out objects, tabs, and apps selectively to different user profiles if you want to allow some users to have access for user acceptance testing.

 Tip: If your organization includes many profiles, use the following strategy for setting up a maintenance window:

   a. Create a new profile named Maintenance with all login hours locked out.
   b. Use the Force.com Data Loader to extract and save a mapping of users and their user profiles. You can download the Data Loader by clicking **Setup ➤ Data Management ➤ Force.com Data Loader** and clicking **Download the Force.com Data Loader**.
   c. At the beginning of the maintenance window, use the Data Loader to change all user profiles *except* the administrator's to the Maintenance profile. Note that it's very important to leave access with the administrator because otherwise all users could remain locked out of the system indefinitely.
   d. At the end of the maintenance window, use the Data Loader to reload the users with their original profiles.

See Also

- *Signing Up for a Free Developer Edition Account* on page 12
- *Creating a Sandbox Organization* on page 35
- *Migrating Metadata Between Two Organizations* on page 38
- *Migrating Apex Between Two Salesforce Organizations* on page 39

Creating a Sandbox Organization

Problem

You want to create a sandbox organization so you can test a new app before deploying it to a Salesforce production organization.

Solution

Create or refresh a sandbox in your Salesforce organization:

1. Click **Setup ➤ Data Management ➤ Salesforce Sandbox**.
2. Select one of the following:

- Click **New Sandbox** to create a new sandbox. Note that Salesforce deactivates the **New Sandbox** button when an organization reaches its sandbox limit. If necessary, contact Salesforce to order more sandboxes for your organization.
- Click **Refresh** to replace an existing sandbox with a new copy. Salesforce only displays the **Refresh** option for sandboxes that are eligible for refreshing. You can refresh your sandbox once every thirty days. The refreshed copy is inactive until you activate it.

3. Enter a name and description for the sandbox. You can only change the name when you create or refresh a sandbox.

   Tip: Choose a name that:

   - Reflects the purpose of this sandbox, such as "QA."
   - Has only a few characters. Salesforce automatically appends the sandbox name to email addresses on user records in the sandbox environment. Names with fewer characters make sandbox usernames easier to type.

4. Optionally, select the **Quick Copy** checkbox to create a quick copy sandbox.

   Quick copy sandboxes copy all of your production organization's reports, dashboards, price books, products, apps, and customizations under **Setup**, but exclude all of your organization's standard and custom object records, documents, and attachments. Creating a quick copy sandbox can decrease the time it takes to create or refresh a sandbox from several hours to just a few minutes.

5. Click **Start Copy**.

   The process may take several hours, depending on the size of your organization and whether you are creating a quick copy.

6. You will receive a notification email when your newly-created or refreshed sandbox is ready for use. Click the link in the notification email to access your sandbox.

   Users can log into the sandbox at https://www.test.salesforce.com/login.jsp by appending `.<sandbox_name>` to their Salesforce username. For example, if your username for your production account is `user1@acme.com`, then your username for a sandbox named "test" is `user1@acme.com.test`.

   Note: Salesforce automatically changes sandbox usernames but does not change passwords.

Discussion

Sandboxes are a great way of testing your new apps in a close-to-production environment without endangering your data. Note the following about sandboxes:

- The following features are disabled and cannot be enabled in sandboxes:

    - Case escalation
    - Opportunity reminders
    - Contract expiration warnings
    - Subscription summary
    - Automated weekly data exports
    - The ability to create sandboxes

     Note: Case escalation, opportunity reminders, and contract expiration warnings are disabled because they automatically send email to contacts and customers who should not interact with sandboxes.

- Sandboxes do not send storage limit email warnings. To check your storage usage and limits, click **Setup ➤ Data Management ➤ Storage Usage** in your sandbox.
- Salesforce has a background process that permanently deletes records in the Recycle Bin that are older than 30 days. The time of the latest execution of this process is available through the `getDeleted()` API call.

    This process runs at different times on different servers, so its timestamp in your sandbox differs from its timestamp in your production organization. Applications and integrations that depend on this timestamp may fail if they are first connected to one environment, such as your production organization, and then later connected to another environment, such as your sandbox. Keep this in mind when developing applications and integrations that depend on this timestamp.

- Sandboxes automatically append `.<sandbox_name>` to email addresses on user records in the sandbox environment. This invalidates all user email addresses and prevents sandboxes from sending email to your production organization's users because Salesforce does not deliver any email with an invalid From address. You can manually correct email addresses in the sandbox user records for users who will use your the sandbox for testing and training.

     Caution: Sandboxes automatically change Salesforce user email addresses, but do not change other email addresses in Salesforce, such as those in contact records. To avoid sending unsolicited email from your sandboxes, manually invalidate or delete all email addresses in your sandboxes that do not belong to users. When testing the generation of outbound email, change contact email addresses to those of testers or an automated test script.

- Only custom links created as relative URLs, such as `/00Oz0000000EVpU&pv0={!Account_ID}` will work in your sandboxes. All custom links created as absolute URLs, such as `https://na1.salesforce.com/00Oz0000000EVpU&pv0={!Account_ID}`, will not work in your organization's sandboxes.

- Customizations to your production organization do not automatically appear in your sandboxes. You must create a new sandbox or refresh an existing one to see the customizations made to your organization since the last time you created or refreshed a sandbox.
- If your sandbox is the same version as the AppExchange, you can:

    - Install and deploy apps from the AppExchange in your sandbox
    - Publish apps from your sandbox to the AppExchange

 Note: The version of your sandboxes may differ from the AppExchange around the time of a Salesforce release. Check the logo in the upper left corner of your sandbox home page for version information.

See Also

- *Signing Up for a Free Developer Edition Account* on page 12
- *Building and Deploying an App* on page 33
- *Migrating Metadata Between Two Organizations* on page 38
- *Migrating Apex Between Two Salesforce Organizations* on page 39

Migrating Metadata Between Two Organizations

Problem

You want to migrate an app from one organization into another.

Solution

Publish the app on the AppExchange as a private or public package. You can then upload it into any other sandbox or production organization as long as they're on the same release as the AppExchange.

 Note: The version of your sandbox and production organizations may differ from the AppExchange around the time of a Salesforce release. Check the logo in the upper left corner of your sandbox home page for version information.

Discussion

Using the AppExchange to migrate an app works best if all components of the app are brand new and do not have the same name as other custom components that already exist in the destination organization. If you need to migrate an app to an organization that already contains some of the app's components and they weren't originally part of a managed package, you need to recreate the app manually.

 Tip: A good tool for making manual migration easier is Snapshot, an app from DreamFactory available on the AppExchange at www.salesforce.com/appexchange/detail_overview.jsp? NavCode__c=&id=a03300000021uE2AAI. Snapshot allows an account administrator to take a picture of the current state of the customizations in their organization and track all changes over time.

See Also

Migrating Apex Between Two Salesforce Organizations

Problem

You want to migrate Apex scripts from one organization to another, such as from a Developer Edition organization to a sandbox, or from a sandbox to an Unlimited Edition production organization.

Solution

Download the Platform Deployment Tool if you want to use a script for deploying Apex from a Developer Edition or sandbox organization to a Salesforce production organization using Apache's Ant build tool.

Discussion

There are three types of organizations where you can run your Apex:

- A *developer* organization: an organization created with a Developer Edition account.
- A *production* organization: an organization that has live users accessing your data.
- A *sandbox* organization: an organization created on your production organization that is a copy of your production organization.

You never want to develop Apex in your Salesforce production organization. Live users accessing the system while you are developing can destabilize your data or corrupt your application. Instead, salesforce.com recommends that you do all your development work in a Developer Edition organization.

To use the Platform Deployment Tool, do the following:

1. Visit java.sun.com/javase/downloads/index.jsp and install Java JDK, Version 6.1 or greater on the deployment machine.
2. Visit ant.apache.org and install Apache Ant, Version 1.6 or greater on the deployment machine.
3. Set up the environment variables (such as `ANT_HOME`, `JAVA_HOME`, and `PATH`) as specified in the Ant Installation Guide at ant.apache.org/manual/install.html.
4. Verify that the JDK and Ant are installed correctly by opening a command prompt and entering `ant -version`. Your output should look something like this:

```
Apache Ant version 1.7.0 compiled on December 13 2006
```

5. Log in to Salesforce on your deployment machine. Click **Setup ➤ Build ➤ Tools**, then click **Platform Deployment Tool**.
6. Unzip the downloaded file to the directory of your choice. The zip file contains the following:

   - A `Readme.html` file that explains how to use the tools.
   - A Jar file containing the ant task: `ant-salesforce.jar`.
   - A sample folder containing:

     - A `Classes` folder that contains `compileAndTest.apex`
     - A `Triggers` folder that contains `phoneSetter.tgr`
     - A sample `build.properties` file that you modify to run the ant task
     - A sample `build.xml` file, that exercises the `compileAndTest` API call

7. Copy the `ant-salesforce.jar` file from the unzipped file into the ant lib directory. The ant lib directory is located in the root folder of your Ant installation.
8. Open the sample subdirectory in the unzipped file.
9. Edit the `build.properties` file:

   a. Enter your Salesforce production organization username and password for the `sf.user` and `sf.password` fields, respectively.

       Note: The username you specify should have the authority to edit Apex.

   b. If you are deploying to a sandbox organization, change the `sf.serverurl` field to `https://test.salesforce.com`.

10. Open a command window in the sample directory.

11. Enter `ant deploy`. This runs the `compileAndTest` API call using the sample class and Account trigger provided with the tool.

The `ant deploy` command calls the following Ant target named `deploy` in the `build.xml` file.

```
<target name="deploy">
        <sf:compileAndTest
            username="${sf.username}"
            password="${sf.password}"
            server="${sf.serverurl}"
            apiversion="10.0"
            baseDir=".">
            <runTests>
                <class>compileAndTest</class>
            </runTests>
        </sf:compileAndTest>
</target>
```

Note: The `compileAndTest` call completes successfully only if all of the following are true:

- 75% of your Apex is covered by unit tests, and all of those test complete successfully.

   Note that when deploying to a production organization, every unit test in your organization namespace is executed.

- Every trigger has some test coverage.
- All classes and triggers compile successfully.

12. To remove the test class and trigger added as part of the execution of `ant deploy`, enter the following in the command window: `ant delete`.

`ant delete` calls the following Ant target named `delete` in the `build.xml` file.

```
<target name="delete">
        <sf:compileAndTest
                        username="${sf.username}"
                        password="${sf.password}"
                        server="${sf.serverurl}"
                        apiversion="10.0">
            <deleteClass>compileAndTest</deleteClass>
            <deleteTrigger>phoneSetter</deleteTrigger>
        </sf:compileAndTest>
</target>
```

If you don't want to use the ant tool to deploy Apex, you can also use `compileAndTest` or the following API calls to deploy your Apex to a development or sandbox organization:

- `compileClasses`
- `compileTriggers`

Both of these calls take an Apex script that contains the class or trigger, as well as the values for any fields that need to be set.

For a sample implementation that takes advantage of these calls, use the Force.com Toolkit for Eclipse. This Eclipse plug-in also allows you to deploy Apex classes and triggers to production organizations.

 Note: You can only use the `compileAndTest` API call to deploy Apex to a Salesforce production organization.

See Also

- *Building and Deploying an App* on page 33
- *Creating a Sandbox Organization* on page 35
- "Deploying Your Apex" in the *Apex Language Reference*, available at www.salesforce.com/us/developer/docs/apexcode/salesforce_apex_language_reference.pdf

Chapter 3

Best Practices for Writing S-Controls

In this chapter ...

- Writing S-Controls in Eclipse
- Writing S-Controls in AJAX Tools
- Using the AJAX Toolkit in an S-Control
- Adding a Flex Application to an S-Control
- Using S-Control Snippets in Other S-Controls
- Using Special Characters in URLs and Custom Links

As you learned in the previous chapter, s-controls are an easy way to leverage HTML and JavaScript to create custom pages and user interface components if you need to manipulate a small set of records or fields, or you want to link to an external server.

In this chapter, you'll learn some best practices to make writing s-controls even easier. We'll show you how to use Eclipse or AJAX Tools to do your development, how to leverage the AJAX Toolkit for easy access to the API, how to incorporate Adobe® Flex™ into your s-controls, and even how to use s-controls in other s-controls. These best practices are tried and true techniques from other platform developers, so you'll be guaranteed success if you follow them.

Writing S-Controls in Eclipse

Problem

You want to create a new s-control for your Salesforce organization in Eclipse.

Solution

Once you've installed the Force.com Toolkit for Eclipse and set up a project, use the Eclipse S-Control wizard:

1. Right-click anywhere in the Eclipse Package Explorer and select **New ➤ Other**.
2. In the Wizard Selection screen, click **Force.com ➤ Force.com Control**, and click **Next**.
3. Specify the name and label for the s-control. The label is used to display the s-control in Salesforce, while the name is a unique identifier that's only used internally.
4. Select the type of s-control you want to define:

    -   `Custom HTML` s-controls consist of HTML and JavaScript. When s-controls of this type are added to a Web tab or displayed inline in a record's detail page, the content of the control is rendered directly by the user's Web browser. These are equivalent to the standard s-controls that are described elsewhere in this book.
    -   `URLs` are links to applications that are hosted on external servers. When a URL s-control is added to a Web tab or displayed inline in a record's detail page, the content of the s-control is rendered by the third-party server and then displayed by the user's Web browser. These are equivalent to the Web controls that are described elsewhere in this book.
    -   `Snippets` are reusable pieces of HTML and JavaScript code that can be referenced by other Custom HTML s-controls.

5. Click **Finish**. A file for your s-control is created in the SControls folder, and the s-control is also saved in your Salesforce organization. You can then edit the content of the s-control in the Eclipse s-control editor.

Discussion

One of the biggest advantages of using the Eclipse Toolkit is that you can enjoy many of the features of the Eclipse development environment while editing your s-controls. The Eclipse Toolkit automatically outlines your code and provides code completion functionality while you type. In addition, right-clicking anywhere in the Eclipse s-control editor allows you to bring up a list of available merge fields and snippets that you can insert with just a click.

Using the Eclipse Toolkit also allows you to leverage the Team features of Eclipse while developing on the platform. If you have a compatible source code control system such as CVS or Perforce, you can add your s-controls and track changes by multiple users. In addition, Eclipse tracks your local edits so you can compare changes and perform rollbacks if necessary.

To save an s-control in Eclipse to your Salesforce organization, simply save the file using any of the typical methods. Once the file is saved (as indicated by the asterisk disappearing from the tab for that editor), your changes are committed to the platform.

See Also

- *Installing the Force.com Toolkit for Eclipse* on page 15
- *Creating a Project in Eclipse* on page 17
- *Deciding When to Use S-Controls, Client Apps, Apex, or Visualforce* on page 30
- *Using the AJAX Toolkit in an S-Control* on page 46
- *Using S-Control Snippets in Other S-Controls* on page 51

Writing S-Controls in AJAX Tools

Problem

You want to create a new s-control for your Salesforce organization in AJAX Tools.

 Note: AJAX Tools is different from the AJAX Toolkit. AJAX Tools is an IDE while the AJAX Toolkit is a JavaScript wrapper for the API that doesn't require a download.

Solution

Once you've installed AJAX Tools from the AppExchange:

1. Select **AJAX Tools** from the app picker menu in the upper right corner of your Salesforce organization.
2. In the AJAX Tools tab, click **Start AJAX Tools**.
3. Click **New** in the toolbar at the top of the page.
4. Select the s-control template you want to use:

   - listview

     Creates an HTML-based s-control that displays a custom list for an object and fields that you specify

   - search inline edit

     Creates an HTML-based s-control that includes a search algorithm for an object you specify

   - simple

Creates a generic HTML-based s-control, with options to include the Dojo or Apex script headers

5. Name your s-control. All s-control names must contain only alphanumeric characters, begin with a letter, and be unique.
6. Specify any additional parameters, according to the template you chose.

Once you create an s-control, it appears in the sidebar on the left.

See Also

- *Installing AJAX Tools* on page 18
- *Using the AJAX Toolkit in an S-Control* on page 46
- *Using S-Control Snippets in Other S-Controls* on page 51

Using the AJAX Toolkit in an S-Control

Problem

You want to write an s-control that queries and updates Salesforce data.

Solution

Add the AJAX Toolkit to your s-control by including the following script reference:

```
<script src="/soap/ajax/10.0/connection.js"
type="text/javascript"></script>
```

Note:

- This script refers to version 10.0 of the AJAX Toolkit released with Salesforce Summer '07. Depending on when you read this book, a more recent version may be available.
- AJAX Tools is different from the AJAX Toolkit. AJAX Tools is an IDE while the AJAX Toolkit is a JavaScript wrapper for the API that doesn't require a download.

Then, issue standard API calls in your JavaScript code by using the `sforce.connection` object. By default, this object is automatically created with the session ID of the user who launches the s-control.

For example, the following sample code queries Account data and displays it on the same tab where the s-control resides:

```html
<html>
  <head>
  <script src="/soap/ajax/10.0/connection.js"
          type="text/javascript"></script>

  <script>
    function setupPage() {
      //Function contains all code to execute after page is
      //rendered

      var state = { //The state that you need when the callback
                    //is called
          output : document.getElementById("output"),
          startTime : new Date().getTime()};

      var callback = {
          //Call layoutResult if the request is successful
          onSuccess: layoutResults,

          //Call queryFailed if the API request fails
          onFailure: queryFailed,
          source: state};

      sforce.connection.query(
          "SELECT Id, Name, Industry FROM Account" +
          "ORDER BY Industry limit 30", callback);
    }

  function queryFailed(error, source) {
    source.output.innerHTML = "An error has occurred: "
                                  + error;
  }

  /**
   * This method is called when the toolkit receives
   * a successful response from the server.
   * @queryResult - result that server returned
   * @source - state passed into the query method call.
   */
  function layoutResults(queryResult, source) {
    if (queryResult.size > 0) {
      var output = "";

      //Get the records array
      var records = queryResult.getArray('records');

      //Loop through the records and construct HTML string
      for (var i = 0; i < records.length; i++) {
        var account = records[i];

        output += account.Id + " " + account.Name +
            " [Industry - " + account.Industry + "]<br>";
```

```
      }

    //Render the generated HTML string
    source.output.innerHTML = output;
    }
  }
  </script>
  </head>

  <body onload="setupPage()">
    <div id="output"> </div>
  </body>
</html>
```

To use this s-control in your own organization:

1. Define the s-control:

   a. Click **Setup ➤ Build ➤ Custom S-Controls**, and click **New Custom S-Control**.

   b. Enter the following values:

      • `Label`: Sample AJAX Toolkit Control
      • `S-Control Name`: Sample_AJAX_Toolkit_Control
      • `Type`: HTML

   c. Copy the preceding code into the body of the s-control.
   d. Click **Save**.

2. Add the s-control to a custom tab:

   a. Click **Setup ➤ Build ➤ Custom Tabs**, and click **New** in the Web Tabs related list.
   b. Select `2 columns with Salesforce sidebar`, and click **Next**.
   c. Enter the following values:

      • `Tab Type`: Custom S-Control
      • `Tab Label`: Sample AJAX
      • `Tab Style`: Choose any style that is not currently used on another tab

   d. Click **Next**.
   e. Select Sample AJAX Toolkit Control, and click **Next**.
   f. Accept the remaining defaults, and click **Save**.

Execute the s-control by clicking on the Sample AJAX tab. A few rows of unformatted data are displayed. For example, a small organization with test data produced the following output:

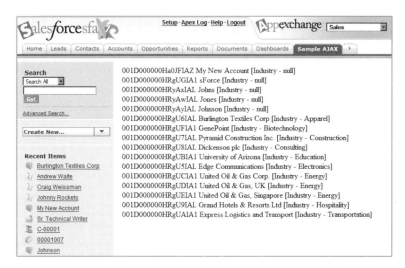

Figure 2: S-Control Output

Discussion

The AJAX Toolkit is a JavaScript wrapper around the API. Any organization that has access to the API can use it in Mozilla Firefox 1.5 and above or Internet Explorer 6 and above. You can execute any call in the API and access any API object that you normally have access to.

The AJAX Toolkit is based on the Partner WSDL. As a result, it can be used in any organization, regardless of the custom objects and fields defined within it. Unlike the API, the AJAX Toolkit also supports both synchronous and asynchronous calls, with callback functions to handle the results.

See Also

- *Using S-Control Snippets in Other S-Controls* on page 51
- The *AJAX Toolkit Developer's Guide* at www.salesforce.com/us/developer/docs/ajax/index.htm

Adding a Flex Application to an S-Control

Problem

You've built a Flex application that leverages the Flex Toolkit for Force.com and you want to display it in an s-control.

"Adding a Flex Application to an S-Control" contributed by Dave Carroll, Principal Developer Evangelist for salesforce.com and author of the Flex Toolkit

Solution

Define an s-control that includes:

- The compiled Flex application (the SWF file) as an attachment to the s-control
- HTML that loads the Flex application as the body of the s-control (included in the Flex Toolkit)

For example, to display the sample Flex application that comes with the Flex Toolkit in an s-control:

1. Run and compile the sample code on your local machine according to the instructions in *Installing the Flex Toolkit for Force.com* on page 21.
2. In your Salesforce organization, click **Setup ➤ Build ➤ Custom S-Controls**, and click **New Custom S-Control**.
3. Name your s-control, and set the `Type` to HTML.
4. In the s-control `Content` text area, add the following code:

```
<!DOCTYPE HTML PUBLIC
        "-//W3C//DTD HTML 4.01 Transitional//EN"
        "http://www.w3.org/TR/html4/loose.dtd">
<html>
<head></head>
<body scroll="no" >

<object classid="clsid:D27CDB6E-AE6D-11cf-96B8-444553540000"
        id="FlexSalesforce" width="100%" height="100%"
        codebase="https://fpdownload.macromedia.com/get/
        flashplayer/current/swflash.cab">
   <param name="movie" value="{!Scontrol.JavaArchive}" />
   <param name="quality" value="high" />
   <param name="play" value="true" />
   <param name="bgcolor" value="#f3f3ec" />
   <param name="allowScriptAccess" value="always" />
   <param name="flashvars"
          value="session_id={!API.Session_ID}&
          server_url={!API.Partner_Server_URL_90}" />

   <embed src="{!Scontrol.JavaArchive}" play="true"
          bgcolor="#f3f3ec" width="100%" height="700"
          name="FlexSalesforce" align="middle"
          flashvars="session_id={!API.Session_ID}&
                  server_url={!API.Partner_Server_URL_90}"

          loop="false" allowScriptAccess="always"
          type="application/x-shockwave-flash"
       pluginspage="http://www.adobe.com/go/getflashplayer">

   </embed>
</object>
</body>
</html>
```

5. In the `Filename` text box, enter the path to the `salesforce.mxml` file that exists in your Flex project.
6. Click **Save**.

Discussion

Notice the following points about the s-control that displays the Flex application:

- The `flashvars` variable passes the critical session and server URL information into the Flex applet, where the information is used to initialize the API connection.
- The s-control's `JavaArchive` parameter is the path to the binary that's specified in the `Filename` text box. It holds the Flex applet, which is loaded on-demand when the user invokes the s-control in Salesforce via a custom link, Web tab, or inline s-control.

See Also

- The ADN's Flex Toolkit information page at wiki.apexdevnet.com/index.php/Flex_Toolkit
- The Flex Toolkit class documentation at www.adnsandbox.com/media/flexsdk/docs/index.html
- Adobe's Flex website at www.flex.org

Using S-Control Snippets in Other S-Controls

Problem

You've written a JavaScript function or HTML code that you want to reuse in several different s-controls.

Solution

Define the code that you want to reuse as an s-control snippet, and then include it in the body of another s-control with the `INCLUDE()` function.

The `INCLUDE()` function has the following syntax:

```
{!INCLUDE(source, [inputs])}
```

Replace *source* with the s-control snippet you want to reference, and replace *inputs* with any information you need to pass to the snippet.

For example, suppose you define the following s-control snippet and name it `Title_Snippet`:

```
<h2 class="{!$Request.titleTheme}.title">{!$Request.titleText}</h2>
```

This snippet requires two input parameters: *titleTheme* and *titleText*. It is reusable HTML code that presents a page title and theme based on input parameters. Next, create an s-control that includes this snippet, and passes in the appropriate parameters:

```
<html>
<head>
</head>
<body>
{! INCLUDE($SControl.Title_Snippet,
[titleTheme = "modern", titleText = "My Sample Title"]) }

<!-- Insert your page specific content here -->

</body>
</html>
```

This s-control uses the snippet titled `Title_Snippet` to display the title of the page "My Sample Title" with a modern theme. Replace *<!-- Insert your page specific content here -->* with your own HTML content and use the s-control as the source of a Web tab to create your own pages.

Discussion

Snippets are great way to store common or identical HTML or JavaScript code that you repeat over and over again in your s-controls, such as a common page header, or a function that all of your s-controls need.

Because the `INCLUDE()` function references an s-control snippet and doesn't copy it, it always runs the latest content of the s-control snippet. Remember when making a change to your s-control snippet that it affects all `INCLUDE` functions that refer to it.

See Also

- *Creating a Roll-Up Summary Field with an S-Control* on page 157
- *Formatting a Currency in an S-Control* on page 154

Using Special Characters in URLs and Custom Links

Problem

You have customers who are using non-English versions of Internet Explorer 6 or another browser, and URL links in s-controls and custom links aren't passing special characters properly. The characters either don't show up, or the entire line of code is copied.

Solution

Encode the URLs with the `encodeURI()` JavaScript function. For example:

```
<script language="JavaScript">
function redirect()
   {parent.frames.location.replace(encodeURI("/003/e?retURL=" +
       "%2F{!Contact.Id}&con4_lkid={!Account.Id}&" +
       "con4{!Account.Name}&00N30000001KqeH=" +
       "{!Account.Account_Name_Localized__c}" +
       "&cancelURL=%2F{!Account.Id}"))}
   redirect();
</script>
```

Chapter 4

Best Practices for Writing Apex

Earlier we introduced you to Apex, the world's first on-demand, multitenant programming language. By now you know that you can use Apex to extend the capabilities of the platform. But what exactly does that mean and what is Apex? What's the syntax of the language? How can you write powerful, yet efficient, code to enhance your on-demand apps?

In this chapter, we'll get you started writing Apex with a simple "Hello World" example. Then you'll learn some of the key concepts of Apex, such as the differences between triggers and classes. We'll also introduce you to best practices for writing Apex—everything from doing bulk processing to avoiding governor limits to creating Web services and writing unit tests.

As you'll see, Apex enables a new class of applications and features to be developed and deployed on the platform by providing the ability to capture business logic and rules. The language uses a combination of Java-like syntax with API functions and SOQL to let you define triggers, classes, and other representations of business logic that can interact with the platform at a low level. Conceptually similar to a stored procedure system, Apex allows almost any kind of transactional, complex logic to be developed and run entirely on demand.

Getting Started with Apex

Problem

You've heard all about Apex but you're unfamiliar with how the language works and you want to learn more.

Solution

Walk through a simple scenario in which we use Apex to update a custom account field named `Hello` with the text "World" every time a new account is created.

 Note: To follow these steps in your own organization, you'll first need to define a custom text field named `Hello` on the Account object. Click **Setup ➤ Customize ➤ Accounts ➤ Fields** and click **New** in the Account Custom Fields & Relationships related list to access the New Custom Field wizard.

To do this we'll first define an Apex class:

1. Click **Setup ➤ Build ➤ Code** and then click **New**.

    Note: You can't make changes to Apex using the Salesforce user interface in a Salesforce production organization. See *Migrating Apex Between Two Salesforce Organizations* on page 39.

2. In the `Body` text box, enter the following code:

```
public class MyHelloWorld {

    // This method updates the Hello field on a list
    // of accounts
    public static void addHelloWorld(Account[] accs){
        for (Account a:accs){
            if (a.Hello__c != 'World')
                a.Hello__c = 'World';
        }
    }

}
```

3. Click **Save**.

Before moving on, let's walk through each line of the code we just wrote:

- ```
  public class MyHelloWorld {
  ```

Apex scripts are generally contained in *classes*. This class is defined as `public`, which means the class is available to other Apex scripts in the same namespace.

- ```
  public static void addHelloWorld(Account[] accs){
  ```

This line is the start of a method definition. The method is called `addHelloWorld`, and is both public and static. Because it's a static method, you don't need to create an instance of the class in order to access the method—you can just use the name of the class followed by a dot (`.`) and the name of the method (for example `MyHelloWorld.addHelloWorld()`). The `addHelloWorld()` method takes one parameter, a list of account records, which is assigned to the variable `accs`.

- ```
  for (Account a:accs){
      if (a.Hello__c != 'World')
          a.Hello__c = 'World';
  }
  ```

This next section of code contains the rest of the method definition. For each account *a* in the list of account records, the code first tests whether the `Hello` field is already populated with the text "World" and, if not, updates the field accordingly.

Notice the `__c` after the field name—`Hello__c`. This indicates that the field is a *custom field*, that is, a field you created. Standard fields that are provided by default in Salesforce are accessed using the same type of dot notation, but without the `__c` (for example, `Account.name`).

To run this piece of code, we'll next have to call it in a component called a *trigger*. A trigger is a piece of code that executes before or after records of a particular type are inserted, updated, or deleted from the database, or after a record is undeleted from the Recycle Bin. Every trigger runs with a set of context variables that provide access to the records that caused the trigger to fire, and all triggers run in bulk mode—that is, they process a list of records at once, rather than just one record at a time.

To run the `addHelloWorld()` method we defined every time a new account is created, we'll need to define a trigger on the Account object:

1. Click **Setup ➤ Customize ➤ Accounts ➤ Triggers**, and then click **New**.
2. In the `Body` text box, enter the following code:

   ```
   trigger helloWorldAccountTrigger on Account
                               (before insert) {
       MyHelloWorld.addHelloWorld(Trigger.new);
   }
   ```
   ```

3. Click **Save**.

The first line of code defines the trigger:

```
trigger helloWorldAccountTrigger on Account (before insert) {
```

It gives the trigger a name, specifies the object on which it operates, and defines the events that cause it to fire. For example, this trigger runs before new account records are inserted into the database.

The next line in the code calls the method `addHelloWorld` in the `MyHelloWorld` class. It passes in a trigger context variable called `Trigger.new`. Trigger context variables such as `Trigger.new` are implicitly defined in all triggers, and provide access to the records that caused the trigger to fire. In this case, `Trigger.new` contains a list of all the new accounts that are about to be inserted.

 Note: Although users typically only create one account record at a time in the Salesforce user interface, a trigger is also fired when a batch of accounts is saved through the API.

```
MyHelloWorld.addHelloWorld(Trigger.new);
```

To test our code, we have to create a new account record. That's because the trigger that calls `addHelloWorld()` runs on the `before insert` trigger event:

1. In the Accounts tab, click **New** to create a new account. The only required field is the name.
2. Click **Save**.

Regardless of what field values you specify when you create the account, the `Hello` field is now populated with the value, World.

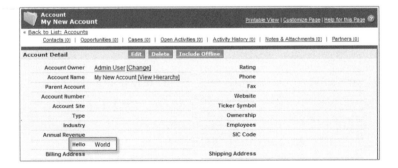

Figure 3: Apex's "Hello World"

- *Choosing Between Classes or Triggers* on page 59
- *Defining an Apex Web Service and Calling It from an S-Control* on page 67

Choosing Between Classes or Triggers

Problem

You're new to writing Apex and you're not sure what the best practices are for coding in classes or triggers.

Solution

While syntactically there's no benefit to putting more of your Apex in a class versus a trigger (or vice versa), stylistically it's far more beneficial to put most of your code's logic into a class and then use triggers as hooks for calling class methods.

Putting code in a class encourages reuse by other developers. If you make a class `public`, any other class or trigger that has access to your organization or its namespace can use that method. Code that runs in a trigger can't be reused.

Additionally, keeping most of your code's logic in classes helps you with organization. It's much harder to understand the logic of an application if it's spread out among several different triggers on several different objects. By organizing your code into a few classes, the logic of your application can be consolidated into a few files, and your class methods can be bundled with the test methods that exercise and verify them.

Although the ability to extend classes is not yet generally available in Apex, the language is, at its heart, an object-oriented programming language. Placing most of your Apex logic in a class rather than a trigger maintains the spirit of that object-oriented approach.

See Also

- *Getting Started with Apex* on page 56
- *Comparing Queries Against Trigger.old and Trigger.new* on page 66
- *Avoiding Apex Governor Limits* on page 70
- *Writing Object-Oriented Apex* on page 87

Writing Apex in Eclipse

Problem

You want to create a new Apex class or trigger for your Salesforce organization in Eclipse.

Solution

Once you've installed the Force.com Toolkit for Eclipse and set up a Force.com project, use the Eclipse Apex wizard:

1. Right-click anywhere in the Eclipse Package Explorer and select **New ➤ Other**.
2. In the Wizard Selection screen, click **Force.com ➤ Apex Trigger** if you're creating a trigger, or **Force.com ➤ Apex Class** if you're creating a class. Click **Next**.
3. Specify the name of the trigger or class. Trigger and class names can't include any spaces.
4. If you're defining a trigger:

    • Select the Salesforce object with which it should be associated.

     Tip: If you're using a namespace, custom objects appear at the bottom of the `Trigger Object` drop-down list. See *Registering a Namespace Prefix* on page 235.

    • Select one or more events that should cause this trigger to execute.

5. Click **Finish**. If you defined a trigger, a file for it is created in the Triggers folder, and the trigger is also saved in your Salesforce organization. If you defined a class, a file for it is created in the Classes folder, as well as your Salesforce organization. You can then edit the content of the trigger or class in the Eclipse s-control editor.

Discussion

One of the biggest advantages of using the Eclipse Toolkit is that you can enjoy many of the features of the Eclipse development environment while editing your Apex class or trigger. The Eclipse Toolkit automatically outlines and highlights your code and allows you to quickly run tests by right-clicking anywhere in a class and selecting **Apex ➤ Run Tests**. You can then easily determine your code coverage percentage—a very useful feature when you're trying to get to the 75% code coverage figure that's required to deploy Apex to a Salesforce production organization.

Using the Eclipse Toolkit also allows you to leverage the Team features of Eclipse while developing on the Force.com platform. If you have a compatible source control system such as CVS or Perforce, you can add your classes and triggers and track changes by multiple users. In addition, Eclipse tracks your local edits so you can compare changes and perform rollbacks if necessary.

To save an Apex class or trigger in Eclipse to your Salesforce organization, simply save the file using any of the typical methods. Once the file is saved (as indicated by the asterisk disappearing from the tab for that editor), your changes are committed to the platform. You can confirm save by right-clicking anywhere in the trigger or class file and selecting **Apex ➤ Show in Salesforce UI**.

See Also

- *Installing the Force.com Toolkit for Eclipse* on page 15
- *Creating a Project in Eclipse* on page 17
- *Deciding When to Use S-Controls, Client Apps, Apex, or Visualforce* on page 30

Bulk Processing Records in a Trigger

Problem

You're new to writing triggers, and whenever you write one it frequently runs into Apex governor limits.

Solution

For efficient bulk processing it's critical that triggers execute only a constant number of database queries, regardless of how many records are being processed. Instead of looping over individual records in the `Trigger.old` or `Trigger.new` lists, use maps to organize records based on their ID or another identifying field, and sets to isolate distinct records.

For example, consider the following lead deduplication trigger, which rejects any new or updated lead that has a duplicate email address:

- The trigger first uses a map to store the updated leads with each lead's email address as the key.
- The trigger then uses the set of keys in the map to query the database for any existing lead records with the same email addresses. For every matching lead, the duplicate record is marked with an error condition.

```
trigger leadDuplicatePreventer on Lead
                        (before insert, before update) {

    Map<String, Lead> leadMap = new Map<String, Lead>();
    for (Lead lead : System.Trigger.new) {

        // Make sure we don't treat an email address that
```

"Bulk Processing Records in a Trigger" contributed by Steve Fisher, Senior Vice President of the Platform Division for salesforce.com

```
        // isn't changing during an update as a duplicate.
        if ((lead.Email != null) &&
            (System.Trigger.isInsert ||
            (lead.Email != System.Trigger.oldMap.
            get(lead.Id).Email))) {

            // Make sure another new lead isn't also a duplicate
            if (leadMap.containsKey(lead.Email)) {
                lead.Email.addError('Another new lead has the '
                                    + 'same email address.');
            } else {
                leadMap.put(lead.Email, lead);
            }
        }
    }

    // Using a single database query, find all the leads in
    // the database that have the same email address as any
    // of the leads being inserted or updated.
    for (Lead lead : [SELECT Email FROM Lead
                    WHERE Email IN :leadMap.KeySet()]) {
        Lead newLead = leadMap.get(lead.Email);
        newLead.Email.addError('A lead with this email '
                                + 'address already exists.');
    }
}
```

 Note: For further discussion of this record deduplication code, see *Preventing Duplicate Records from Saving* on page 118.

See Also

- *Controlling Recursive Triggers* on page 62
- *Comparing Queries Against Trigger.old and Trigger.new* on page 66
- *Avoiding Apex Governor Limits* on page 70
- *Getting Started with Apex* on page 56

Controlling Recursive Triggers

Problem

You want to write a trigger that creates a new record as part of its processing logic; however, that record may then cause another trigger to fire, which in turn will cause another to fire, and so on. You don't know how to stop that recursion.

Solution

Use a static variable in an Apex class to avoid an infinite loop. Static variables are local to the context of a Web request (or test method during a call to `runTests()`), so all triggers that fire as a result of a user's action have access to it.

For example, consider the following scenario: frequently a Salesforce user wants to follow up with a customer the day after logging a call with that customer. Because this is such a common use case, you want to provide your users with a helpful checkbox on a task that allows them to automatically create a follow-up task scheduled for the next day.

You can use a `before insert` trigger on Task to insert the follow-up task, but this, in turn, refires the `before insert` trigger before the follow-up task is inserted. To exit out of this recursion, set a static class boolean variable during the first pass through the trigger to inform the second trigger that it should not insert another follow-up task:

 Note: For this Apex script to work properly, you first must define a custom checkbox field on Task. In this example, this field is named `Create_Follow_Up_Task__c`.

The following code defines the class with the static class variable:

```
public class FollowUpTaskHelper {

    // Static variables are local to the context of a Web request
    // (or testMethod during a runTests call)
    // Therefore, this variable will be initialized as false
    // at the beginning of each Web request which accesses it.

    private static boolean alreadyCreatedTasks = false;


    public static boolean hasAlreadyCreatedFollowUpTasks() {
        return alreadyCreatedTasks;
    }


    // By setting the variable to true, it maintains this
    // new value throughout the duration of the request
    // (or testMethod)
    public static void setAlreadyCreatedFollowUpTasks() {
        alreadyCreatedTasks = true;
    }


    public static String getFollowUpSubject(String subject) {
        return 'Follow Up: ' + subject;
    }

}
```

This code defines the trigger:

```
trigger AutoCreateFollowUpTasks on Task (before insert) {
    // Before cloning and inserting the follow-up tasks,
    // make sure the current trigger context isn't operating
    // on a set of cloned follow-up tasks.
    if (!FollowUpTaskHelper.hasAlreadyCreatedFollowUpTasks()) {

        List<Task> followUpTasks = new List<Task>();

        for (Task t : Trigger.new) {
            if (t.Create_Follow_Up_Task__c) {

                // False indicates that the ID should NOT
                // be preserved
                Task followUpTask = t.clone(false);
                System.assertEquals(null, followUpTask.id);

                followUpTask.subject = FollowUpTaskHelper.
                        getFollowUpSubject(followUpTask.subject);
                if (followUpTask.ActivityDate != null) {
                    followUpTask.ActivityDate =
                        followUpTask.ActivityDate + 1; //The day after
                }
                followUpTasks.add(followUpTask);
            }
        }
        FollowUpTaskHelper.setAlreadyCreatedFollowUpTasks();
        insert followUpTasks;
    }
}
```

This code defines the test methods:

```
// This class includes the test methods for the
// AutoCreateFollowUpTasks trigger.

public class FollowUpTaskTester {
    private static integer NUMBER_TO_CREATE = 4;
    private static String UNIQUE_SUBJECT =
                                'Testing follow-up tasks';

    static testMethod void testCreateFollowUpTasks() {
        List<Task> tasksToCreate = new List<Task>();
        for (Integer i = 0; i < NUMBER_TO_CREATE; i++) {
            Task newTask = new Task(subject = UNIQUE_SUBJECT,
                    ActivityDate = System.today(),
                    Create_Follow_Up_Task__c = true );
            System.assert(newTask.Create_Follow_Up_Task__c);
            tasksToCreate.add(newTask);
        }

        insert tasksToCreate;
        System.assertEquals(NUMBER_TO_CREATE,
```

```
                               [select count()
                                from Task
                                where subject = :UNIQUE_SUBJECT
                                and ActivityDate = :System.today()]);

        // Make sure there are follow-up tasks created
        System.assertEquals(NUMBER_TO_CREATE,
                               [select count()
                                from Task
                                where subject = :FollowUpTaskHelper.
                                     getFollowUpSubject(UNIQUE_SUBJECT)
                                and ActivityDate = :System.today()+1]);
    }

    static testMethod void assertNormalTasksArentFollowedUp() {
        List<Task> tasksToCreate = new List<Task>();
        for (integer i = 0; i < NUMBER_TO_CREATE; i++) {
            Task newTask = new Task(subject=UNIQUE_SUBJECT,
                               ActivityDate = System.today(),
                               Create_Follow_Up_Task__c = false);
            tasksToCreate.add(newTask);
        }

        insert tasksToCreate;
        System.assertEquals(NUMBER_TO_CREATE,
                               [select count()
                                from Task
                                where subject=:UNIQUE_SUBJECT
                                and ActivityDate =:System.today()]);

        // There should be no follow-up tasks created
        System.assertEquals(0,
                               [select count()
                                from Task
                                where subject=:FollowUpTaskHelper.
                                     getFollowUpSubject(UNIQUE_SUBJECT)
                                and ActivityDate =:(System.today() +1)]);

    }

}
```

See Also

- *Bulk Processing Records in a Trigger* on page 61
- *Comparing Queries Against Trigger.old and Trigger.new* on page 66
- *Avoiding Apex Governor Limits* on page 70

Comparing Queries Against Trigger.old and Trigger.new

Problem

You're writing a `before update` or `before delete` trigger and need to issue a SOQL query to get related data for records in the `Trigger.new` and `Trigger.old` lists.

Solution

Correlate records and query results with the `Trigger.newMap` and `Trigger.oldMap` ID-to-SObject maps.

For example, this trigger uses `Trigger.oldMap` to create a set of unique IDs (`Trigger.oldMap.keySet()`). The set is then used as part of a query to create a list of job applications associated with the candidates being processed by the trigger. For every job application returned by the query, the related candidate is retrieved from `Trigger.oldMap` and prevented from being deleted.

```
trigger candidateTrigger on Candidate__c (before delete) {
    for (Job_Application__c jobApp : [SELECT Candidate__c
                                      FROM Job_Application__c
                                      WHERE Candidate__c
                                      IN :Trigger.oldMap.keySet()]) {

        Trigger.oldMap.get(jobApp.Candidate__c).addError(
                'Cannot delete candidate with a job application');

    }
}
```

Discussion

It's a better practice to use `Trigger.newMap` and `Trigger.oldMap` because you can't assume that directly querying the `Trigger.new` and `Trigger.old` lists will return the same number of records in the same order. Even though these lists are sorted by ID, external operations might change the number of records that are returned and make parallel list processing dangerous.

See Also

- *Bulk Processing Records in a Trigger* on page 61
- *Controlling Recursive Triggers* on page 62
- *Avoiding Apex Governor Limits* on page 70

Defining an Apex Web Service and Calling It from an S-Control

Problem

You want to use Apex in an s-control.

Solution

Use the `webService` keyword to designate an Apex method as a Web service. You can then use the AJAX Toolkit to call this method directly from any s-control that has access to the method's class.

For example, the following procedure shows how you can define a simple "Hello World" Web service and use it in an s-control that's displayed in a Web tab. This Web service also includes a simple test method that exercises the code:

1. Create the class and the Web service method:

   a. Click **Setup ➤ Build ➤ Code**, and then click **New**.

       Note: You can't make changes to Apex using the Salesforce user interface in a Salesforce production organization. See *Migrating Apex Between Two Salesforce Organizations* on page 39.

   b. Enter the following code in the `Body` text box:

```
global class HelloWorld2 {

    // The WebService keyword makes this a public
    // WebService method. WebService methods must
    // always be static, and must also be contained
    // in a global class.
    WebService static String sayHelloWorld(String arg)
    {
        return 'Hello ' + arg;
    }

    // The following is a simple unit test for the
    // sayHelloWorld method. Unit test methods take
    // no arguments, commit no data to the database,
    // and are flagged with the testMethod keyword
    // in the definition.
    static testMethod void testHelloWorld() {
        System.assertEquals('Hello to you!',
                sayHelloWorld('to you!'));
    }

}
```

"Defining an Apex Web Service and Calling It from an S-Control" contributed by Chris Fry, Senior Director of Platform Development for salesforce.com

  c. Click **Save**.

2. Create the s-control that calls this method:

  a. Click **Setup ➤ Build ➤ Custom S-Controls**, and then click **New Custom S-Control**.

  b. Specify the following values:

- `Label`: HelloWorld
- `S-Control Name`: HelloWorld
- `Type`: HTML

  c. Enter the following content in the body of the s-control:

```html
<html>
<head>
<script type="text/javascript"
src="/js/functions.js"></script>
<script src="/soap/ajax/10.0/connection.js"></script>
<script src="/soap/ajax/10.0/apex.js"></script>
<script>
function demo() {

    // The apex.execute() command in the AJAX Toolkit
    // allows the s-control to access the specified
    // Apex class and method.
    var result = sforce.apex.execute('HelloWorld2' ,
               'sayHelloWorld',
               {arg:"new Apex user!"});

    // The next block of code runs any testMethods
    // you've written for the HelloWorld2 class
    sforce.apex.debug=true;
    var request = new sforce.RunTestsRequest();
    request.allTests = false;
    request.classes = ['HelloWorld2'];
    var result_2= sforce.apex.runTests(request);

    // Alternatively you can uncomment this block to run

    // all of the testMethods you've written.
    //    sforce.apex.debug=true;
    //    var request = new sforce.RunTestsRequest();
    //    request.allTests = true;
    //    var result_2 = sforce.apex.runTests(request);

    // Now display the final result, including the test
    // results.
    document.getElementById('userNameArea').innerHTML =
           'Congratulations! ' + result +
           '<p>Tests Run = ' + result_2.numTestsRun +
           ';Test Failures = ' + result_2.numFailures +
           '</p>';
```

```
        // Or uncomment the following block to display the
        // entire debug log.
        //document.getElementById('userNameArea').innerHTML=

        //  'Congratulations! ' + result +
        //  '<p>Tests Run = ' + result_2.numTestsRun +
        //  '; Test Failures = ' + result_2.numFailures +
        //  '</p><p> Full print out = ' + result_2 + '</p>';
    }
    </script>
    </head>

    <body onload=demo()>
        <div id=userNameArea>
        </div>
    </body>
    </html>
```

    d. Click **Save**.

3. Create the Web tab that displays the s-control:

    a. Click **Setup ➤ Build ➤ Custom Tabs**, and click **New** in the Web Tabs related list.

    b. Select `2 columns with Salesforce sidebar`, and click **Next**.

    c. Specify the following values:

       • `Tab Type`: Custom S-Control

       • `Tab Label`: Hello World

    d. Next to `Tab Style` click 🔍 to choose a color and icon for the tab. Then click **Next**.

    e. From the `Custom S-Control` drop-down list, select HelloWorld, and then click **Next**.

    f. Accept the remaining defaults, and click **Save**.

4. Click the Hello World tab to view the results.

The s-control associated with the tab calls the Apex class `HelloWorld2`, then the method `sayHelloWorld`. For the argument, it passes in the string "new Apex user!"

The `HelloWorld2` class returns the string with the word "Hello" added to the beginning. The s-control then adds the word "Congratulations!" to the start of the string and displays it on the page.

Figure 4: The "Hello World" Tab

Discussion

Apex Web service methods can also be called by external applications. To generate the appropriate WSDL, click **Setup ➤ Build ➤ Code**, and click **WSDL** next to the name of the class with the Web service method.

See Also

- *Getting Started with Apex* on page 56
- *Creating a Button with Apex* on page 141
- *Avoiding Apex Governor Limits* on page 70

Avoiding Apex Governor Limits

Problem

You're writing Apex in a high-volume environment, and you want to avoid running into the execution governor limits.

Solution

Use the following strategies when writing Apex scripts:

- Make sure that database statements such as `insert()`, `update()`, and `delete()` operate in bulk
- Use `Limits.getDMLRows()` for error handling
- Limit queries by using static class variables to store query results
- Test bulk behavior

To illustrate these strategies, consider the following inefficient solution for updating contact records every time a related account record's shipping address changes. It's inefficient because it not only issues a SOQL query for every account record in `Trigger.new`, but also makes a call to `update()` for every contact record associated with those accounts:

```
trigger INEFFICIENTMassUpdateContactsOnAccountChange
                            on Account (after update) {
    for (Integer i = 0; i < Trigger.new.size(); i++) {
        if    ((Trigger.old[i].ShippingCity !=
                Trigger.new[i].ShippingCity)
        || (Trigger.old[i].ShippingCountry !=
                Trigger.new[i].ShippingCountry)
        || (Trigger.old[i].ShippingPostalCode !=
                Trigger.new[i].ShippingPostalCode)
        || (Trigger.old[i].ShippingState !=
                Trigger.new[i].ShippingState)
        || (Trigger.old[i].ShippingStreet !=
                Trigger.new[i].ShippingStreet))   {
        for (Contact c : [select id, accountId, MailingCity,
                            MailingCountry, MailingPostalCode,
                            MailingState, MailingStreet
                        from contact
                        where accountId =
                            :Trigger.new[i].Id]) {
        c.MailingCity = Trigger.new[i].ShippingCity;
        c.MailingCountry = Trigger.new[i].ShippingCountry;
        c.MailingPostalCode =
            Trigger.new[i].ShippingPostalCode;
        c.MailingState = Trigger.new[i].ShippingState;
        c.MailingStreet = Trigger.new[i].ShippingStreet;
        update c;
    }
    }
    }
}
```

This inefficient trigger runs into a "Too many DML statements" governor limit when editing an account with lots of contacts. To fix this, we can rewrite the trigger to operate over `Trigger.new` and populate a list of records to update. We start by identifying only those records with an address that has changed, and then place the records in a map of IDs to accounts. This map then can be used in the following ways:

- We can use `map.keySet()` to query the set of contacts to update.
- When we query the contacts, we can select for the Account ID to allow us to identify the new values for each individual contact field in constant time. Without the map, we'd either have to do a query for each account, or we'd have to iterate over `Trigger.new` to find the account that matches each contact—an $O(n^2)$ operation.

Once we generate a complete list of updated contacts, we only need one DML statement in the trigger:

```
trigger BETTERMassUpdateContactsOnAccount on Account (after update) {


    //The map allows us to keep track of the accounts
    //that actually have new addresses
    Map<Id, Account> accountsWithNewAddresses =
                                new Map<Id, Account>();


    //Trigger.new is an array of Accounts containing the updated
    //value. This loop iterates over the list, and adds any that
    //have new addresses to the accountsWithNewAddresses Map
    for (Integer i = 0; i < Trigger.new.size(); i++) {
        if (    (Trigger.old[i].ShippingCity !=
                    Trigger.new[i].ShippingCity)
            || (Trigger.old[i].ShippingCountry !=
                    Trigger.new[i].ShippingCountry)
            || (Trigger.old[i].ShippingPostalCode !=
                    Trigger.new[i].ShippingPostalCode)
            || (Trigger.old[i].ShippingState !=
                    Trigger.new[i].ShippingState)
            || (Trigger.old[i].ShippingStreet !=
                    Trigger.new[i].ShippingStreet))   {
            accountsWithNewAddresses.put(Trigger.old[i].id,
                                Trigger.new[i]);
        }
    }

 List<Contact> updatedContacts = new List<Contact>();

    //Here we can see two syntatic features of Apex:
    //  1) iterating over an embedded SOQL query
    //  2) binding an array directly to a SOQL query with 'in'
 for (Contact c : [select id, accountId, MailingCity,
                    MailingCountry, MailingPostalCode,
                    MailingState, MailingStreet
                from contact
                where accountId
                in :accountsWithNewAddresses.keySet()]) {
   Account parentAccount = accountsWithNewAddresses.get
                                (c.accountId);
   c.MailingCity = parentAccount.ShippingCity;
   c.MailingCountry = parentAccount.ShippingCountry;
   c.MailingPostalCode = parentAccount.ShippingPostalCode;
   c.MailingState = parentAccount.ShippingState;
   c.MailingStreet = parentAccount.ShippingStreet;

        //Rather than insert the contacts individually, add the
        //contacts to an array and bulk insert the array.
        //This makes the trigger run faster and allows us to
        //avoid hitting the governor limit on DML statements
    updatedContacts.add(c);
 }
```

```
  update updatedContacts;
}
```

This version of the trigger is better, but it still doesn't scale infinitely. The total number of records processed as a result of DML statements is restricted to 100 for a trigger. Consequently, any account with more than 100 contacts will cause this trigger to hit a governor limit.

With that in mind, it's a good idea to add some custom error handling so that the trigger can fail gracefully. In this case, we can provide the user with a helpful error message. By using `Limits.getDMLRows()` we can ensure that the trigger code can still take advantage of the higher limits that are available during Web service calls. For example:

```
if (updatedContacts.size() + Limits.getDMLRows()
                         > Limits.getLimitDMLRows()) {

    //If the user is attemting to edit multiple accounts at once,
    //instruct them to try again on a smaller set
    if ( Trigger.new.size() == 1) {

        //Note that it might make sense to simply not attempt
        //the update in this situation, rather than telling
        //the user she is out of luck.
        //Alternately you could add a checkbox to the account
        //to make updating the contacts optional.
        Trigger.new[0].addError('You are attempting to update
                the addresses of an account with too many
                contacts.');
    } else {
        for (Account a: Trigger.new) {
            a.addError('You are attempting to update the
                        addresses of too many accounts at
                        once. Please try again with fewer
                        accounts.');
        }
    }
}
```

But wait! There's one extra hurdle we have to deal with: we want to add the error messages during a `before` trigger to prevent records from being saved, but it's only possible to execute DML statements during an `after` trigger. Consequently, we need to split up the code into two triggers, and, to save our code from having to issue the contact query in both triggers, we can also define a helper class to store the results.

The following code defines the `before update` trigger:

```
trigger BESTMassUpdateContactsOnAccountBefore
                            on Account (before update) {

    //The map allows us to keep track of the accounts
    //that actually have new addresses
```

```
    Map<Id, Account> accountsWithNewAddresses =
                            new Map<Id, Account>();

    //Trigger.new is an array of accounts containing the updated
    //value. This loop iterates over the list, and adds any that
    //have new addresses to the accountsWithNewAddresses Map
    for (Integer i = 0; i < Trigger.new.size(); i++) {
        if (   (Trigger.old[i].ShippingCity !=
                    Trigger.new[i].ShippingCity)
            || (Trigger.old[i].ShippingCountry !=
                    Trigger.new[i].ShippingCountry)
            || (Trigger.old[i].ShippingPostalCode !=
                    Trigger.new[i].ShippingPostalCode)
            || (Trigger.old[i].ShippingState !=
                    Trigger.new[i].ShippingState)
            || (Trigger.old[i].ShippingStreet !=
                    Trigger.new[i].ShippingStreet))  {
            accountsWithNewAddresses.put(Trigger.old[i].id,
                                Trigger.new[i]);
        }
    }

List<Contact> updatedContacts = new List<Contact>();

    //Here we can see two syntatic features of Apex:
    //  1) iterating over an embedded SOQL query
    //  2) binding an array directly to a SOQL query with 'in'
for (Contact c : [select id, accountId, MailingCity,
                    MailingCountry, MailingPostalCode,
                    MailingState, MailingStreet
                from contact
                where accountId
                in :accountsWithNewAddresses.keySet()]) {
  Account parentAccount = accountsWithNewAddresses.get
                                        (c.accountId);
  c.MailingCity = parentAccount.ShippingCity;
  c.MailingCountry = parentAccount.ShippingCountry;
  c.MailingPostalCode = parentAccount.ShippingPostalCode;
  c.MailingState = parentAccount.ShippingState;
  c.MailingStreet = parentAccount.ShippingStreet;

    //Rather than insert the contacts individually, add the
    //contacts to an array and bulk insert the array.
    //This makes the trigger run faster and allows us to
    //avoid hitting the governor limit on DML statements
 updatedContacts.add(c);
}

    //We can proactively detect if we will hit a governor limit,
    // and react accordingly
    if (updatedContacts.size() + Limits.getDMLRows()
                        > Limits.getLimitDMLRows()) {

        //If the user is attemting to edit multiple accounts at
        //once, instruct them to try again on a smaller set
        if ( Trigger.new.size() == 1) {
```

```
                    //Note that it might make sense to simply not attempt
                    //the update in this situation, rather than telling
                    //the user she is out of luck.
                    //Alternately you could add a checkbox to the account
                    //to make updating the contacts optional.
                    Trigger.new[0].addError('You are attempting to '
                            + 'update the addresses of an account with '
                            + 'too many contacts.');
            } else {
                for (Account a: Trigger.new) {
                    a.addError('You are attempting to update the '
                            + 'addresses of too many accounts at '
                            + 'once. Please try again with fewer '
                            + 'accounts.');
                }
            }
        }

    MassUpdateContactsHelper.rememberContactsForUpdate
                                        (updatedContacts);
}
```

This code defines the helper class:

```
public class MassUpdateContactsHelper {

    //Static variables are local to the context of a Web request
    //or testMethod during a runTests call.
    //Therefore, we can set this static variable in the before
    //trigger when we validate, and insert the proporsed changes
    //during the after trigger
    private static List<Contact> contactsToRemember = null;

    public static void rememberContactsForUpdate
                                    (List<Contact> contacts) {
        contactsToRemember = contacts;
    }

    public static List<Contact> getContactsForUpdate() {
        return contactsToRemember;
    }
}
```

And this code defines the `after update` trigger:

```
//This trigger updates contacts whenever the shipping address
//on the account changes
trigger BESTMassUpdateContactsOnAccountAfter
                            on Account (after update) {
    List<Contact> contactsForUpdate =
            MassUpdateContactsHelper.getContactsForUpdate();
    update contactsForUpdate;
}
```

Finally, no Apex script is complete without test methods. When writing tests:

- Identify how many records on which your users need to operate. Remember that Apex runs during API calls as well. In addition, be particularly aware of how any nightly batch loading might affect your requirements.
- Add error handling at the limits your code can support
- Use `Test.startTest()` and `Test.stopTest()` to build a robust set of tests that push the limits identified previously.

By building these limits into your test suite, you'll ensure that:

- Your code performs as you expect.
- Performance doesn't degrade during future deployment.
- Your customers will be able to identify negative interactions with other applications at install-time, rather than after deployment.

 Note: In the following test code, we know with certainty that the application runs on accounts with up to 100 contacts, which is hard-coded into the test methods. The triggers themselves actually only require an average of 100 contacts per account. That is, if a user batch updates one account with 200 contacts and 20 accounts with one contact, the update will succeed.

```
public class UpdateContactOnAccountChangeTester {

    private static integer MAX_CONTACTS_PER_ACCOUNT = 100;


    static testMethod void accountUpdateSyncToContacts() {
        //Create an account
        Account theAthletics = new Account(name = 'Oakland A\'s',
                            ShippingCity = 'Oakland',
                            ShippingCountry = 'USA',
                            ShippingPostalCode = '94621',
                            ShippingState = 'CA',
                            ShippingStreet = '7000 Coliseum Way');
        insert theAthletics;

        //Insert a list of contacts, but do not set the
        //addresses yet
        Contact[] pitchers = new Contact[0];
        pitchers.add(new Contact(AccountId = theAthletics.id,
                            FirstName = 'Joe',
                            LastName = 'Blanton'));
        pitchers.add(new Contact(AccountId = theAthletics.id,
                            FirstName = 'Dallas',
                            LastName = 'Branden'));
        pitchers.add(new Contact(AccountId = theAthletics.id,
                            FirstName = 'Kiko',
                            LastName = 'Calero'));
        insert pitchers;
```

```
    //Updating the account fires the trigger to update the
    //addresses for all of the contacts
    theAthletics.shippingCity = 'Fremont';
    update theAthletics;

    Integer i = 0;

    //Now iterate over the pitchers and assert the address
    //fields are properly set
    for (Contact player : [select id, MailingCity, MailingCountry,

                                    MailingPostalCode, MailingState,

                                        MailingStreet
                            from Contact
                            where accountId = :theAthletics.id]) {

        System.assertEquals(theAthletics.ShippingCity,
                            player.MailingCity);
        System.assertEquals(theAthletics.ShippingCountry,
                            player.MailingCountry);
        System.assertEquals(theAthletics.ShippingPostalCode,
                            player.MailingPostalCode);
        System.assertEquals(theAthletics.ShippingState,
                            player.MailingState);
        System.assertEquals(theAthletics.ShippingStreet,
                            player.MailingStreet);
        i++;
    }

    //Ensure that the query returned the expected number of
    //contacts.
    System.assertEquals(pitchers.size(), i);
}


static testMethod void testAccountWithManyContacts() {
    Account a = createAccountWithNContacts(
                            MAX_CONTACTS_PER_ACCOUNT);
    a.shippingCity = 'Fremont';
    update a;
}


static testMethod void testBulkAccountEdit() {
    Account[] acctsToUpdate = new Account[0];
    for (Integer i = 0; i < 25; i++) {
        Account a = createAccountWithNContacts(10);
        a.shippingCity = 'Fremont';
        acctsToUpdate.add(a);
    }
    update acctsToUpdate;
}


static testMethod void testBulkAccountEditTooManyChildren() {
```

```
        Account[] acctsToUpdate = new Account[0];
        for (Integer i = 0; i < 2; i++) {
            Account a = createAccountWithNContacts(
                                MAX_CONTACTS_PER_ACCOUNT + 1);
            a.shippingCity = 'Fremont';
            acctsToUpdate.add(a);
        }

        boolean caughtException = false;
        Test.startTest();
        try {
            update acctsToUpdate;
        } catch(System.DmlException e) {
            System.assert(e.getMessage().contains('Please try' +
                                ' again with fewer accounts'));
            caughtException = true;
        }
        Test.stopTest();
        System.assert(caughtException);
    }

    static testMethod void testAccountWithTooManyContacts() {
        Account a = createAccountWithNContacts(
                            MAX_CONTACTS_PER_ACCONT + 1);
        a.shippingCity = 'Fremont';
        boolean caughtException = false;

        Test.startTest();
        try {
            update a;
        } catch(System.DmlException e) {
            System.assert(e.getMessage().contains('You are trying'
                        + ' to update the addresses of an account'
                        + ' with too many contacts.'));
            caughtException = true;
        }
        Test.stopTest();
        System.assert(caughtException);
    }

    //a utility method used for bulk testing
    static Account createAccountWithNContacts(Integer n) {
        Account theAs = new Account(name = 'Oakland A\'s',
                            shippingCity = 'Oakland',
                            ShippingCountry = 'USA',
                            ShippingPostalCode = '94621',
                            ShippingState = 'CA',
                            ShippingStreet = '7000 Coliseum Way');
        insert theAs;
        List<Contact> players = new List<Contact>();
        for (Integer i = 0; i < n; i++) {
            players.add(new Contact(AccountId = theAs.id,
                                FirstName = 'player',
                                LastName = 'number ' + i));
        }
        insert players;
```

```
        return theAs;
    }

}
```

Discussion

Apex execution governor limits enforce the statistics outlined in the following table. If a script ever exceeds a limit, the associated governor issues a runtime exception that cannot be handled.

Table 4: Apex Script Execution Limits

Limit	Trigger	Anonymous Block or WSDL Method	RunTests[1]
Total number of SOQL queries issued[2]	20	1,000	100
Total number of records retrieved through SOQL queries	1,000	10,000	100
Total number of DML statements issued (`insert`, `update`, `upsert`, `merge`, or `delete`)	20	100	20
Total number of records processed as a result of DML statements	100	10,000	100
Total number of executed script statements[3]	10,000[4]	10,000	10,000
Total heap size[3]	100,000 bytes	1,000,000 bytes	500,000 bytes
Total stack depth for any Apex invocation that does not result in additional triggers firing due to `insert`, `update`, or `delete` statements	100	100	100
Total stack depth for any Apex invocation that recursively fires triggers due to `insert`, `update`, or `delete` statements[5]	16	16	16
Total number of characters for a single String	32,000	32,000	32,000
For loop array batch size	n/a	200	n/a
Total number of elements in a single List, Set, or Map[3]	1,000	1,000	1,000

[1]RunTests limits apply individually to each `testMethod`.

[2]In a SOQL query with parent-child relationship sub-queries, each parent-child relationship counts as an additional query. These types of queries have a limit of three times the number for top-level queries. The record counts from these relationship queries contribute to the record counts of the overall script execution.

[3]These limits scale with trigger batch size as follows:

- For 1-40 records, the normal limits apply.
- For 41-80 records, two times the normal limits apply.
- For 81-120 records, three times the normal limits apply.
- For 121-160 records, four times the normal limits apply.
- For 161 or more records, five times the normal limits apply.

[4]Trigger context is 10,000 statements plus 200 times the number of records in the top level call. For example, a DML statement that processes 200 records is subject to a limit of 10,000 + 200*200, which equals 50,000 statements. For a Web Service call, the limit is 200,000 statements.

[5]Recursive Apex that does not fire any triggers with `insert`, `update`, or `delete` statements exists in a single invocation, with a single stack. Conversely, recursive Apex that fires a trigger spawns the trigger in a new Apex invocation, separate from the invocation of the code that caused it to fire. Because spawning a new invocation of Apex is a more expensive operation than a recursive call in a single invocation, there are tighter restrictions on the stack depth of these types of recursive calls.

See Also

- *Getting Started with Apex* on page 56
- *Writing Unit Tests for Apex* on page 80

Writing Unit Tests for Apex

Problem

You want to write unit tests that verify your Apex code works properly during development and from release to release.

Solution

Use the `testMethod` keyword to flag a unit test method in an Apex class. For example:

```
public class myClass {
    static testMethod void myTest() {
```

```
        // Unit test code here
    }
}
```

Discussion

Apex test methods are class methods that verify whether a particular piece of code is working properly. Test methods take no arguments and commit no data to the database if they're executed by the `runTests()` API call (either via the command line or in an Apex IDE, such as Eclipse with the Eclipse Toolkit). After each test method executes, all changes to the database are automatically rolled back, so two test methods in the same class do not affect one another.

Test methods are used both by developers for debugging purposes and also by salesforce.com for testing before upgrades to new versions of the platform or Apex.

 Important: You must define test methods for any Apex script that you wish to upload as a managed package on the AppExchange.

Good test methods should do the following:

- Cover as many lines of code as possible, and, in the case of conditional logic (including ternary operators), execute each branch of code logic

   Tip: If you want to deploy your Apex scripts to a production organization, make sure you reach at least 75% code coverage and have at least some coverage for every trigger.

- Make calls to methods with both valid and invalid inputs
- Complete successfully without throwing any exceptions, unless those errors are expected and caught in a `try...catch` block
- Liberally make use of `System.assert()` methods to prove that code behaves properly
- Cause all relevant triggers to execute, preferably in bulk

For example, the following class includes tests for the lead deduplication trigger described in *Preventing Duplicate Records from Saving* on page 118:

```
public class leadDupePreventerTests{
  static testMethod void testLeadDupPreventer() {

      // First make sure there are no leads already in the system
      // that have the email addresses used for testing
      Set<String> testEmailAddress = new Set<String>();
      testEmailAddress.add('test1@duptest.com');
      testEmailAddress.add('test2@duptest.com');
      testEmailAddress.add('test3@duptest.com');
      testEmailAddress.add('test4@duptest.com');
      testEmailAddress.add('test5@duptest.com');
```

```
System.assert([SELECT count() FROM Lead
                WHERE Email IN :testEmailAddress] == 0);

// Seed the database with some leads, and make sure they can
// be bulk inserted successfully.
Lead lead1 = new Lead(LastName='Test1', Company='Test1 Inc.',
                       Email='test1@duptest.com');
Lead lead2 = new Lead(LastName='Test2', Company='Test2 Inc.',
                       Email='test4@duptest.com');
Lead lead3 = new Lead(LastName='Test3', Company='Test3 Inc.',
                       Email='test5@duptest.com');
Lead[] leads = new Lead[] {lead1, lead2, lead3};
insert leads;

// Now make sure that some of these leads can be changed and
// then bulk updated successfully. Note that lead1 is not
// being changed, but is still being passed to the update
// call. This should be OK.
lead2.Email = 'test2@duptest.com';
lead3.Email = 'test3@duptest.com';
update leads;

// Make sure that single row lead duplication prevention works
// on insert.
Lead dup1 = new Lead(LastName='Test1Dup',
                      Company='Test1Dup Inc.',
                      Email='test1@duptest.com');
try {
   insert dup1;
   System.assert(false);
} catch (System.DmlException e) {
   System.assert(e.getNumDml() == 1);
   System.assert(e.getDmlIndex(0) == 0);
   System.assert(e.getDmlFields(0).size() == 1);
   System.assert(e.getDmlFields(0)[0] == 'Email');
   System.assert(e.getDmlMessage(0).indexOf(
      'A lead with this email address already exists.') > -1);
}

// Make sure that single row lead duplication prevention works
// on update.
dup1 = new Lead(Id = lead1.Id, LastName='Test1Dup',
                 Company='Test1Dup Inc.',
                 Email='test2@duptest.com');
try {
   update dup1;
   System.assert(false);
} catch (System.DmlException e) {
   System.assert(e.getNumDml() == 1);
   System.assert(e.getDmlIndex(0) == 0);
   System.assert(e.getDmlFields(0).size() == 1);
   System.assert(e.getDmlFields(0)[0] == 'Email');
   System.assert(e.getDmlMessage(0).indexOf(
      'A lead with this email address already exists.') > -1);
}
```

```
// Make sure that bulk lead duplication prevention works on
// insert. Note that the first item being inserted is fine,
// but the second and third items are duplicates. Note also
// that since at least one record insert fails, the entire
// transaction will be rolled back.
dup1 = new Lead(LastName='Test1Dup', Company='Test1Dup Inc.',
                Email='test4@duptest.com');
Lead dup2 = new Lead(LastName='Test2Dup',
                     Company='Test2Dup Inc.',
                     Email='test2@duptest.com');
Lead dup3 = new Lead(LastName='Test3Dup',
                     Company='Test3Dup Inc.',
                     Email='test3@duptest.com');
Lead[] dups = new Lead[] {dup1, dup2, dup3};
try {
   insert dups;
   System.assert(false);
} catch (System.DmlException e) {
   System.assert(e.getNumDml() == 2);
   System.assert(e.getDmlIndex(0) == 1);
   System.assert(e.getDmlFields(0).size() == 1);
   System.assert(e.getDmlFields(0)[0] == 'Email');
   System.assert(e.getDmlMessage(0).indexOf(
      'A lead with this email address already exists.') > -1);
   System.assert(e.getDmlIndex(1) == 2);
   System.assert(e.getDmlFields(1).size() == 1);
   System.assert(e.getDmlFields(1)[0] == 'Email');
   System.assert(e.getDmlMessage(1).indexOf(
      'A lead with this email address already exists.') > -1);
}

// Make sure that bulk lead duplication prevention works on
// update. Note that the first item being updated is fine,
// because the email address is new, and the second item is
// also fine, but in this case it's because the email
// address doesn't change. The third case is flagged as an
// error because it is a duplicate of the email address of the
// first lead's value in the database, even though that value
// is changing in this same update call. It would be an
// interesting exercise to rewrite the trigger to allow this
// case. Note also that since at least one record update
// fails, the entire transaction will be rolled back.
dup1 = new Lead(Id=lead1.Id, Email='test4@duptest.com');
dup2 = new Lead(Id=lead2.Id, Email='test2@duptest.com');
dup3 = new Lead(Id=lead3.Id, Email='test1@duptest.com');
dups = new Lead[] {dup1, dup2, dup3};
try {
   update dups;
   System.assert(false);
} catch (System.DmlException e) {
   System.debug(e.getNumDml());
   System.debug(e.getDmlMessage(0));
   System.assert(e.getNumDml() == 1);
   System.assert(e.getDmlIndex(0) == 2);
   System.assert(e.getDmlFields(0).size() == 1);
   System.assert(e.getDmlFields(0)[0] == 'Email');
```

```
      System.assert(e.getDmlMessage(0).indexOf(
         'A lead with this email address already exists.') > -1);
}

// Make sure that duplicates in the submission are caught when
// inserting leads. Note that this test also catches an
// attempt to insert a lead where there is an existing
// duplicate.
dup1 = new Lead(LastName='Test1Dup', Company='Test1Dup Inc.',
                Email='test4@duptest.com');
dup2 = new Lead(LastName='Test2Dup', Company='Test2Dup Inc.',
                Email='test4@duptest.com');
dup3 = new Lead(LastName='Test3Dup', Company='Test3Dup Inc.',
                Email='test3@duptest.com');
dups = new Lead[] {dup1, dup2, dup3};
try {
   insert dups;
   System.assert(false);
} catch (System.DmlException e) {
   System.assert(e.getNumDml() == 2);
   System.assert(e.getDmlIndex(0) == 1);
   System.assert(e.getDmlFields(0).size() == 1);
   System.assert(e.getDmlFields(0)[0] == 'Email');
   System.assert(e.getDmlMessage(0).indexOf(
      'Another new lead has the same email address.') > -1);
   System.assert(e.getDmlIndex(1) == 2);
   System.assert(e.getDmlFields(1).size() == 1);
   System.assert(e.getDmlFields(1)[0] == 'Email');
   System.assert(e.getDmlMessage(1).indexOf(
      'A lead with this email address already exists.') > -1);
}

// Make sure that duplicates in the submission are caught when
// updating leads. Note that this test also catches an attempt
// to update a lead where there is an existing duplicate.
dup1 = new Lead(Id=lead1.Id, Email='test4@duptest.com');
dup2 = new Lead(Id=lead2.Id, Email='test4@duptest.com');
dup3 = new Lead(Id=lead3.Id, Email='test2@duptest.com');
dups = new Lead[] {dup1, dup2, dup3};
try {
   update dups;
   System.assert(false);
} catch (System.DmlException e) {
   System.assert(e.getNumDml() == 2);
   System.assert(e.getDmlIndex(0) == 1);
   System.assert(e.getDmlFields(0).size() == 1);
   System.assert(e.getDmlFields(0)[0] == 'Email');
   System.assert(e.getDmlMessage(0).indexOf(
      'Another new lead has the same email address.') > -1);
   System.assert(e.getDmlIndex(1) == 2);
   System.assert(e.getDmlFields(1).size() == 1);
   System.assert(e.getDmlFields(1)[0] == 'Email');
   System.assert(e.getDmlMessage(1).indexOf(
      'A lead with this email address already exists.') > -1);
}
```

```
    }
}
```

See Also

- *Determining Apex Test Coverage* on page 85
- *Avoiding Apex Governor Limits* on page 70
- *Debugging Apex in Salesforce* on page 229
- *Debugging Apex in Eclipse* on page 229

Determining Apex Test Coverage

Problem

You want to determine how much test coverage you have for a particular Apex class or trigger.

Solution

Examine the results of the `runTests()` system method. In Eclipse you can do this by:

1. Opening the project for the organization that contains your Apex scripts.
2. Opening the Apex class file that contains the test methods you want to execute.
3. Right-clicking anywhere in the file and selecting **Force.com ➤ Run Tests**.

This action opens the Run Test Results work area, showing the test coverage for the class in question. The lines of code that aren't tested are listed for each class and trigger in the organization, along with the percentage of total coverage.

For example, if you ran the test in the following simple Apex class:

```
/*
 * Sample test coverage
 */
public class util{
    private Account a;
    void testingCoverage(String foo) { foo = 'bar'; }

    static testMethod void tryTest () {
        System.debug('a');
        testingCoverage('sample');
        // Uncomment the line below for 100% coverage:
        // a = null;
    }
}
```

The Run Test Results area displays the following result:

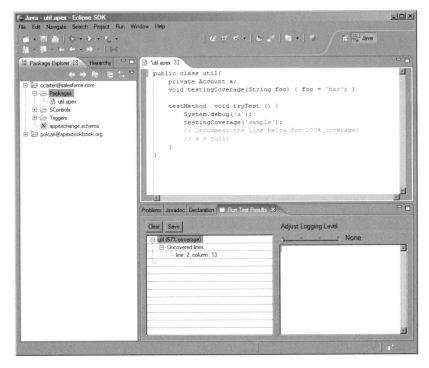

Figure 5: The Run Test Results Area in Eclipse

Because there's no coverage for the variable `private Account a;` (which should be assigned to an Account object or the value null), there's less than 100% coverage. If you uncomment the line `a = null;`, the Run Test Results area reports 100% coverage.

Discussion

While 100% code coverage is difficult to achieve in large code bases, the peace of mind that comes with improving your test coverage is well worth the time invested. Indeed, test methods are a requirement for uploading any Apex scripts to the AppExchange as part of a managed package.

See Also

- *Writing Unit Tests for Apex* on page 80
- *Installing the Force.com Toolkit for Eclipse* on page 15
- *Debugging Apex in Salesforce* on page 229
- *Debugging Apex in Eclipse* on page 229

Writing Object-Oriented Apex

Problem

You prefer to write code using an object-oriented programming paradigm, but while Apex supports classes, it doesn't yet support extending them.

Solution

Contact your salesforce.com representative to request participation in beta tests for future Apex enhancements.

Discussion

Apex is the world's first on-demand, multitenant programming language, and as such, salesforce.com rigorously tests new functionality before releasing it to ensure that it won't adversely impact existing Salesforce users and applications. Salesforce.com is currently evaluating and testing object-oriented functionality for Apex.

The following sample code shows a preview of functionality that is currently available as a beta release for select partners. It shows how Apex classes can be extended, as well as examples of interfaces, overridden methods, and use of the `virtual` and `abstract` keywords.

The code implements a simple service-level agreement module where companies are serviced differently based on whether they're categorized as Bronze or Gold accounts.

 Important: As of September 2007, the following Apex is not currently valid, nor may it ever be valid. It is provided merely as an illustration of how Apex might be enhanced in the future.

```
public class Sla {

    //
    // Sla Constructor
    // We make this constructor private to ensure that no one can
    // create this outer class externally. It's not necessary
    // because the class consists only of static methods and
    // variables.
    //
    // Note that in Apex, the "private" keyword is not actually
    // necessary because all declarations are private by default.
    //
    private Sla() {}

    //
```

"Writing Object-Oriented Apex" contributed by Craig Weissman, Chief Software Architect for salesforce.com and the creator of Apex

```
// These class-level variables enumerate the two available service
// levels. By declaring them as public static final, they're
// essentially constant values.
//
public static final Integer GOLD = 1;
public static final Integer BRONZE = 0;


//
// This static method returns the appropriate Service Provider
// based on business rules.
//
public static ServiceProvider getProvider(Account a) {
  if (a.isGold__c) {
    return new GoldServiceProvider(a);
  } else {
    return new BronzeServiceProvider(a);
  }
}


//
// This interface encapsulates the general idea of a service
// provider. Outside the Sla class only this type is exposed,
// along with the methods that can be called. The code that
// implements each method is hidden in the other classes
// below.
//
public interface ServiceProvider {

  // Escalate an issue
  void escalate();

  // Return the level of this provider
  Integer getLevel();
}


//
// The abstract keyword means that this is an internal
// implementation of the ServiceProvider interface, but that
// it must be extended by other classes.
//
abstract class BaseServiceProvider implements ServiceProvider {

  //
  // This class variable stores the account id
  //
  protected final Id accountId;

  BaseServiceProvider(Id accountId) {
    this.accountId = accountId;
  }

  //
  // This declaration adds a method for notifying the site that
```

```
  // something is wrong.
  // Because it's abstract, the method must be implemented by
  // each sub-class that extends BaseServiceProvider.
  //
  abstract void notifySite();

  //
  // This method defines a default implementation of the escalate
  // method -- it creates a task.
  // Because it's virtual, it can be overridden by each sub-class
  // of BaseServiceProvider, but it doesn't have to be.
  //
  public virtual void escalate() {
    insert new Task(whatId = accountId,
                subject = 'Normal Escalation');
  }
}


//
// This class extends BaseServiceProvider to define the Bronze
// Service Provider level. Because the class doesn't implement
// escalate(), it's using the default version that was defined
// in BaseServiceProvider.
//
class BronzeServiceProvider extends BaseServiceProvider {

  //
  // To construct a BronzeServiceProvider, pass in the account
  // id to the default constructor in BaseServiceProvider
  // (accessible by making a call to 'super()')
  //
  BronzeServiceProvider(Account a) {
    super(a.id);
  }

  //
  // We don't notify the sites for Bronze providers, so we
  // leave the implementation empty.
  //
  override void notifySite() {}

  public Integer getLevel() {
    return BRONZE;
  }
}


//
// This class extends BaseServiceProvider to define the Gold
// Service Provider level.
//
class GoldServiceProvider extends BaseServiceProvider {

  //
  // This private variable is set during initialization, and then
```

```
    // can't be changed.
    //
    private final Double minutesUntilEscalation;

    //
    // To construct a GoldServiceProvider, pass in the account
    // id to the default constructor in BaseServiceProvider
    // (accessible by making a call to 'super()' as the first
    // line of the method). This method also sets the
    // minutesUntilEscalation parameter.
    //
    GoldServiceProvider(Account a) {
      super(a.id);
      this.minutesUntilEscalation = a.minutesUntilEscalation__c;
    }

    //
    // In this future, this method could notify the account site
    // that something is wrong, for example. In the meanwhile, it's
    // left blank.
    //
    override void notifySite() {
      // To be implemented...
    }

    public Integer getLevel() {
      return GOLD;
    }

    //
    // Override the escalate() method to add a row to a queue table.
    // It can then be polled for sending emails when the
    // minutesUntilEscalation time expires.
    // Notice the use of 'this.accountId' to access the protected
    // variable in the BaseServiceProvider parent class.
    //
    public override void escalate() {
      insert new MyQueue__c(
                    account__c = this.accountId,
        minutesUntilEscalation__c = this.minutesUntilEscalation);
    }
}


//
// This test method exercises the entire module. No Apex
// class is complete without a testMethod.
//
static testMethod void testAll() {

    //
    // Create different types of accounts
    //
    Account a1 = new Account(name = 'gold', isGold__c = true,
                             minutesUntilEscalation__c = 5);
    Account a2 = new Account(name = 'bronze', isGold__c = false);
```

```
        insert new Account[]{a1, a2};

        //
        // Test the Gold Service Provider
        //
        ServiceProvider sp = getProvider(a1);
        System.assertEquals(GOLD, sp.getLevel());
        sp.escalate();
        System.assertEquals(1, [select count() from MyQueue__c
                                where account__c = :a1.id]);

        //
        // Test the Bronze Service Provider
        //
        sp = getProvider(a2);
        System.assertEquals(BRONZE, sp.getLevel());
        sp.escalate();
        System.assertEquals(1, [select count() from Task
                                where WhatId = :a2.id]);
    }
}
```

See Also

- *Getting Started with Apex* on page 56
- *Choosing Between Classes or Triggers* on page 59
- *Writing Unit Tests for Apex* on page 80

Chapter 5

Searching and Querying Data

Truly useful, on-demand business apps include business logic and processes that help companies run their businesses efficiently. As we've mentioned, the Force.com platform gives you the power to write code and develop components to incorporate business logic, such as data validation, into your app. Pretty much any business process you write for your app will require your code to search, query, and examine sets of records upon which the business process will operate. So what's the best way to do that?

In this chapter, you'll learn how to examine your app's objects, relationships, and fields in a graphical way. You'll also learn the difference between SOQL and SOSL and how to use them to construct queries that examine sets of records in your app. Then you'll see how to use SOQL to query related objects using their relationship associations and how to filter your queries by a relative date or the division of a record. These examples and best practices are a great way to get started developing your own queries to manipulate the data in ways that are unique to your app.

Using the Force.com Explorer to Examine Your Data Model

Problem

You want to browse through the fields, attributes, and relationships of every object in your Salesforce organization, and you're on a Windows platform.

Solution

Use the Force.com Explorer, an open-source C#.Net client application available on the Apex Developer Network (see *Installing the Force.com Explorer (for Windows)* on page 19).

After installing the Force.com Explorer, open the application and log in by clicking the **Login** button and entering your standard Salesforce username and password. At this point the Force.com Explorer issues a `describeGlobal()` call to the API to populate the interactive list of objects in the right sidebar.

 Tip: The permissions associated with your login affect the visibility of objects and fields in the Force.com Explorer. Be sure that your login has access to the data you need to explore—a user with the "Modify All Data" permission typically works best.

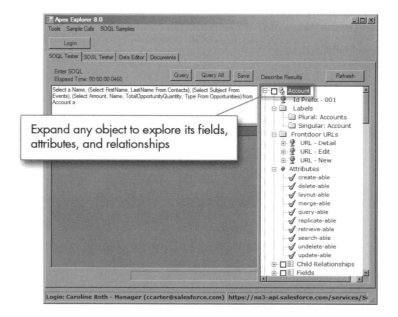

Figure 6: The Force.com Explorer

Once you've logged in, you can expand any object to explore its fields, attributes, and relationships. For example, the following information is available if you expand the Account object:

Id Prefix

The first three characters of the Salesforce ID for records of this object type. For example, the ID of any account record always starts with `001`. Likewise, contact records always start with `003`.

Labels

The labels that are used to display this object in both singular and plural form.

Frontdoor URLs

The URLs that can be used to reach detail, edit, and list pages for the object in a Web browser. See *Redirecting a User to an Edit, Detail, or List Page* on page 139.

Attributes

A list of actions that you can perform on the object. See www.salesforce.com/us/developer/docs/api/index_CSH.htm# sforce_api_calls_describesobjects_describesobjectresult.htm

Child Relationships

The relationships that have been defined on other objects that reference this object as the "one" side of a one-to-many relationship. For example, if you expand the Child Relationships node under the Account object, contacts, opportunities, and tasks are included in this list.

 Note: Relationships that are defined on this object so that it represents the "many" side of a one-to-many relationship (for example, the Parent Account relationship on the Account object) are included in the list of fields.

Fields

The fields that are available on this object. These, too, have associated attributes, relationships, a label, and a field type that you can expand for more information. For example, if you expand the Account object's `CreatedById` field:

- **Attributes** indicate what actions can be performed on the field. For example, `CreatedById` can't be created, updated, or set to null because it is `defaulted on create`. However, it can be used in SOQL query filters and to sort a list of records.
- **CreatedBy** represents the name of the relationship that's used to access the user record to which `CreatedById` refers. For example, you can use `CreatedBy.<fieldName>` to select User data in SOQL queries.
- **label** specifies the label that's used to display the field in Salesforce.
- **Type** indicates the type of field, including its length, number of digits, and precision. For this example, `CreatedById` is a reference field because it represents a lookup relationship to the User object.

Note: Standard objects are listed by their standard names, even if you've renamed them.

Discussion

If you want to connect to a different instance of Salesforce, such as your sandbox or a pre-release instance, click **Tools ➤ Options**, and set the domain name of the `Endpoint` to the appropriate server. For example, if you wanted to point to a sandbox organization, change:

```
https://www.salesforce.com/services/Soap/u/10.0
```

To:

```
https://test.salesforce.com/services/Soap/u/10.0
```

You can also use the `Endpoint` parameter to change to a different version of the API. For example, to have the Force.com Explorer use Version 10 of the API, change your `Endpoint` to:

```
https://www.salesforce.com/services/Soap/u/10.0
```

See Also

- *Installing the Force.com Explorer (for Windows)* on page 19
- *Constructing SOQL and SOSL Queries in the Force.com Explorer* on page 100
- *Redirecting a User to an Edit, Detail, or List Page* on page 139

Using SoqlXplorer to Examine Your Data Model

Problem

You want to browse through the fields, attributes, and relationships of every object in your Salesforce organization, and you're on the Mac OS X platform.

Solution

Use SoqlXplorer, a free client application available from Simon Fell's PocketSOAP website (see *Installing SoqlXplorer (for Mac OS X)* on page 20).

After installing SoqlXplorer, open the application and log in by entering your standard Salesforce username and password and specifying the server to which you want to connect. Choose www.salesforce.com to connect to the normal production servers, or test.salesforce.com to connect to a sandbox organization.

After you click **Login**, SoqlXplorer issues a `describeGlobal()` call to the API to populate the interactive list of objects in the right sidebar.

 Tip: The permissions associated with your login affect the visibility of objects and fields in the Force.com Explorer. Be sure that your login has access to the data you need to explore—a user with the "Modify All Data" permission typically works best.

You can expand any object to explore its fields and relationships. To view attributes for an object, toggle the **Details** button to On in the bottom right corner of the window. If you select an object field, the **Details** popup shows properties for the field instead.

 Note: Standard objects are listed by their standard names, even if you've renamed them.

Figure 7: Viewing Object Attributes in SoqlXplorer

Two views are available in the main window: SOQL and Schema.

- Use **SOQL** view to open a SOQL query editor where you can construct and execute SOQL queries. The queries you write use syntax-highlighting to improve legibility, and you can double-click an object's name to automatically build a query that selects all available fields. You can also double-click any result data to copy and paste it elsewhere.

- Use **Schema** view to open an interactive entity relationship diagram (ERD) of the objects in your organization. Select any object in the right sidebar to view that object's parent relationships (in blue) and child relationships (in orange). You can expand the fields of any object by clicking the + toggle button in the upper right corner of any object, and you can double-click an object to move it to the center of the view.

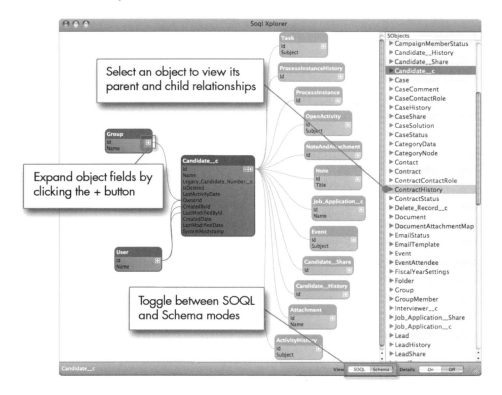

Figure 8: Schema View in SoqlXplorer

 Tip: Simon Fell frequently adds new functionality to SoqlXplorer. To automatically check for updates, click **SoqlXplorer ➤ Preferences** and select `Check for updates at startup`.

See Also

- *Installing SoqlXplorer (for Mac OS X)* on page 20
- *Constructing SOQL and SOSL Queries in the Force.com Explorer* on page 100

Choosing Between SOQL and SOSL

Problem

You know that the platform supports Salesforce Object Query Language (SOQL) and Salesforce Object Search Language (SOSL), but you don't know what the difference is between the two, or when to use one over the other.

Solution

A SOQL query is the equivalent of a SELECT clause in a SQL statement. Use SOQL with a call to `query()` when:

- You know in which objects or fields the data resides
- You want to retrieve data from a single object or from multiple objects that are related to one another
- You want to count the number of records that meet particular criteria
- You want to sort your results as part of the query
- You want to retrieve data from number, date, or checkbox fields

A SOSL query is a programmatic way of performing a text-based search. Use SOSL with a call to `search()` when:

- You don't know in which object or field the data resides and you want to find it in the most efficient way possible
- You want to retrieve multiple objects and fields efficiently, and the objects may or may not be related to one another
- You want to retrieve data for a particular division in an organization with Divisions, and you want to find it in the most efficient way possible

 Tip: Although SOQL was previously the only one of the two query languages that allowed condition-based filtering with WHERE clauses, as of the Summer '07 release SOSL supports this functionality as well.

See Also

- *Constructing SOQL and SOSL Queries in the Force.com Explorer* on page 100
- *Finding Data Based on Division* on page 111
- "Sforce Object Query Language (SOQL)" at www.salesforce.com/us/developer/docs/api/index_CSH.htm#sforce_api_calls_soql.htm
- "Sforce Object Search Language (SOSL)" at www.salesforce.com/us/developer/docs/api/index_CSH.htm#sforce_api_calls_sosl.htm

Constructing SOQL and SOSL Queries in the Force.com Explorer

Problem

You want to construct a SOQL or SOSL query, but you don't want to type all the object and field names by hand.

Solution

Use the Force.com Explorer to build and test SOQL and SOSL queries with point-and-click functionality. Building SOQL and SOSL queries in the Force.com Explorer saves you time if you're learning SOQL and SOSL syntax, or if you're looking for an easy way to test queries before implementing them in an s-control or integration.

 Note: This recipe describes how to create SOQL and SOSL queries in the Force.com Explorer, but other metadata explorer tools such as SoqlXplorer for Mac OS X, or the SOQL Explorer in the Force.com Toolkit for Eclipse work in a similar manner.

After logging in to the Force.com Explorer, the Describe Results pane displays an interactive list of selectable fields for each object in your Salesforce organization. Selecting one or more fields from this pane automatically creates a SOQL query in the SOQL Tester pane on the left.

For example, the following screenshot shows a SOQL query that was automatically generated after selecting the `MailingCity` and `MailingState` fields of the Contact object.

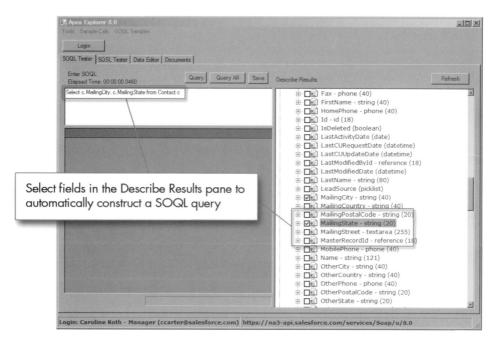

Figure 9: Constructing SOQL Queries in the Force.com Explorer

- If you want to include a field from a related object in a query, expand the `Child Relationships` element under the parent object, expand the child object you want to query, and then expand its `Child Fields`. You can add a child field to your query just by selecting its checkbox.
- If you want to filter the results by any additional values, enter the `WHERE` clause for the SOQL query by hand.

Once the query is constructed, click **Query** to execute it against the database. Results appear in the lower pane.

If you want to save the query for future use, click **Save** and enter a label. Saved queries are stored in **SOQL Samples ➤ Saved Queries**.

The Force.com Explorer also allows you to construct SOSL queries in the same way:

1. In the SOSL Tester tab enter a `Search Query` according to the same rules that you use for entering queries in the search text box in the Salesforce user interface. For example, *acme**, or *jerry g.*
2. In the `Search Group` drop-down list, specify whether you want to search all possible fields or restrict your search to just name, email, or phone fields.

3. Optionally, specify the objects and fields that you want returned by your SOSL query in the `Return Field Spec` text area. For example:

```
Lead(Name, Phone ORDER BY Name DESC), Contact(Name, Phone WHERE
    createddate = THIS_FISCAL_QUARTER)
```

4. Click **Send Request**.

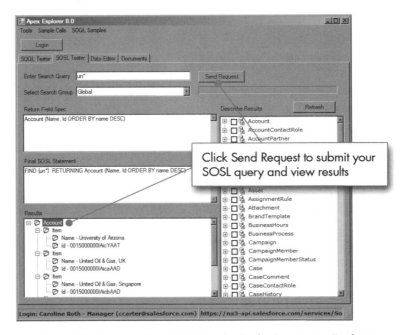

Figure 10: Constructing SOSL Queries in the Force.com Explorer

See Also

- *Installing the Force.com Explorer (for Windows)* on page 19
- *Using the Force.com Explorer to Examine Your Data Model* on page 94
- *Installing SoqlXplorer (for Mac OS X)* on page 20
- *Using SoqlXplorer to Examine Your Data Model* on page 96
- *Choosing Between SOQL and SOSL* on page 99
- "Sforce Object Query Language (SOQL)" at www.salesforce.com/us/developer/docs/api/index_CSH.htm#sforce_api_calls_soql.htm
- "Sforce Object Search Language (SOSL)" at www.salesforce.com/us/developer/docs/api/index_CSH.htm#sforce_api_calls_sosl.htm

Traversing Object Relationships through the API

Problem

You want to use as few SOQL queries as possible to access data from multiple related objects.

Solution

Use SOQL relationship syntax to pull data from related records in a single query.

For each of the following examples, the child object is the object on which the relationship field (the foreign key) is defined, and the parent is the object that the child references:

Basic Child-to-Parent (Foreign Key) Traversal

To traverse a relationship from a child to a parent, use standard dot notation off the name of the relationship. For example, this SOQL query retrieves information about contacts from the Contact object, along with the name of each contact's related account (the parent object):

```
SELECT Id, LastName, FirstName, Account.Name
FROM Contact
```

`Account` is the name of the relationship that's defined by the `AccountId` lookup field on the Contact object. Using dot notation, this SOQL query retrieves the `Name` field on the account that is related through the `Account` relationship.

Expanded Child-to-Parent (Foreign Key) Traversal

Child-to-parent traversals can extend up to five levels from the original root object. For example, the last selected field in this SOQL statement extends two levels from the root contact record by retrieving the name of the parent account on the account associated with the contact:

```
SELECT Id, LastName, FirstName, Account.Name,
    Account.Parent.Name
FROM Contact
```

Basic Parent-to-Child (Aggregate) Traversal

To traverse a relationship from a parent to a set of children, use a nested query. For example, this SOQL query retrieves opportunities and the opportunity products associated with each opportunity:

```
SELECT Id, Name, Amount,
    (SELECT Quantity, UnitPrice, TotalPrice
     FROM OpportunityLineItems)
FROM Opportunity
```

Using the nested query, we're specifying that for each opportunity we want the respective set of OpportunityLineItem records that are related through the OpportunityLineItems child relationship.

Combined Child-to-Parent and Parent-to-Child Traversal

Foreign key and aggregate traversals can also be combined in a single query. For example:

```
SELECT Id, Name, Account.Name,
       (SELECT Quantity, UnitPrice, TotalPrice,
               PricebookEntry.Name,
               PricebookEntry.Product2.Family
        FROM OpportunityLineItems)
FROM Opportunity
```

See Also

- *Constructing SOQL and SOSL Queries in the Force.com Explorer* on page 100
- "Relationship Queries" at www.salesforce.com/us/developer/docs/api/ index_CSH.htm#sforce_api_calls_soql_relationships.htm
- "Sforce Object Query Language (SOQL)" at www.salesforce.com/us/developer/ docs/api/index_CSH.htm#sforce_api_calls_soql.htm

Finding a Contact, Lead, or Person Account

Problem

You want to write a query to find a person, but you don't know whether this person is stored as a lead, as a contact, or as a person account.

Solution

Perform the search with one SOSL query, rather than multiple SOQL queries. For example:

- To look for *Joe* in all searchable text fields in the system, and return the IDs of the records where *Joe* is found in a case-insensitive search:

```
FIND {Joe}
```

- To look for all email fields that start with *jo* or end in *acme.com*, and return the IDs of the records where those fields are found:

```
FIND {"jo*" OR "*acme.com"}
IN EMAIL FIELDS
```

Tip: If you know you're looking for a name, an email address, or a phone number, it's more efficient to narrow your search scope to only name fields, email fields, or phone fields, respectively, rather than searching every field.

- To look for the name *Joe Smith* or *Joe Smythe* in the name field on a lead or contact only, and return the name and phone number of any matching record that was also created in the current fiscal quarter:

```
FIND {"Joe Smith" OR "Joe Smythe"}
IN NAME FIELDS
RETURNING
    lead(name, phone WHERE createddate = THIS_FISCAL_QUARTER),
    contact(name, phone WHERE createddate = THIS_FISCAL_QUARTER)
```

If you want to search for records based on a query string that was entered by a user, first escape any special characters that were entered by the user, and then construct the appropriate SOSL string. For example, the following s-control searches leads, contacts, and accounts for any instance of a record named "Phil Degauss":

```
<html>
<head>
<script src="/soap/ajax/10.0/connection.js"></script>
<script type="text/javascript">
function init() {
    var who = "phil degauss";

    // These special characters must be preceded by a backslash
    // before they can be used in a SOSL query.
    who = who.replace(/([\&\|\!\(\)\{\}\[\]\^~\:\\\+\-])/g, "\\$1");

    var sstr = "find {" + who + "} in NAME FIELDS RETURNING " +
               "Lead (id, firstname, lastname), " +
               "Contact(id, firstname, lastname), " +
               "Account(id, name)";

    // Issue the SOSL query using the AJAX Toolkit.
    var sr = sforce.connection.search(sstr);
    var m = document.getElementById('main');

    // Write out the results.
    if (sr) {
        var list = sr.getArray('searchRecords');
        for (var i = 0; i < list.length; i++ ) {
            m.innerHTML += "<p>Search results : " +
            list[i].toString();
        }
    } else {
        m.innerHTML += "<p>No search results";
    }
}
</script>
</head>
```

```
<body onload="init();">
<div id="main"></div>
</body>
</html>
```

Discussion

You can make this solution even more robust by making use of the * wildcard character. For example, the solution here only searches for exact matches of the name "Phil Degausse." If you wanted this solution to also return a record named "Philip Degausse," or "Phil Degaussey," modify the user's search string by appending * after each token in the string:

```
var who = "phil* degauss*";
```

Note that it's still important to maintain the space between the two names, so that each token `phil*` and `degauss*` will match individual name fields in the objects that are queried.

See Also

- *Choosing Between SOQL and SOSL* on page 99
- "Sforce Object Search Language (SOSL)" at www.salesforce.com/us/developer/ docs/api/index_CSH.htm#sforce_api_calls_sosl.htm

Filtering Data Based on a Relative Date

Problem

You want to retrieve records based on a relative date, such as "before last year" or "during the next fiscal quarter."

Solution

Use a date literal in the WHERE clause of your SOQL or SOSL statement. For example:

- This SOQL statement returns all opportunities that closed yesterday:

    ```
    SELECT Id FROM Opportunity WHERE CloseDate = YESTERDAY
    ```

- This SOQL statement returns all opportunities that closed prior to the beginning of the last fiscal quarter:

    ```
    SELECT Id FROM Opportunity WHERE CloseDate < LAST_FISCAL_QUARTER
    ```

- This SOQL statement returns all opportunities with a close date that is more than 15 days away:

```
SELECT Id FROM Opportunity WHERE CloseDate > NEXT_N_DAYS:15
```

Discussion

When you specify a date in a SOQL or SOSL query, it can be a specific date or dateTime field, or it can be an expression that uses a date literal—a keyword that represents a relative range of time such as *last month* or *next year*. To construct an expression that returns date or dateTime values within the range, use =. To construct an expression that returns date or dateTime values that fall on either side of the range, use > or <.

Salesforce provides the following date literals:

Date Literal	Range	Example
YESTERDAY	Starts 12:00:00 the day before and continues for 24 hours.	`SELECT Id FROM Account WHERE CreatedDate = YESTERDAY`
TODAY	Starts 12:00:00 of the current day and continues for 24 hours.	`SELECT Id FROM Account WHERE CreatedDate > TODAY`
TOMORROW	Starts 12:00:00 after the current day and continues for 24 hours.	`SELECT Id FROM Opportunity WHERE CloseDate = TOMORROW`
LAST_WEEK	Starts 12:00:00 on the first day of the week before the most recent first day of the week and continues for seven full days. First day of the week is determined by your locale.	`SELECT Id FROM Account WHERE CreatedDate > LAST_WEEK`
THIS_WEEK	Starts 12:00:00 on the most first day of the week before the current day and continues for seven full days. First day of the week is determined by your locale.	`SELECT Id FROM Account WHERE CreatedDate < THIS_WEEK`
NEXT_WEEK	Starts 12:00:00 on the most recent first day of the week after the current day and continues for seven full days. First day of the week is determined by your locale.	`SELECT Id FROM Opportunity WHERE CloseDate = NEXT_WEEK`

Date Literal	Range	Example
LAST_MONTH	Starts 12:00:00 on the first day of the month before the current day and continues for all the days of that month.	SELECT Id FROM Opportunity WHERE CloseDate > LAST_MONTH
THIS_MONTH	Starts 12:00:00 on the first day of the month that the current day is in and continues for all the days of that month.	SELECT Id FROM Account WHERE CreatedDate < THIS_MONTH
NEXT_MONTH	Starts 12:00:00 on the first day of the month after the month that the current day is in and continues for all the days of that month.	SELECT Id FROM Opportunity WHERE CloseDate = NEXT_MONTH
LAST_90_DAYS	Starts 12:00:00 of the current day and continues for the last 90 days.	SELECT Id FROM Account WHERE CreatedDate = LAST_90_DAYS
NEXT_90_DAYS	Starts 12:00:00 of the current day and continues for the next 90 days.	SELECT Id FROM Opportunity WHERE CloseDate > NEXT_90_DAYS
LAST_N_DAYS:n	For the number n provided, starts 12:00:00 of the current day and continues for the last n days.	SELECT Id FROM Account WHERE CreatedDate = LAST_N_DAYS:365
NEXT_N_DAYS:n	For the number n provided, starts 12:00:00 of the current day and continues for the next n DAYS.	SELECT Id FROM Opportunity WHERE CloseDate > NEXT_N_DAYS:15
THIS_QUARTER	Starts 12:00:00 of the current quarter and continues to the end of the current quarter.	SELECT Id FROM Account WHERE CreatedDate = THIS_QUARTER
LAST_QUARTER	Starts 12:00:00 of the previous quarter and continues to the end of that quarter.	SELECT Id FROM Account WHERE CreatedDate > LAST_QUARTER
NEXT_QUARTER	Starts 12:00:00 of the next quarter and continues to the end of that quarter.	SELECT Id FROM Account WHERE CreatedDate < NEXT_QUARTER
NEXT_N_QUARTERS:n	Starts 12:00:00 of the next quarter and continues to the end of the nth quarter.	SELECT Id FROM Account WHERE CreatedDate < NEXT_N_QUARTERS:2

Date Literal	Range	Example
LAST_N_QUARTERS:n	Starts 12:00:00 of the previous quarter and continues to the end of the previous nth quarter.	`SELECT Id FROM Account WHERE CreatedDate > LAST_N_QUARTERS:2`
THIS_YEAR	Starts 12:00:00 on January 1 of the current year and continues through the end of December 31 of the current year.	`SELECT Id FROM Opportunity WHERE CloseDate = THIS_YEAR`
LAST_YEAR	Starts 12:00:00 on January 1 of the previous year and continues through the end of December 31 of that year.	`SELECT Id FROM Opportunity WHERE CloseDate > LAST_YEAR`
NEXT_YEAR	Starts 12:00:00 on January 1 of the following year and continues through the end of December 31 of that year.	`SELECT Id FROM Opportunity WHERE CloseDate < NEXT_YEAR`
NEXT_N_YEARS:n	Starts 12:00:00 on January 1 of the following year and continues through the end of December 31 of the nth year.	`SELECT Id FROM Opportunity WHERE CloseDate < NEXT_N_YEARS:5`
LAST_N_YEARS:n	Starts 12:00:00 on January 1 of the previous year and continues through the end of December 31 of the previous nth year.	`SELECT Id FROM Opportunity WHERE CloseDate > LAST_N_YEARS:5`
THIS_FISCAL_QUARTER	Starts 12:00:00 on the first day of the current fiscal quarter and continues through the end of the last day of the fiscal quarter. The fiscal year is defined in the company profile at **Setup ➤ Company Profile ➤ Fiscal Year**.	`SELECT Id FROM Account WHERE CreatedDate = THIS_FISCAL_QUARTER`
LAST_FISCAL_QUARTER	Starts 12:00:00 on the first day of the last fiscal quarter and continues through the end of the last day of that fiscal quarter. The fiscal year is defined in the company profile at **Setup ➤ Company Profile ➤ Fiscal Year**.	`SELECT Id FROM Account WHERE CreatedDate > LAST_FISCAL_QUARTER`

Date Literal	Range	Example
NEXT_FISCAL_QUARTER	Starts 12:00:00 on the first day of the next fiscal quarter and continues through the end of the last day of that fiscal quarter. The fiscal year is defined in the company profile at **Setup ➤ Company Profile ➤ Fiscal Year**.	`SELECT Id FROM Account WHERE CreatedDate < NEXT_FISCAL_QUARTER`
NEXT_N_FISCAL_QUARTERS:*n*	Starts 12:00:00 on the first day of the next fiscal quarter and continues through the end of the last day of the *n*th fiscal quarter. The fiscal year is defined in the company profile at**Setup ➤ Company Profile ➤ Fiscal Year**.	`SELECT Id FROM Account WHERE CreatedDate < NEXT_N_FISCAL_QUARTERS:6`
LAST_N_FISCAL_QUARTERS:*n*	Starts 12:00:00 on the first day of the last fiscal quarter and continues through the end of the last day of the previous *n*th fiscal quarter. The fiscal year is defined in the company profile at **Setup ➤ Company Profile ➤ Fiscal Year**.	`SELECT Id FROM Account WHERE CreatedDate > LAST_N_FISCAL_QUARTERS:6`
THIS_FISCAL_YEAR	Starts 12:00:00 on the first day of the current fiscal year and continues through the end of the last day of the fiscal year. The fiscal year is defined in the company profile at **Setup ➤ Company Profile ➤ Fiscal Year**.	`SELECT Id FROM Opportunity WHERE CloseDate = THIS_FISCAL_YEAR`
LAST_FISCAL_YEAR	Starts 12:00:00 on the first day of the last fiscal year and continues through the end of the last day of that fiscal year. The fiscal year is defined in the company profile at **Setup ➤ Company Profile ➤ Fiscal Year**.	`SELECT Id FROM Opportunity WHERE CloseDate > LAST_FISCAL_YEAR`
NEXT_FISCAL_YEAR	Starts 12:00:00 on the first day of the next fiscal year and continues through the end of the last day of that fiscal year. The fiscal year is defined in the company profile at	`SELECT Id FROM Opportunity WHERE CloseDate < NEXT_FISCAL_YEAR`

Date Literal	Range	Example
	Setup ➤ Company Profile ➤ Fiscal Year.	

`NEXT_N_FISCAL_YEARS:`*n*	Starts 12:00:00 on the first day of the next fiscal year and continues through the end of the last day of the *n*th fiscal year. The fiscal year is defined in the company profile at **Setup ➤ Company Profile ➤ Fiscal Year**.	`SELECT Id FROM Opportunity`
		`WHERE CloseDate <`
		`NEXT_N_FISCAL_YEARS:3`

`LAST_N_FISCAL_YEARS:`*n*	Starts 12:00:00 on the first day of the last fiscal year and continues through the end of the last day of the previous *n*th fiscal year. The fiscal year is defined in the company profile at **Setup ➤ Company Profile ➤ Fiscal Year**.	`SELECT Id FROM Opportunity`
		`WHERE CloseDate >`
		`LAST_N_FISCAL_YEARS:3`

Remember that date and dateTime field values are stored as Greenwich Mean Time (GMT) or Coordinated Universal Time (UTC). When one of these values is returned in Salesforce, it's automatically adjusted for the time zone specified in your organization preferences.

See Also

- *Constructing SOQL and SOSL Queries in the Force.com Explorer* on page 100
- "Sforce Object Query Language (SOQL)" at www.salesforce.com/us/developer /docs/api/index_CSH.htm#sforce_api_calls_soql.htm
- "Sforce Object Search Language (SOSL)" at www.salesforce.com/us/developer /docs/api/index_CSH.htm#sforce_api_calls_sosl.htm
- "Date Formats and Date Literals" in the *Force.com Web Services API Developer's Guide* at www.salesforce.com/us/developer/docs/api/index_CSH.htm# sforce_api_calls_soql_select_dateformats.htm

Finding Data Based on Division

Problem

You want to retrieve data for a particular division.

Solution

Use the WITH clause in a SOSL query to filter on division before any other filters are applied. Although you can also filter on an object's Division field within a WHERE clause, using WITH is more efficient because it filters all records based on division before applying other filters. For example:

```
FIND {test} RETURNING Account (id where name like 'Smith'),
                      Contact (id where name like 'Smith')
             WITH DIVISION = 'Global'
```

Notice that the WITH clause filters based on the Division name field, rather than its ID. If you filter on division in a WHERE clause, you need to use the division ID instead.

See Also

- *Constructing SOQL and SOSL Queries in the Force.com Explorer* on page 100
- "Sforce Object Query Language (SOQL)" at www.salesforce.com/us/developer/docs/api/index_CSH.htm#sforce_api_calls_soql.htm
- "Sforce Object Search Language (SOSL)" at www.salesforce.com/us/developer/docs/api/index_CSH.htm#sforce_api_calls_sosl.htm

Previewing Query Results

Problem

Your solution gives users a chance to build a query or set up a filter for a query that you've already written. You want to offer users a "preview" of what data will be returned from their query, including the total number of records that will be returned.

Solution

Run two SOQL queries: one that uses COUNT() to return the total number of records that will be returned, and one that uses LIMIT to quickly return 25 random records that match the query.

Discussion

If your solution allows a user to build a query or set up a filter for an existing query, there's a chance that the user might execute a long-running query that uses query() or queryMore() in a loop. This query could easily take a lot longer than the user expects.

To avoid this issue, it's a good idea to give users a preview of their query results if the result set is going to be greater than 1,000 records, including the total number of records that will be returned and a sample of what the resulting data will look like. You can then prompt them with a question such as, "Are you sure?" before proceeding with the full query.

Although running the normal `query()` call returns the total result size, it also returns a batch of up to 2,000 records, depending on your configured batch size. If you want your application to be faster, it's a good idea to run a `COUNT()` query and a `LIMIT` query instead.

For example, the following SOQL query returns the total number of accounts in the organization, without any filters. You can use this value in a prompt to the user to ask if they're sure they want to proceed with the query:

```
SELECT COUNT() FROM Account
```

Then you can use the following SOQL query to return a random subset of the total data to the user. The user might decide that he or she requires additional fields before the full query should run:

```
SELECT Name, BillingCity FROM Account LIMIT 25
```

See Also

- *Implementing the Query/Query More Pattern* on page 191
- *Constructing SOQL and SOSL Queries in the Force.com Explorer* on page 100
- "Sforce Object Query Language (SOQL)" at www.salesforce.com/us/developer/ docs/api/index_CSH.htm#sforce_api_calls_soql.htm

Sorting Query Results

Problem

You've issued a SOQL or SOSL query and want the results sorted by the value of one or more fields.

Solution

Use the `ORDER BY` clause in your SOQL or SOSL statement to efficiently receive results in the order that you prefer.

> **Note:** You can't use the `ORDER BY` clause in any Apex query if it also uses locking. Those query results, however, are always ordered by ID.

For example, this SOQL query:

```
SELECT Name FROM Contact ORDER BY FirstName
```

Returns a list of contacts sorted alphabetically by first name:

- Andy Young
- Ashley James
- Jack Bond
- Jill Jazzy
- Stella Pavlov
- Zebidiah Jazzy

This SOQL query:

```
SELECT Name FROM Contact ORDER BY LastName DESC,
                         FirstName DESC
```

Returns a list of contacts sorted in reverse-alphabetical order by last name and then in reverse-alphabetical order by first name:

- Andy Young
- Stella Pavlov
- Zebidiah Jazzy
- Jill Jazzy
- Ashley James
- Jack Bond

This SOSL query:

```
FIND {Ja*} RETURNING Contact (Name ORDER BY LastName)
```

Returns a list of contacts that include "Ja" in the name, sorted alphabetically by last name:

- Jack Bond
- Ashley James
- Jill Jazzy
- Zebidiah Jazzy

This SOSL query:

```
FIND {Ja*} RETURNING Contact (Name ORDER BY LastName,
                                   FirstName DESC),
                 Lead (Name ORDER BY FirstName)
```

Returns a list of contacts and leads that include "Ja" in the name, where contacts are sorted alphabetically by last name and then reverse-alphabetically by first name, and where leads are sorted alphabetically by first name:

- (Contact) Jack Bond
- (Contact) Ashley James
- (Contact) Zebidiah Jazzy
- (Contact) Jill Jazzy
- (Lead) Jack Rodgers
- (Lead) Tom Jamison

Discussion

ORDER BY is the best solution for sorting because the Force.com platform server does the work and your code doesn't need to do anything else after receiving the data.

You can sort your query results by any of the specified object's fields that is not a long text area or multi-select picklist field, even if the field is not one of the query fields that you want returned.

 Note: If you attempt to sort by a long text area or multi-select picklist field, you'll receive a "malformed query" error message.

The ORDER BY clause for SOQL and SOSL includes a number of features:

- Sort by Multiple Fields

  You can sort your query by multiple fields, so that records that have the same value for the first field are then ordered by the value of a second field. For example, the following query returns contacts sorted first by LastName and then by FirstName:

```
SELECT Name FROM Contact ORDER BY LastName,
                                  FirstName
```

- Sort in Ascending and Descending Order

  You can specify whether values should be sorted in ascending or descending order by adding the modifiers ASC or DESC to any sort field. For example, the following query returns contacts in reverse-alphabetical order:

```
SELECT Name FROM Contact ORDER BY LastName DESC,
                                   FirstName DESC
```

  When this value is not specified, results are sorted in ascending order by default.

- Sort Null Values

You can also specify whether null values should be sorted at the beginning (FIRST) or end (LAST) of the list of results. For example, the following query places null values at the end of a list of contact mailing cities and states that's organized by state in reverse-alphabetical order:

```
SELECT MailingCity, MailingState FROM Contact
                    ORDER BY MailingState DESC NULLS LAST
```

ORDER BY always follows the WHERE clause in a SOQL or SOSL statement. For example:

```
SELECT Name FROM Contact WHERE Name like 'Ja%'
                    ORDER BY LastName, FirstName
```

 Note: SOQL query sorting is case insensitive. If you require case sensitive sorting, you'll need to implement this in your own code.

See Also

- *Choosing Between SOQL and SOSL* on page 99
- *Constructing SOQL and SOSL Queries in the Force.com Explorer* on page 100
- "Sforce Object Query Language (SOQL)" at www.salesforce.com/us/developer/docs/api/index_CSH.htm#sforce_api_calls_soql.htm
- "Sforce Object Search Language (SOSL)" at www.salesforce.com/us/developer/docs/api/index_CSH.htm#sforce_api_calls_sosl.htm

Chapter 6

Improving Data Quality

In the previous chapter, you learned how to use SOQL and SOSL to query and search sets of records. Now that you know how to do that, you're ready to start manipulating that data. In this chapter, you'll see some different ways you can work with data to automate business processes. Whether it's Apex that prevents users from creating duplicate records or a method for updating contacts when a parent account record changes, you'll greatly enhance the usefulness of your on-demand by including these types of business logic.

Preventing Duplicate Records from Saving

Problem

You want to prevent users from saving duplicate records based on the value of one or more fields.

Solution

If you can determine whether a record is a duplicate based on the value of a single custom field, select the `Unique` and `Required` checkboxes on that field's definition:

- To edit a field on a standard object, click **Setup ➤ Customize**, select the link for the desired object, and click **Fields**. Then click **Edit** next to the name of the appropriate field.
- To edit a field on a custom object, click **Setup ➤ Build ➤ Custom Objects**, click the name of the object on which the field appears, and then click **Edit** next to the name of the field in the Custom Fields and Relationships related list.

If you need to require uniqueness based on the value of two or more fields, or a single standard field, write an Apex `before insert` and `before update` trigger. For example, the following trigger prevents leads from being saved if they have a matching `Email` field:

- The trigger first uses a map to store the updated leads with each lead's email address as the key.
- The trigger then uses the set of keys in the map to query the database for any existing lead records with the same email addresses. For every matching lead, the duplicate record is marked with an error condition.

```
trigger leadDuplicatePreventer on Lead
                        (before insert, before update) {

  Map<String, Lead> leadMap = new Map<String, Lead>();
  for (Lead lead : System.Trigger.new) {

    // Make sure we don't treat an email address that
    // isn't changing during an update as a duplicate.
    if ((lead.Email != null) &&
          (System.Trigger.isInsert ||
          (lead.Email != System.Trigger.oldMap.
          get(lead.Id).Email))) {

      // Make sure another new lead isn't also a duplicate
      if (leadMap.containsKey(lead.Email)) {
        lead.Email.addError('Another new lead has the '
                            + 'same email address.');
```

"Preventing Duplicate Records from Saving" contributed by Steve Fisher, Senior Vice President of the Platform Division for salesforce.com

```
            } else {
                leadMap.put(lead.Email, lead);
            }
        }
    }

    // Using a single database query, find all the leads in
    // the database that have the same email address as any
    // of the leads being inserted or updated.
    for (Lead lead : [SELECT Email FROM Lead
                        WHERE Email IN :leadMap.KeySet()]) {
        Lead newLead = leadMap.get(lead.Email);
        newLead.Email.addError('A lead with this email '
                            + 'address already exists.');
    }
}
```

The following class can be used to test the trigger for both single- and bulk-record inserts and updates.

```
public class leadDupePreventerTests{
 static testMethod void testLeadDupPreventer() {

    // First make sure there are no leads already in the system
    // that have the email addresses used for testing
    Set<String> testEmailAddress = new Set<String>();
    testEmailAddress.add('test1@duptest.com');
    testEmailAddress.add('test2@duptest.com');
    testEmailAddress.add('test3@duptest.com');
    testEmailAddress.add('test4@duptest.com');
    testEmailAddress.add('test5@duptest.com');
    System.assert([SELECT count() FROM Lead
                    WHERE Email IN :testEmailAddress] == 0);

    // Seed the database with some leads, and make sure they can
    // be bulk inserted successfully.
    Lead lead1 = new Lead(LastName='Test1', Company='Test1 Inc.',
                        Email='test1@duptest.com');
    Lead lead2 = new Lead(LastName='Test2', Company='Test2 Inc.',
                        Email='test4@duptest.com');
    Lead lead3 = new Lead(LastName='Test3', Company='Test3 Inc.',
                        Email='test5@duptest.com');
    Lead[] leads = new Lead[] {lead1, lead2, lead3};
    insert leads;

    // Now make sure that some of these leads can be changed and
    // then bulk updated successfully. Note that lead1 is not
    // being changed, but is still being passed to the update
    // call. This should be OK.
    lead2.Email = 'test2@duptest.com';
    lead3.Email = 'test3@duptest.com';
    update leads;

    // Make sure that single row lead duplication prevention works
    // on insert.
```

```
Lead dup1 = new Lead(LastName='Test1Dup',
                     Company='Test1Dup Inc.',
                     Email='test1@duptest.com');
try {
   insert dup1;
   System.assert(false);
} catch (System.DmlException e) {
   System.assert(e.getNumDml() == 1);
   System.assert(e.getDmlIndex(0) == 0);
   System.assert(e.getDmlFields(0).size() == 1);
   System.assert(e.getDmlFields(0)[0] == 'Email');
   System.assert(e.getDmlMessage(0).indexOf(
      'A lead with this email address already exists.') > -1);
}

// Make sure that single row lead duplication prevention works
// on update.
dup1 = new Lead(Id = lead1.Id, LastName='Test1Dup',
                Company='Test1Dup Inc.',
                Email='test2@duptest.com');
try {
   update dup1;
   System.assert(false);
} catch (System.DmlException e) {
   System.assert(e.getNumDml() == 1);
   System.assert(e.getDmlIndex(0) == 0);
   System.assert(e.getDmlFields(0).size() == 1);
   System.assert(e.getDmlFields(0)[0] == 'Email');
   System.assert(e.getDmlMessage(0).indexOf(
      'A lead with this email address already exists.') > -1);
}

// Make sure that bulk lead duplication prevention works on
// insert. Note that the first item being inserted is fine,
// but the second and third items are duplicates. Note also
// that since at least one record insert fails, the entire
// transaction will be rolled back.
dup1 = new Lead(LastName='Test1Dup', Company='Test1Dup Inc.',
                Email='test4@duptest.com');
Lead dup2 = new Lead(LastName='Test2Dup',
                     Company='Test2Dup Inc.',
                     Email='test2@duptest.com');
Lead dup3 = new Lead(LastName='Test3Dup',
                     Company='Test3Dup Inc.',
                     Email='test3@duptest.com');
Lead[] dups = new Lead[] {dup1, dup2, dup3};
try {
   insert dups;
   System.assert(false);
} catch (System.DmlException e) {
   System.assert(e.getNumDml() == 2);
   System.assert(e.getDmlIndex(0) == 1);
   System.assert(e.getDmlFields(0).size() == 1);
   System.assert(e.getDmlFields(0)[0] == 'Email');
   System.assert(e.getDmlMessage(0).indexOf(
      'A lead with this email address already exists.') > -1);
```

```
            System.assert(e.getDmlIndex(1) == 2);
            System.assert(e.getDmlFields(1).size() == 1);
            System.assert(e.getDmlFields(1)[0] == 'Email');
            System.assert(e.getDmlMessage(1).indexOf(
                'A lead with this email address already exists.') > -1);
        }

        // Make sure that bulk lead duplication prevention works on
        // update. Note that the first item being updated is fine,
        // because the email address is new, and the second item is
        // also fine, but in this case it's because the email
        // address doesn't change. The third case is flagged as an
        // error because it is a duplicate of the email address of the
        // first lead's value in the database, even though that value
        // is changing in this same update call. It would be an
        // interesting exercise to rewrite the trigger to allow this
        // case. Note also that since at least one record update
        // fails, the entire transaction will be rolled back.
        dup1 = new Lead(Id=lead1.Id, Email='test4@duptest.com');
        dup2 = new Lead(Id=lead2.Id, Email='test2@duptest.com');
        dup3 = new Lead(Id=lead3.Id, Email='test1@duptest.com');
        dups = new Lead[] {dup1, dup2, dup3};
        try {
            update dups;
            System.assert(false);
        } catch (System.DmlException e) {
            System.debug(e.getNumDml());
            System.debug(e.getDmlMessage(0));
            System.assert(e.getNumDml() == 1);
            System.assert(e.getDmlIndex(0) == 2);
            System.assert(e.getDmlFields(0).size() == 1);
            System.assert(e.getDmlFields(0)[0] == 'Email');
            System.assert(e.getDmlMessage(0).indexOf(
                'A lead with this email address already exists.') > -1);
        }

        // Make sure that duplicates in the submission are caught when
        // inserting leads. Note that this test also catches an
        // attempt to insert a lead where there is an existing
        // duplicate.
        dup1 = new Lead(LastName='Test1Dup', Company='Test1Dup Inc.',
                    Email='test4@duptest.com');
        dup2 = new Lead(LastName='Test2Dup', Company='Test2Dup Inc.',
                    Email='test4@duptest.com');
        dup3 = new Lead(LastName='Test3Dup', Company='Test3Dup Inc.',
                    Email='test3@duptest.com');
        dups = new Lead[] {dup1, dup2, dup3};
        try {
            insert dups;
            System.assert(false);
        } catch (System.DmlException e) {
            System.assert(e.getNumDml() == 2);
            System.assert(e.getDmlIndex(0) == 1);
            System.assert(e.getDmlFields(0).size() == 1);
            System.assert(e.getDmlFields(0)[0] == 'Email');
            System.assert(e.getDmlMessage(0).indexOf(
```

```
            'Another new lead has the same email address.') > -1);
        System.assert(e.getDmlIndex(1) == 2);
        System.assert(e.getDmlFields(1).size() == 1);
        System.assert(e.getDmlFields(1)[0] == 'Email');
        System.assert(e.getDmlMessage(1).indexOf(
            'A lead with this email address already exists.') > -1);
    }

    // Make sure that duplicates in the submission are caught when
    // updating leads. Note that this test also catches an attempt
    // to update a lead where there is an existing duplicate.
    dup1 = new Lead(Id=lead1.Id, Email='test4@duptest.com');
    dup2 = new Lead(Id=lead2.Id, Email='test4@duptest.com');
    dup3 = new Lead(Id=lead3.Id, Email='test2@duptest.com');
    dups = new Lead[] {dup1, dup2, dup3};
    try {
        update dups;
        System.assert(false);
    } catch (System.DmlException e) {
        System.assert(e.getNumDml() == 2);
        System.assert(e.getDmlIndex(0) == 1);
        System.assert(e.getDmlFields(0).size() == 1);
        System.assert(e.getDmlFields(0)[0] == 'Email');
        System.assert(e.getDmlMessage(0).indexOf(
            'Another new lead has the same email address.') > -1);
        System.assert(e.getDmlIndex(1) == 2);
        System.assert(e.getDmlFields(1).size() == 1);
        System.assert(e.getDmlFields(1)[0] == 'Email');
        System.assert(e.getDmlMessage(1).indexOf(
            'A lead with this email address already exists.') > -1);
    }
  }
}
```

Discussion

The first and most important lesson to learn from this recipe is that you should generally take advantage of native Force.com Builder functionality if it can solve your problem, rather than writing code. By using the point-and-click tools that are provided, you leverage the power of the platform. Why reinvent the wheel if you can take advantage of a native feature that performs the same functionality? As a result, we indicate in this recipe that you should first determine whether you can simply use the Unique and Required checkboxes on a single custom field definition to prevent duplicates.

 Note: The Unique and Required checkboxes are only available on custom fields. If you want to check for uniqueness based on the value of a single standard field and your edition can't use Apex, you can also use the following workaround:

1. Create a custom field with the same type and label as the standard field. Select the Unique and Required checkboxes on the custom field's definition page.
2. Replace the standard field with your new custom field on all page layouts.

3. Use field-level security to make the standard field read-only for all user profiles. This prevents any user from mistakenly modifying the standard field through the API, unless the user has the "Modify All Data" profile permission.

4. Define a workflow rule that automatically updates the value of the standard field with the value of the custom field whenever the custom field changes. This ensures that any application functionality that relies on the value of the standard field will continue to work properly. (For example, the **Send An Email** button on the Activity History related list relies on the standard `Email` field for a lead or contact.)

Because this is a less-elegant solution than using Apex, creating a trigger on lead is the preferred solution for Unlimited Edition and Developer Edition.

If you do need to check for duplicates based on the value of a single standard field, or more than one field, Apex is the best way to accomplish this. Because Apex runs natively on the Force.com platform servers, it's far more efficient than a deduplication algorithm that runs in an s-control or Web control. Additionally, Apex can execute every time a record is inserted or updated in the database, regardless of whether the database operation occurs as a result of a user clicking **Save** in the user interface or as a result of a bulk `upsert` call to the API. S-controls and Web controls can only be triggered when a record is saved through the user interface.

The included trigger is production-ready because it meets the following criteria:

- The trigger only makes a single database query, regardless of the number of leads being inserted or updated.
- The trigger catches duplicates that are in the list of leads being inserted or updated.
- The trigger handles updates properly. That is, leads that are being updated with email addresses that haven't changed are not flagged as duplicates.
- The trigger has full unit test coverage, including tests for both single- and bulk-record inserts and updates.

See Also

- *Deciding When to Use S-Controls, Client Apps, Apex, or Visualforce* on page 30
- *Writing Unit Tests for Apex* on page 80
- *Determining Apex Test Coverage* on page 85

Populating a Contact Edit Page with Default Values from an Account

Problem

You want to auto-populate field values for a new contact with values from the account record from which the contact is created. For example, if a user is on the Acme account detail page and clicks **New** on the Contacts related list, the new contact record's mailing address has the values auto-populated from the Acme record.

Solution

Override the **New** account button with an s-control that redirects the user to the standard New Contact page, but with default field values specified in the URL. For example, by inspecting the names of the input text fields in the New Contact page, we can determine that the name of the `Billing City` input field is `con19city`. We can then use a merge field to provide a value for this field from the parent account record.

 Note: While you can manually inspect the HTML of the contact page to find the names of the input text fields, it's much easier to do this with a tool like Firebug.

For example, the following HTML s-control auto-populates a contact's `Account`, `Mailing Street`, `Mailing City`, `Mailing State/Province`, `Mailing Zip/Postal Code`, and `Mailing Country` fields:

```
<html>
<head>
<title></title>
<script>
//First construct the new URL
var newUrl = "{!URLFOR( $Action.Contact.NewContact, null,
            [con4=Account.Name,
             con19city= Account.BillingCity,
             con19state=Account.BillingState,
             con19street= Account.BillingStreet,
             con19zip=Account.BillingPostalCode,
             con19country= Account.BillingCountry,
             retURL=$Request.retURL] ,true)}";

//Then redirect the user to it
window.parent.location.replace(newUrl);
</script>
</head>
```

To replace the **New** contact button with this s-control, first create the s-control via **Setup ➤ Build ➤ Custom S-Controls**. Then, click **Setup ➤ Customize ➤ Contacts ➤ Buttons and**

Links, and click **Override** next to the **New** button. Select the s-control from the `Custom S-Control` picklist, and click **Save**.

Discussion

Once the **New** button is overridden, this s-control is used whenever a new contact is created, regardless of whether the New Contact edit page is accessed from a parent account record, from the Contacts tab, or even from the Create New drop-down list in the sidebar. When there's no reference account that the s-control can access, the field values are left blank and the user doesn't notice any difference.

See Also

- *Overriding a Standard Button with an S-Control* on page 139
- *Redirecting a User to an Edit, Detail, or List Page* on page 139
- *Passing Parameters into a Custom Button or Link* on page 137
- *Debugging S-Controls with Firebug* on page 219

Creating a Default Interviewer Record When a Position is Created

Problem

You want to automatically create a new child interviewer record when you create a parent position record. The interviewer record should be populated with default values from the position.

Solution

Use an Apex trigger to automatically create the child interviewer record when a new position record is created.

For this example, let's automatically create a new interviewer record for the specified hiring manager whenever a new position is created:

```
trigger AutoCreateInterviewer on Position__c (after insert) {
    List<Interviewer__c> interviewers = new List<Interviewer__c>();

    //For each position processed by the trigger, add a new
    //interviewer record for the specified hiring manager.
    //Note that Trigger.New is a list of all the new positions
    //that are being created.
    for (Position__c newPosition: Trigger.New) {
        if (newPosition.Hiring_Manager__c != null) {
```

```
                interviewers.add(new Interviewer__c(
                                Name = '1',
                                Position__c = newPosition.Id,
                                Employee__c = newPosition.
                                              Hiring_Manager__c,
                                Role__c = 'Managerial'));
        }
    }
    insert interviewers;
}
```

See Also

- *Bulk Processing Records in a Trigger* on page 61
- *Avoiding Apex Governor Limits* on page 70

Mass Updating Contacts When an Account Changes

Problem

You want to update the address of all contacts associated with an account whenever the account's address changes.

Solution

Write a trigger in Apex that updates associated contacts when an account is updated:

```
trigger updateContactsOnAddressChange on Account
                                    (before update) {

    // The map allows us to keep track of the accounts that have
    // new addresses
    Map<Id, Account> acctsWithNewAddresses = new Map<Id, Account>();

    // Trigger.new is a list of the Accounts that will be updated
    // This loop iterates over the list, and adds any that have new
    // addresses to the acctsWithNewAddresses map.
    for (Integer i = 0; i < Trigger.new.size(); i++) {
        if (   (Trigger.old[i].ShippingCity != Trigger.new[i].
                                                ShippingCity)
            || (Trigger.old[i].ShippingCountry != Trigger.new[i].
                                                ShippingCountry)
            || (Trigger.old[i].ShippingPostalCode != Trigger.new[i].
                                                ShippingPostalCode)
            || (Trigger.old[i].ShippingState != Trigger.new[i].
                                                ShippingState)
            || (Trigger.old[i].ShippingStreet != Trigger.new[i].
                                                ShippingStreet)) {
            acctsWithNewAddresses.put(Trigger.old[i].id,
```

```
                                         Trigger.new[i]);
        }
    }

    List<Contact> updatedContacts = new List<Contact>();

    //Here we can see two syntatic features of Apex:
    //  1) iterating over an embedded SOQL query
    //  2) binding an array directly to a SOQL query with 'in'

    for (Contact c : [SELECT id, accountId, MailingCity,
                            MailingCountry, MailingPostalCode,
                            MailingState, MailingStreet
                      FROM contact
                      WHERE accountId in :acctsWithNewAddresses.
                                            keySet()]) {
        Account parentAccount = acctsWithNewAddresses.
                                get(c.accountId);
        c.MailingCity = parentAccount.ShippingCity;
        c.MailingCountry = parentAccount.ShippingCountry;
        c.MailingPostalCode = parentAccount.ShippingPostalCode;
        c.MailingState = parentAccount.ShippingState;
        c.MailingStreet = parentAccount.ShippingStreet;

        // Rather than insert the contacts individually, add the
        // contacts to a list and bulk insert it. This makes the
        // trigger run faster and allows us to avoid hitting the
        // governor limit on DML statements
        updatedContacts.add(c);
    }
    update updatedContacts;
}
```

See Also

- *Bulk Processing Records in a Trigger* on page 61
- *Avoiding Apex Governor Limits* on page 70

Chapter 7

Customizing Buttons and Links

The Salesforce user interface is known for its ease-of-use and usability. End users easily navigate from page to page by clicking buttons and links to accomplish the tasks they need to do. For example, to create a new account, a user simply clicks the **New** button on the Accounts tab and a new account record page displays for the user to fill in the necessary information. But what if your app needs something more than the standard functionality? Perhaps you want to add a custom button to a list view to give users the ability to update all of the records in the list at one time, or perhaps you want to add some additional functionality when a user clicks the **Save** button on an account. And of course, after you've customized these aspects of your app, you want to give users some custom documentation that describes how to use it. All of this is possible, and easy to do, on the Force.com platform!

In this chapter, you'll learn how to create custom buttons, such as a **Mass Delete** and a **Mass Update** button, override the action of a standard Salesforce button, pass parameters into your custom button or link code, redirect users to a different URL when they go to a standard Salesforce page, and provide custom help documentation with your app. We'll use a combination of native and composite platform features to create these customizations easily and quickly.

Creating a Custom Detail Page Button

Problem

You want to add a custom button to the account detail page.

Figure 11: A Custom Button on an Account Detail Page

Solution

First define the button, then add it to the appropriate page layout. For example, the following procedure creates a simple button that, when clicked, displays a popup dialog with a welcome message:

1. Define the button:

   a. Click **Setup ➤ Customize ➤ Accounts ➤ Buttons and Links**.

       Tip: For a new button on a custom object, navigate to **Setup ➤ Build ➤ Custom Objects**, and click the name of the object.

   b. In the Custom Buttons and Links related list, click **New**.

   c. Name the button and set its attributes as follows:

      - `Label`: Welcome!
      - `Name`: Welcome
      - `Display Type`: Detail Page Button
      - `Behavior`: Execute JavaScript
      - `Content Source`: OnClick JavaScript

Tip: Since there's a limited amount of space in the button bar, keep the button label as short as possible.

    d. In the body of the button, enter the following JavaScript code:

```
alert ("Hello {!User.FirstName}");
```

    e. Click **Save**.

2. Add the button to the Account page layout:

    a. Click **Setup ➤ Customize ➤ Accounts ➤ Page Layouts**.

 Tip: For a new button on a custom object, navigate to **Setup ➤ Build ➤ Custom Objects**, and click the name of the object.

    b. Click **Edit** next to page layout you want to customize.
    c. From the Button Section, double-click the Detail Page Buttons item to edit it.
    d. Select the Welcome! button in the Available buttons list and click **Add**.
    e. Click **OK** to close the popup.
    f. Click **Save** on the page layout. Your changes are not saved until you do so.

Discussion

Custom buttons allow you to build custom actions directly into Salesforce. A button can navigate to a URL, display a custom s-control, or simply execute JavaScript when a user clicks it. It can open a new window, display in the existing window, or just perform an action behind the scenes.

 Tip: If you define a button that displays in a new window, you can control the properties of that window by clicking **Window Open Properties** in the button's detail page.

Because buttons are more recognizable and easy to find on a page than custom links, use them for your most important value-add functionality.

See Also

- *Creating a Mass Delete Button* on page 132
- *Creating a Mass Update Button* on page 135
- *Overriding a Standard Button with an S-Control* on page 139
- "Getting Started with Custom Buttons and Links," a Breeze presentation available at salesforce.breezecentral.com/buttonsandlinks

- "Embedded Mash-Up Samples," a PDF available at blogs.salesforce.com/features/files/salesforce_useful_scontrols.pdf
- "Operators and Functions" in the Salesforce online help
- "Understanding Global Variables" in the Salesforce online help

Creating a Mass Delete Button

Problem

You want to add a button to the top of the Contacts related list in an account detail page that allows users to select multiple contacts in the list and delete all of them at once.

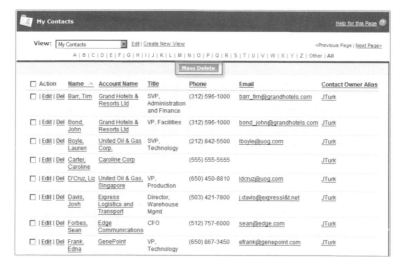

Figure 12: A Mass Delete Button on a Contacts List View

Solution

Create a new button on Contact, and then add the button to the related list on the Account page layout.

To do this:

1. Click **Setup ➤ Customize ➤ Contacts ➤ Buttons and Links**.

     Tip: For a new button on a custom object, navigate to **Setup ➤ Build ➤ Custom Objects**, and click the name of the object.

2. In the Custom Buttons and Links related list, click **New**. Assign it the following attributes:

   - `Label`: Mass Delete
   - `Name`: Mass_Delete_Contacts
   - `Display Type`: List Button
   - `Behavior`: Execute JavaScript
   - `Content Source`: OnClick JavaScript

3. In the code for the button, use the `GETRECORDIDs()` function to acquire the Ids of the contacts that the user selects. The code then performs the appropriate logic, updates the database using the AJAX Toolkit, and refreshes the page as confirmation to the user.

   For example:

```
// Include and initialize the AJAX Toolkit javascript library
//
{!REQUIRESCRIPT("/soap/ajax/10.0/connection.js")}


// Get the list of accounts that should be deleted.
// Use the $ObjectType merge field to indicate the type of
// record Ids that are expected.
//
var idsToDelete = {!GETRECORDIDS( $ObjectType.Contact )};
var deleteWarning = 'Are you sure you wish to delete ' +
                    idsToDelete.length + ' contacts?';

if (idsToDelete.length && (window.confirm(deleteWarning))) {

    // Delete the records, and pass a function into the call
    // so that the toolkit refreshes the current page
    // asynchronously when the call succeeds.
    //
    sforce.connection.deleteIds(idsToDelete,
          function() {navigateToUrl(window.location.href);});

} else if (idsToDelete.length == 0) {
    alert("Please select the contacts you wish to delete.");
}
```

4. Click **Save**.
5. Add the button to the Contacts related list on the Account page layout:

   a. Click **Setup ➤ Customize ➤ Accounts ➤ Page Layouts**.

   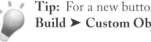 **Tip:** For a new button on a custom object, navigate to **Setup ➤ Build ➤ Custom Objects**, and click the name of the object.

b. Click **Edit** next to page layout you want to customize.

c. From the Related Lists Section, double-click the Contacts related list to edit it.

d. In the Custom Buttons section, select the Mass Delete button in the Available buttons list and click **Add**.

e. Click **OK** to close the popup.

f. Click **Save** on the page layout. Your changes are not saved until you do so.

Discussion

The GETRECORDIDs() function is the crucial call in any mass action list button. It returns an array of string record IDs for the selected records in the list view or related list. It always takes a single $ObjectType merge field with the specified type of the records that are included in the list (for example, $ObjectType.Case or $ObjectType.Position__c).

If you're creating a mass delete button for a list of activities, you must specify whether the activities are tasks or events. If tasks, use $ObjectType.Task in your call to GETRECORDIDs(). If events, use $ObjectType.Event instead.

Note: Both the GETRECORDIDs() function and the $ObjectType merge field are only available in custom buttons, links, and s-controls.

Tip: If you'd rather not go to the trouble of creating this button yourself, install it free and others like it by going to the AppExchange and searching for the Mass Delete app. Installing this package includes a mass delete custom button for each standard object. The custom list button for activity lists also deletes all selected tasks or events at once.

See Also

- *Creating a Mass Update Button* on page 135
- *Passing Parameters into a Custom Button or Link* on page 137
- "Getting Started with Custom Buttons and Links," a Breeze presentation available at salesforce.breezecentral.com/buttonsandlinks
- "Embedded Mash-Up Samples," a PDF available at blogs.salesforce.com/features/files/salesforce_useful_scontrols.pdf
- "Operators and Functions" in the Salesforce online help
- "Understanding Global Variables" in the Salesforce online help

Creating a Mass Update Button

Problem

You want to add a button to the top of a list of records that allows users to select multiple items in the list and perform the same updates on all of them.

Solution

Create a custom mass action list button on the object that's associated with the records that appear in the list.

To illustrate this solution, we'll enhance the sample Recruiting application by giving users a quick way to close multiple job applications after a position has closed. Instead of forcing users to open each job application and change its `Stage` and `Status` fields, we'll set up a list button called **Reject Applications** to do this for us.

To implement this solution on your own, use the same general procedure for creating a list button as was described in the recipe for *Creating a Mass Delete Button* on page 132. Instead of using the JavaScript code for the mass delete button, though, swap in the following code:

 Note: For this code sample to work, you must have the Recruiting app metadata in your organization. See *The Sample Recruiting App* on page 9.

```
// Include and initialize the AJAX Toolkit javascript library
//
{!REQUIRESCRIPT("/soap/ajax/10.0/connection.js")}

// Get the list of job applications that should be closed by using the
// $ObjectType merge field to indicate the type of record Ids that
// are expected.
//
var jobAppIdArr = {!GETRECORDIDS( $ObjectType.Job_Application__c )};

if (jobAppIdArr == null || jobAppIdArr.length == 0) {
    alert("Please select the job applications you wish to reject.");

} else {

    // Retrieving the job applications that should be deleted from
    // the database is inefficient and unnecessary. Instead, create
    // new job application records for each job application that
    // should be updated, store them in an array, and then use the
    // update API call.
    //
    var jobApps = new Array();

    for (var i = 0; i < jobAppIdArr.length; i++) {
        var jobApp = new sforce.SObject("Job_Application__c");
```

```
        // Since we'll be using the update call, we must set the id
        // on the new job application record.
        //
        jobApp.Id = jobAppIdArr[i];

        // Next set the appropriate fields to reject the
        //application.
        //
        jobApp.Status__c = "Closed";
        jobApp.Stage__c = "Closed - Rejected";

        // Finally add the record to our array.
        //
        jobApps.push(jobApp);
    }

    // Now make the update API call in a try statement so we can
    // catch any errors. Save the resulting array so we can also
    // check for problems with individual records.
    //
    var callCompleted = false;
    try {
        var result = sforce.connection.update(jobApps);
        callCompleted = true;

    } catch(error) {
      alert("Failed to update Job Applications with error: " + error);

    }

    // Now check for problems with individual records.
    //
    if (callCompleted) {
        for (var i = 0; i < result.length; i++) {
            if (!result[i].getBoolean("success")) {
                alert("Job Application (id='" + jobAppIdArr[i] +
                    "') could not be updated with error: " +
                    result[i].errors);
            }
        }

        // Finally, refresh the browser to provide confirmation
        // to the user that the job applications were rejected.
        //
        window.location.reload(true);
    }
}
```

See Also

- *The Sample Recruiting App* on page 9
- *Creating a Mass Delete Button* on page 132
- *Passing Parameters into a Custom Button or Link* on page 137

- "Getting Started with Custom Buttons and Links," a Breeze presentation available at salesforce.breezecentral.com/buttonsandlinks
- "Embedded Mash-Up Samples," a PDF available at blogs.salesforce.com/features/files/salesforce_useful_scontrols.pdf
- "Operators and Functions" in the Salesforce online help
- "Understanding Global Variables" in the Salesforce online help

Passing Parameters into a Custom Button or Link

Problem

You want to use one s-control as the source logic for two or more different custom buttons or links, but to do so you need to pass in a parameter that indicates which button or link was clicked.

Solution

Use the URLFOR() function in the s-control or OnClick JavaScript associated with the button or link to generate a relative URL for a second s-control that executes the logic. URLFOR() allows you to add one or more optional parameters to this relative URL. Within the s-control, you can then use the $Request merge variable to receive the parameters that you passed in.

For example, the following code is associated with a button or link and uses URLFOR() to pass a parameter named action to an s-control, myScontrol, which performs the logic:

```
<html>
    <head>
    </head>
    <body>
        <script type="text/javascript">
            window.location.href = "{!URLFOR($SControl.myScontrol,
                                    Account.Id, [action="attach"])}";
        </script>
    </body>
</html>
```

Inside the s-control (myScontrol), the value for the action parameter is retrieved using the $Request merge variable:

```
var action = "{!$Request.action}";
if ( action == 'attach' ) {
    // Code that should execute only when the action parameter
    // is set to 'attach'
    //
}
```

Discussion

`URLFOR()` allows you to generate the link that will execute any action or custom s-control that you want. You can pass an unlimited number of parameters to the targeted action or custom s-control with the following syntax:

```
{!URLFOR(target, id, [optParam1="value1", optParam2="value2", ...],
        optNoOverride)}
```

Where:

- *target* is the action or the s-control that should execute. In the earlier example, we used the `$SControl` merge variable to access a custom s-control named `myScontrol`. We could have also performed a standard action by using the `$Action` merge variable. For example, using `$Action.Case.CloseCase` for the target generates a relative link that executes the logic for closing a case.
- *id* is the ID of the record that should be affected by the target action.
- `[`*optParam1="value1"*, *optParam2="value2"*, ...`]` is an optional list of parameter-value pairs that can be of any length. You can use any alphanumeric string values for the parameters and the values that you want. For example, if you want to pass in a parameter "foo" with value "bar," and a second parameter "alpha" with value "beta," the syntax is: `[foo="bar", alpha="beta"]`. When the URL is ultimately generated, the parameters are passed in as follows:

  ```
  https://....&foo=bar&alpha=beta
  ```

- *optNoOverride* is an optional Boolean argument that specifies whether a standard Salesforce page should be displayed, regardless of whether you've defined an override for it elsewhere. If left unspecified, the default value for this option is false.

Once you've passed parameters into an s-control, you can use the `$Request` merge variable to examine their values. The syntax is `$Request.<paramName>`, where *paramName* is the name of a parameter that was passed in.

Based on the earlier example, "`{!$Request.foo}`" and "`{!$Request.alpha}`" would evaluate to "bar" and "beta," respectively.

If you want to check for an unspecified parameter, simply test it against an empty string. For example:

```
if ("{!$Request.foo}" == "" )  // No foo parameter passed
```

See Also

- *Redirecting a User to an Edit, Detail, or List Page* on page 139
- *Overriding a Standard Button with an S-Control* on page 139

Redirecting a User to an Edit, Detail, or List Page

Problem

You want to write an s-control that redirects a user to the edit, detail, or list view page for a particular object.

Solution

Use the `$Action` merge variable in a `URLFOR()` function to generate the link to which the user should be redirected. For example, to redirect a user to the edit page for an Account, use the following in a `<script>` tag of an s-control:

```
var newURL = "{!URLFOR($Action.Account.Edit, Account.Id, null, false)}";
window.parent.location.replace(newURL);
```

For additional information on `URLFOR()`, see *Passing Parameters into a Custom Button or Link* on page 137.

See Also

- *Passing Parameters into a Custom Button or Link* on page 137
- *Overriding a Standard Button with an S-Control* on page 139
- *Populating a Contact Edit Page with Default Values from an Account* on page 124

Overriding a Standard Button with an S-Control

Problem

You want to override a standard button, such as **New** or **Edit**, with your own custom s-control.

Solution

To override a button on a standard object:

1. Click **Setup ➤ Customize**, select the name of the object, and then click **Buttons and Links**.
2. In the Standard Buttons and Links related list, click **Override** next to the name of the button you want to change, select a custom s-control, and click **Save**.

To override a button on a custom object:

1. Click **Setup ➤ Build ➤ Custom Objects** and select the name of the object.

139

2. Scroll down to the Standard Buttons and Links related list and click **Override** next to the name of the button you want to change. Select a custom s-control, and click **Save**.

Discussion

For standard and custom objects in the application, you can override the object's tab and the following standard buttons:

- New
- View
- Edit
- Delete
- Clone
- Accept

Additionally, some standard objects also have special actions. For example, Leads have Convert, Change Status, Add to Campaign, and others.

Overriding a tab overrides what a user sees when he or she clicks on the tab. Overriding a standard button overrides its functionality in all parts of theSalesforce user interface. For example, if you override a **New** button for contacts, it overrides the **New** button on the Contacts tab, the **New** button on any Contacts related list, and the **Contact** option in the Create New drop-down list in the sidebar.

However, because s-controls are only available through the Salesforce user interface, overriding the **New** button for contacts has no effect on new contacts that are created via Apex or theAPI.

You can use any custom HTML or URL s-control to override a standard button. As a result, you can either create a brand new page with a new look and feel, or you can leverage an existing Salesforce page and simply add default values for one or more fields.

 Note: You can only override standard buttons that appear on an object's detail page or list views. Buttons that only appear on an edit page or in reports can't be overridden.

As a final note, button overrides shouldn't be confused with Apex triggers, which execute in tandem with the typical behavior. Button overrides replace the standard behavior entirely. For example, if you override the **Delete** button on Accounts and a user attempts to delete an account, it won't necessarily be deleted. Instead, the user is forwarded on to the URL of your choosing, which may or may not include code to delete the account. If you define an Apex delete trigger on Accounts, however, the normal delete behavior still occurs, as long as the trigger doesn't prevent deletion by adding an error to the record.

See Also

- *Populating a Contact Edit Page with Default Values from an Account* on page 124
- *Redirecting a User to an Edit, Detail, or List Page* on page 139
- *Passing Parameters into a Custom Button or Link* on page 137

Creating a Button with Apex

Problem

You want to create a new button that executes logic written in Apex.

Solution

Define a `webService` method in Apex and then call it using the AJAX Toolkit in a button.

For example, suppose you want to create a **Mass Add Notes** button on accounts:

1. Define the Web service method in Apex by clicking **Setup ➤ Build ➤ Code**, clicking **New**, and adding the following code into the body of your new class:

```
global class MassNoteInsert{

  WebService static Integer insertNotes(String iTitle,
                                        String iBody,
                                        Id[] iParentIds) {
    Note[] notes = new Note[0];
    for (Id iParentId : iParentIds) {
        notes.add(new Note(parentId = iParentId,
                           title = iTitle, body = iBody));
    }
    insert notes; //Bulk Insert
    return notes.size();
  }

}
```

 Note: You can't make changes to Apex using the Salesforce user interface in a Salesforce production organization. See *Migrating Apex Between Two Salesforce Organizations* on page 39.

2. Then, click **Setup ➤ Customize ➤ Accounts ➤ Buttons and Links**, and click **New** in the Custom Buttons and Links related list.
3. Name the button and assign it the following attributes:

   - `Display Type`: List Button
   - `Behavior`: Execute JavaScript

- Content Source: OnClick JavaScript

4. In the code for the button, enter

```
{!REQUIRESCRIPT("/soap/ajax/10.0/connection.js")}
{!REQUIRESCRIPT("/soap/ajax/10.0/apex.js")}


var idsToInsert= {!GETRECORDIDS( $ObjectType.Account )};
var noteTitle = prompt("Please enter the title of the note");
var noteBody = prompt("Please enter the body of the note");

if (idsToInsert.length) {

   // Now make a synchronous call to the Apex Web service
   // method
   var result = sforce.apex.execute(
     "MassNoteInsert",        // class
     "insertNotes",           // method
     {iTitle : noteTitle,     // method arguments
      iBody: noteBody,
      iParentIds: idsToInsert });

   alert(result[0] + " notes inserted!"); //response
} else if (idsToInsert.length == 0) {
   alert("Please select the accounts to which" +
         " you would like to add notes.");
}
```

5. Click **Save**.
6. Click **Setup ➤ Customize ➤ Accounts ➤ Search Layouts** and add the button to the Accounts List View layout.

To test this new button, visit the Accounts tab and click **Go!** to view a list of accounts. Select one or more accounts and click **Mass Add Notes**.

See Also

- *Creating a Mass Delete Button* on page 132
- *Creating a Mass Update Button* on page 135
- *Getting Started with Apex* on page 56
- *Defining an Apex Web Service and Calling It from an S-Control* on page 67

Creating Custom Help for a Custom Object

Problem

You want to add help for a custom object so that users can learn about objects or procedures that are specific to your company. You want the help to be available on the custom object's list, detail, and edit pages, and on any related lists and views.

Solution

Create an HTML s-control that displays the help, and then link it to the custom object via the object's definition page:

1. Click **Setup ➤ Build ➤ Custom S-Controls**, click **New Custom S-Control**, and then define an HTML s-control that displays your help.

    For example, this simple help page uses the same style sheet as the Salesforce online help to create help text that fits in with the rest of the Salesforce user interface:

    ```
    <!DOCTYPE HTML PUBLIC
                "-//W3C//DTD HTML 4.01 Transitional//EN"
                "http://www.w3.org/TR/html4/loose.dtd">
    <html>
    <head>

    <!-- The link to the standard Salesforce stylesheet -->
    <link  href="/sCSS/Theme2/default/help.css"
           type="text/css" rel="stylesheet" >
    </head>

    <body>
    <h3> My Custom Help Title</h3>
    <p>Here is the first help topic. This can show a custom
    procedure or description for your application or company.</p>
    </body>

    </html>
    ```

     Tip: Rather than editing the help HTML by hand, write the help in an HTML editor and then save it as raw HTML. You can then paste that HTML into the body of the s-control.

2. Add the custom help s-control to the appropriate object:

    a. Click **Setup ➤ Build ➤ Custom Objects** and click **Edit** next to the name of the object.
    b. Next to the `Context Sensitive Help Setting` field, select "Open a window using a custom S-Control" and choose the help s-control that you defined.

    c. Click **Save**.

Discussion

Integrated custom help for custom objects and custom fields is a new feature in the Summer '07 release. To add help for a custom field, edit the `Help Text` field on any custom field definition. The help text you define displays to users on any record detail or edit page when a user mouses over the help indicator next to the custom field.

See Also

* *Mimicking the Salesforce Look-and-Feel in an S-Control* on page 146

Chapter 8

Customizing Salesforce Pages and Fields

In this chapter ...

- Mimicking the Salesforce Look-and-Feel in an S-Control
- Displaying Fields from a Related Record on a Detail Page
- Formatting a Currency in an S-Control
- Creating a Roll-Up Summary Field with an S-Control
- Allowing Users to Subscribe to Record Update Notifications

In the previous chapter, you learned how to combine native point-and-click platform features with more advanced composite functionality to customize buttons and links in the Salesforce user interface. You can take your app even further by customizing the standard Salesforce pages and fields.

In this chapter, you'll learn how to easily create pages that have the Salesforce styles, how to display fields from a related object on a record detail page, how to format currency data, how to aggregate data from related records, and how to create customized email alerts when records are updated.

Again in this chapter, you'll see the importance of leveraging the platform's native point-and-click tools whenever possible to make developing your apps easier.

Mimicking the Salesforce Look-and-Feel in an S-Control

Problem

You want to build an s-control that matches the Salesforce user interface.

Solution

First make sure that you can't build what you want with a Visualforce page instead of an s-control. Visualforce make mimicking the Salesforce look-and-feel very easy, but as of September 2007, they are only available as a Developer Edition preview. See *Chapter 8: Customizing Salesforce Pages and Fields* on page 249.

If you can't use Visualforce, make sure your s-control meets the following requirements:

- The first line of your s-control must be exactly:

```
<!DOCTYPE HTML PUBLIC "-//W3C//DTD HTML 4.01 Transitional//EN"
 "http://www.w3.org/TR/html4/loose.dtd">
```

- The `<head>` of your s-control must include the Salesforce cascading style sheet (CSS) files. You can easily include them with the `writeCss()` helper function as shown here:

```
<head>
    <script>
        parent.DynamicCss.writeCss('10.0', document);
    </script>
</head>
```

Or you can include them as follows:

```
<head>
<title>My New Page</title>

<!-- Include the Salesforce style sheets -->
<link href="/sCSS/Theme2/en/common.css"
      media="handheld,print,projection,screen,tty,tv"
      rel="stylesheet" type="text/css" />
<link href="/sCSS/10.0/Theme2/allCustom.css"
      media="handheld,print,projection,screen,tty,tv"
      rel="stylesheet" type="text/css" />
</head>
```

- The HTML in your s-control must be well-formed, with closing tags for each opening tag.

Then use a tool like Firebug (as described in *Debugging S-Controls with Firebug* on page 219) to inspect the HTML that renders an element you want to mimic.

Firebug allows you to highlight the relevant code just by hovering over the related list element on the account detail page. You can then add and remove classes from particular tags to determine their effect on how the list appears. Once you're familiar with how the element is constructed and how the classes work, you can use this code as a model for any related list that you want add to a custom s-control.

For example, the following HTML can be used to display an empty Contacts related list on an account detail page:

```
<!DOCTYPE HTML PUBLIC "-//W3C//DTD HTML 4.01 Transitional//EN"
 "http://www.w3.org/TR/html4/loose.dtd">

<html>
<head><title>My S-Control</title>

<script>
   parent.DynamicCss.writeCss('10.0', document);
</script>
</head>

<!-- Setting the body tag's class attribute to 'accountTab' sets the
     color for the entire page to blue. -->
<body class="accountTab">

   <!-- Setting the div tag's class to 'listRelatedObject' signals
        that this is a related list, while also setting it to
        'contactBlock' specifies that the contacts icon should be
        displayed. -->
   <div class="listRelatedObject contactBlock">

   <!-- Setting the next div tag's class to 'bPageBlock' adds the
        border that goes around the related list, while also setting
        it to 'secondaryPalette' applies the appropriate color (in
        this case, standard account blue because we set the body
        class to 'accountTab'. -->
   <div class="bPageBlock secondaryPalette">

   <!-- Now we're writing the header for the related list.-->
   <div class="pbHeader">
      <table cellspacing="0" cellpadding="0" border="0">
         <tr>
            <td class="pbTitle">
               <img width="1" height="1" title=""
                    class="minWidth" alt=""
                    src="/s.gif"/>

               <!-- This next image sets the icon for
                    the related list. -->
               <img title="" class="relatedListIcon"
                    alt="" src="/s.gif"/>
               <h3>Contacts</h3>
            </td>

            <!-- Here we're adding the 'New' button. -->
```

```
            <td class="pbButton">
                <input value=" New " class="btn"
                        name="newContact" onclick="navigateToUrl(
                        '/003/e?retURL=%2F001D000000HRgU6' +
                        '&accid=001D000000HRgU6');"
                        title="New Contact" type="button" />
            </td>

            <!-- And here we're adding the 'Contacts Help'
                link. -->
            <td class="pbHelp">
                <span title="Contacts Help (New Window)"
                        class="help">
                    <a class="linkCol"
                        href="javascript:openPopupFocusEscapePounds(
                            '/help/doc/user_ed.jsp?loc=help' +
                            '&target=contactroles_edit.htm' +
                            '&section=Contact_Roles','Help',
                            700, 600, 'width=700, height=600,' +
                            ' resizable=yes, toolbar=yes, status=no,' +

                            ' scrollbars=yes, menubar=yes,' +
                            ' directories=no, location=no,' +
                            ' dependant=no', false, false);">

                        <span class="linkSpan">Contacts Help</span>
                        <img title="Contacts Help (New Window)"
                            class="helpIcon" alt="Contacts Help
                            (New Window)" src="/s.gif"/>
                    </a>
                </span>
            </td>
        </tr>
    </table>
</div>

<!-- Next we specify the body of the list. Since we do not
    want to display any records, we can just leave a
    message in the header row that there are no records to
    display. -->
<div class="pbBody">
    <table cellspacing="0" cellpadding="0" border="0"
        class="list">
      <tr class="headerRow">
        <th class="noRowsHeader" scope="col">
            No records to display</th>
      </tr>
    </table>
</div>

<!-- Finally we close the related list with the bottom
    border. -->
<div class="pbFooter secondaryPalette">
<div class="bg"/>
</div>
</div>
```

```
</div>
</body>
</html>
```

To use this HTML in your own organization, add it to an s-control and then display the
s-control in an Account page layout:

1. Click **Setup ➤ Build ➤ Custom S-Controls**, then click **New Custom S-Control**.
2. Specify the following values:

   - `Label`: Empty Related List
   - `S-Control Name`: Empty_Related_List
   - `Type`: HTML

3. Cut and paste the preceding HTML into the `Body` text area, and click **Save**.
4. Click **Setup ➤ Customize ➤ Accounts ➤ Page Layouts** and click **Edit** next to
   the Accounts page layout you want to modify.
5. From the `View` drop-down on the right, select Custom S-Controls.
6. Drag the Empty Related List s-control onto a one-column-wide page layout section
   and click **Save**.
7. In the Accounts tab, open an account record to view the empty Contacts related list.

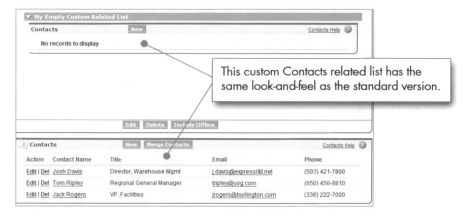

Figure 13: A Custom Related List with the Salesforce Look-and-Feel

Discussion

The HTML tags that are used to display Salesforce pages have few attributes other than `class`
or `id`. That's because the look and feel of Salesforce is generated entirely with cascading style
sheet (CSS) files. CSS files contain all of the information relevant to color, font, borders, and
images that are displayed in the Salesforce user interface.

Even if you're unfamiliar with how the Salesforce `.css` files are constructed, you can still use
the styles they define within your own s-controls by studying existing Salesforce pages. For

example, in the HTML for the Contacts related list shown previously, there are a few things you can discover by removing and replacing classes on different tags:

- If you remove `contactBlock` from the `listRelatedObject` <div> tag, the Contacts icon disappears from the top left corner of the list.
- If you remove `secondaryPalette` from the `bPageBlock` <div> tag, the color is removed from the related list border, but the form of the list remains intact.
- If you remove `pPageBlock`, `pbHeader`, or `pbBody` from their respective <div> tags, the related list is no longer formatted correctly. All three of these styles are critical to the related list structure.

Regardless of the way you assign styles, your s-controls will not have the Salesforce look-and-feel unless you set the `DOCTYPE` parameter in the very first line of your s-control. Setting the `DOCTYPE` at the top of the page tells the browser to use *standards* mode when rendering the s-control. If you forget this step, or if you don't used well-formed HTML in the body of your s-control, the browser reverts to *quirks* mode and won't display text and other elements correctly.

Quirks mode exists in all browser implementations as a way of supporting legacy Web pages that rely on Web browsers' incomplete or incorrect implementations of HTML and CSS to display properly. In standards mode, browsers respect all parts of the HTML and CSS language specifications.

See Also

- *Displaying Fields from a Related Record on a Detail Page* on page 150
- *Debugging S-Controls with Firebug* on page 219
- "Cascading Style Sheets: Learning CSS," available at www.w3.org/Style/CSS/learning.

Displaying Fields from a Related Record on a Detail Page

Problem

You want to show fields from a related object on another object's detail page. Although standard Salesforce functionality allows you to display a related record's name, you also want to show additional fields.

Solution

Use an inline s-control to retrieve and display the information.

For example, in the Recruiting application, a Job Application object links a Candidate to a Position. When a user views a job application record, standard Salesforce functionality only allows the candidate's number to be displayed (for example, C-0007). To also show the related candidate's name, phone number, and email address, use the following HTML:

 Note: For this code sample to work, you must have the Recruiting app metadata in your organization. See *The Sample Recruiting App* on page 9.

```html
<!DOCTYPE HTML PUBLIC
   "-//W3C//DTD HTML 4.01 Transitional//EN"
   "http://www.w3.org/TR/html4/loose.dtd">
<html>
<head>
<title>Candidate</title>

<!-- Include the Salesforce style sheets -->
<link href="/sCSS/Theme2/en/common.css"
media="handheld,print,projection,screen,tty,tv" rel="stylesheet"
type="text/css" />
<link href="/sCSS/10.0/Theme2/allCustom.css"
media="handheld,print,projection,screen,tty,tv" rel="stylesheet"
type="text/css" />

<!-- Get the AJAX Toolkit -->
<script src="/soap/ajax/10.0/connection.js"></script>

<script>

//
// Use a global variable to capture the Id of the Candidate record
// whose data should be retrieved. Use a merge field to access this
// information.
//
var candidateId= "{!Job_Application__c.CandidateId__c}";

//
// Set up a method to write errors to the body of the s-control
// asynchronously.
//
function failure(error) {
   document.body.innerHTML += "Error retrieving candidate info";
   document.body.innerHTML += "<br>API Error: " + error;
}

//
// This function is called when the page loads
//
function initPage() {

   try{

   //
   // Use the retrieve call and the candidateId variable to
   // asynchronously retrieve the desired fields.
   //
   // Note that while the retrieve call used to be more efficient
```

```
    // than the query call, the two calls are now comparable.
    //
        var result= sforce.connection.retrieve("Name, First_Name__c,
                    Last_Name__c,Phone__c,Mobile__c,Email__c",
                    "Candidate__c", [candidateId],
                    {onSuccess: render, onFailure: failure});

    } catch (e) {
      document.body.innerHTML += "Error retrieving candidate info";
      document.body.innerHTML += "<br>Fault code: " + e.faultcode;
      document.body.innerHTML += "<br>Fault string: " + e.faultstring;

    }

}


//
// This method is called asynchronously on success.
// It renders the results on the page.
//
function render(result) {

    try {

        //
        // We'll only get a single result, so get the record
        // from the first element of the result array
        //
        var record = result[0];

        //
        // Now generate HTML output for the body of this page
        //

        //
        // Leverage standard Salesforce detail page styles
        //
       var output = "<div class='bPageBlock secondaryPalette' id='ep'>";

        output += "<div class='pbHeader'>";
        output += "<div class='pbBody'>";
        output += "<div class='pbSubsection' style='display: block;'>"

        //
        // Output Candidate data into a detailList table
        //
        output += "<table class='detailList' cellpadding='0'
                    cellspacing='0' border='0'>";
        output += "<tr>";
        output +="<td class='labelCol'>Candidate</td>"
        output += "<td class='dataCol col02'><a target='_top' href=/"
                    + candidateId + ">" + record.Name + "</a></td>
                    <td class='labelCol empty'> </td>
                    <td class='dataCol empty'> </td>";
        output += "</tr>";
```

```
      output += "<tr>";
      output += "<td class='labelCol'>Name </td>";
      output += "<td class='dataCol col02'>" + record.First_Name__c
              + " " + record.Last_Name__c + "</td>";
      output += "<td class='labelCol'>Phone </td>";
      output += "<td class='dataCol'>" + record.Phone__c + "</td>";
      output += "</tr>";
      output += "<tr><td class='labelCol last'>Email </td>";
      output += "<td class='dataCol col02 last'><a href='mailto:"
              + record.Email__c + "'>" + record.Email__c
              + "</a></td>";
      output += "<td class='labelCol last'>Mobile </td>";
      output += "<td class='dataCol last'>" + record.Mobile__c
              + "</td>";
      output += "</tr></table>";
      output += "</div></div></div><div class='pbFooter
              secondaryPalette'><div class='bg'/></div></div>";

      document.body.innerHTML += output;

   } catch (e) {
      document.body.innerHTML += "Error retrieving candidate
                          information";
      document.body.innerHTML += "<br>Fault code: "
                          + e.faultcode;
      document.body.innerHTML += "<br>Fault string: "
                          + e.faultstring;
}

}

</script>
</head>


<!--Use the custom tab class to match the look of Job Application
    page -->

<body class="Custom79Tab detailPage" onload="initPage();">
   <!-- Candidate data is written here -->
</body>
</html>
```

To use this HTML in your own organization, add it to an s-control and then display the s-control in the Job Application page layout:

1. Click **Setup ➤ Build ➤ Custom S-Controls**, then click **New Custom S-Control**.
2. Specify the following values:

   - `Label`: Candidate Information
   - `S-Control Name`: Candidate_Information
   - `Type`: HTML

3. Cut and paste the preceding HTML into the `Body` text area, and click **Save**.

4. Click **Setup ➤ Build ➤ Custom Objects**, click the Job Application object, and then click **Edit** next to the Job Application page layout you want to modify.

5. From the View drop-down list on the right, select Custom S-Controls.

6. Drag the Candidate Information s-control onto a one-column-wide page layout section, and click **Save**.

7. In the Job Applications tab, open a job application record to view the additional candidate data.

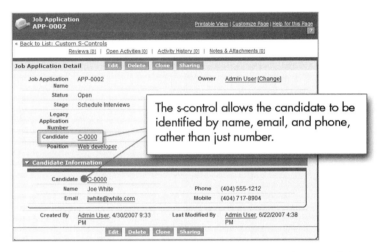

Figure 14: Candidate Information on a Job Application Detail Page

See Also

- *Mimicking the Salesforce Look-and-Feel in an S-Control* on page 146
- *The Sample Recruiting App* on page 9

Formatting a Currency in an S-Control

Problem

You want to display a currency value in a custom s-control, but the API doesn't return currencies in a formatted state.

Solution

Use a code snippet to format currency values properly in JavaScript. The `formatCurrency()` function in the following snippet performs the following checks and manipulations:

- Ensures the value passed to the function is a number

- Adds decimal indicators and two numbers to represent decimal values if there are less than two decimals in the value
- Separates the integer value into chunks of three digits, which are then placed in an array and combined with a separator

```
<script type="text/javascript">
    // The formatCurrency() function adds 2 decimal places and
    // commas to a number using Javascript.
    function formatCurrency(amount) {
        // First check to make sure the amount parameter is a
        // number. If the amount is not a number, return 0.00
        if(isNaN(amount)) { i = 0.00; }

        // Create a string from the amount as a starting point.
        // This string will also be returned with the properly
        // formatted currency amount.
        s = new String(amount);

        // If there is no decimal then add a decimal point and
        // two zeroes
        if(s.indexOf('.') < 0) { s += '.00'; }

        // If there is a decimal and there are not two decimal
        // places, add the zero in the hundreths position.
        if(s.indexOf('.') == (s.length - 2)) { s += '0'; }

        // This is an optional delimiter. Some locales may not
        // like comma as the 1,000 separator, but the comma could be
        // replaced, as could the decimal indicator, above, based
        // on a user's locale.
        var delimiter = ",";

        // Split the string so we are only looking at the left of
        // the decimal for inserting the delimiter(s).
        var a = s.split('.',2)

        // This is the part of the string to the right of the
        // decimal indicator.
        var d = a[1];

        // This is the part of the string to the left of the decimal
        // indicator and is the placeholder we use to process each
        // part into the array.
        var n = a[0];

        // This is the array that will hold each block of the number
        // that will be delimited.
        var a = [];
        while(n.length > 3) {
            // Take the last three characters of the string.
            var block = n.substr(n.length-3);

            // Put the last three characters at the start of the
            // string.
```

```
            a.unshift(block);

            // Now remove the last three characters so processing
            // can continue.
            n = n.substr(0,n.length-3);
        }

        // If there is anything left in our place holder, place it
        // at the beginning of the array.
        if(n.length > 0) { a.unshift(n); }

            // Re-construct the left side of the currency amount by
            // joining the array elements with the specified
            // delimiter.
            n = a.join(delimiter);

            // Put the left and right sides of the '.' together and
            // return the string.
            return s = n + '.' + d;

    }
</script>
```

Discussion

By defining this function in an s-control of type Snippet, the function can be reused by any other s-control with the INCLUDE() function. For example, to include this snippet in another s-control, use the following line in the other s-control:

```
{!INCLUDE($Scontrol.Format_Number_as_Currency)}
```

You can see an example of this usage in *Creating a Roll-Up Summary Field with an S-Control* on page 157, which calculates summary values and then displays the result.

 Note: This INCLUDE line assumes that the name of the s-control (as opposed to its label) is Format_Number_as_Currency.

This function formats currency based on the standard notation used in the United States. If you want to alter the function so that it changes the format based on a user's locale, you can retrieve this information by making a call to the getUserInfo() AJAX Toolkit function.

See Also

- *Using S-Control Snippets in Other S-Controls* on page 51
- *Creating a Roll-Up Summary Field with an S-Control* on page 157

Creating a Roll-Up Summary Field with an S-Control

Problem

You want to see a summary of related records on a record detail page—for example, a summary on an account that totals all closed opportunities in the last year. You want to solve this problem by defining a new field, or using an s-control.

Solution

If the relationship you want to use as the basis for the summary is a master-detail relationship between two custom objects, and you can filter the summarized detail records by the value of another field on the object, create a new roll-up summary custom field using the custom field wizard. This field type is new in the Summer '07 release.

However, if any of the following statements is true:

*   The relationship you want to use as the basis for the summary is not a master-detail relationship between two custom objects
*   You want to filter the summarized detail records by a value in a related object
*   You want to filter the summarized detail records by a dynamic value, such as a relative period of time

Then you can't use the native custom field wizard to create your roll-up summary. Instead, implement the summary by defining an s-control that uses a SOQL query to retrieve the data that you want to summarize, and then calculates and displays the result.

For example, the following s-control sums the total of all opportunities closed and won in the last four quarters:

 Note: The following s-control does not work unless you've already defined the Format_Number_as_Currency s-control described in *Formatting a Currency in an S-Control* on page 154.

```
<html>
<head>
<script type="text/javascript" src="/js/functions.js"></script>
<script src="/soap/ajax/10.0/connection.js"></script>
<style>
       .data {
          font-family:'Arial','Helvetica','sans-serif';
          font-size:12px;
          padding: 2px 0px;
          background-color: #F0F0F0;
       }
</style>
<script type="text/javascript">
```

```
 /* The getTotal() function contains all of the code that should
    execute after the page is rendered.  The function's
    separation allows the query processing to be performed
    asynchronously. */
function getTotal() {

    /* This establishes the state that you need when the
       callback is called. */
    var state = {
        output : document.getElementById("total"),

        /* This code is part of the standard AJAX toolkit
           code, but startTime is not used in this example. */
        startTime : new Date().getTime()
    };

    /* This is the callback handler, which tells the function
       what to do when the response from the query comes back. */

    var callback = {
        //call calculateResult if the request is successful
        onSuccess: calculateResults,
        //call queryFailed if the api request fails
        onFailure: queryFailed,
        source: state
    };

/* This next call is the key to the function. The
   'LAST_N_QUARTERS:4' string literal in the where clause
   allows the query to dynamically filter opportunities that
   closed in the last year each time the query runs.
   The second argument is the callback handler.

   Since this code is part of an s-control, there's no need to
   log in to Salesforce before executing this call--the
   context is already established. Also notice the use of the
   Account.Id merge field, which is populated from the context
   of the page on which this s-control resides. */
   sforce.connection.query("SELECT Amount, Name, Id" +
                      " FROM Opportunity" +
                      " WHERE AccountId = '{!Account.Id}'" +
                      "  AND CloseDate = LAST_N_QUARTERS:4" +
                      "  AND IsClosed = true" +
                      "  AND isWon = true" +
                      "  AND Amount <> 0",callback);

}
/* The calculateResults() function processes the results if the
   query is successful. The first argument is the response from the
   sforce query and the second argument is the handle to the state
   variable which includes the section of the page to write to. */
   function calculateResults(queryResult, source) {

    //Declare and initialize the variable that holds
    //the total.
```

```
      var total = 0;

      //Assign the results of the query to an array.
      records = queryResult.getArray('records');

      //Iterate over the results and sum the total.
      for(var n in records) {
         var opp = records[n];

         //Add the current premium's amount to the running total.
         total += opp.getFloat('Amount');
      }

      //Get the appropriate currency symbol using the
      //getUserInfoResult utility call
      var guir = sforce.connection.getUserInfo();

      //Assign the value to the output area if there was no error.
      //The formatCurrency() function is called here (see the
      //preceding recipe).
      source.output.innerHTML = guir.currencySymbol +
                                formatCurrency(total);
   }

   //The queryFailed() function assigns an error message if the
   //SOQL query failed.
   function queryFailed(error, source) {
      source.output.innerHTML = "ERROR!";
      alert(error);
   }

</script>


<!-- This syntax pulls in an s-control snippet that formats the
     Javascript number into the appropriate currency display
     (commas and 2 decimal places). See the preceding recipe
     for details. -->
{!INCLUDE($Scontrol.Format_Number_as_Currency)}

</head>

<!-- The onLoad event calls the getTotal() function to process the
     calculation -->
<body onLoad="getTotal();">
<!-- This element is initialized with an informational message which
     is asynchronously updated with the value we want. -->
<div class="data" id="total">Loading...</div>
</body>
</html>
```

Discussion

Using an s-control to implement this summary has advantages and disadvantages over using a standard roll-up summary field. One advantage is that you can write any SOQL you want to retrieve the records for summary. You can also easily reuse this code to create other summaries, perhaps by creating an s-control snippet that takes a SOQL statement as a parameter.

However, one of the drawbacks of using an s-control to define the summary is that its logic is generated outside of the native platform in a user's browser. Consequently, you can't use the results in other reports or formula fields, or access the data through the API. You also can't use the value for validation rules or to trigger workflow rules.

Although you might consider using a custom currency field and Apex to circumvent these issues, Apex is not suitable for filtering records by a dynamic date. To do that, the code would need to execute each time the field was queried, either through a page view or via the API. Because Apex doesn't have the equivalent of a "before query" trigger, there's no guarantee the field value would be up-to-date.

See Also

- *Formatting a Currency in an S-Control* on page 154
- *Using S-Control Snippets in Other S-Controls* on page 51
- *Filtering Data Based on a Relative Date* on page 106
- *Deciding When to Use S-Controls, Client Apps, Apex, or Visualforce* on page 30

Allowing Users to Subscribe to Record Update Notifications

Problem

You want to let users subscribe to email alerts every time a record is updated.

Solution

Use a combination of a new custom object, an Apex trigger, an email template, and a workflow email update to implement this functionality.

For example, the following procedure shows how to implement record subscriptions for the Account object:

1. Create a custom object named Account_Subscriber that has a master-detail relationship with Account. This object represents a user who has subscribed to a designated account:

    a. Click **Setup ➤ Build ➤ Custom Objects**, and click **New Custom Object**.

    b. Enter the following information:

    - `Label`: Account Subscriber

- Plural Label: Account Subscribers

c. Accept the remaining defaults, and click **Save**.

d. In the Custom Fields & Relationships related list, click **New** and define a field with the following attributes:

- Data Type: Master-Detail Relationship
- Related To: Account
- Field Label: Account
- Field Name: Account
- Field-Level Security: Visible for all profiles
- Add Related List: On all page layouts

e. In the Custom Fields & Relationships related list, click **New** and define a second field with the following attributes:

- Data Type: Date/Time
- Field Label: Last Email Sent
- Field Name: Last_Email_Sent
- Field-Level Security: Hidden from all profiles
- Add Field: Hidden from all page layouts
-

2. Create an Apex trigger on Account so that each time an account is updated, the Last Email Sent field is updated on all related Account Subscribers to the current date and time:

a. Click **Setup ➤ Customize ➤ Accounts ➤ Triggers**, and click **New**.

 Note: You can't make changes to Apex using the Salesforce user interface in a Salesforce production organization. See *Migrating Apex Between Two Salesforce Organizations* on page 39.

b. Enter the following code:

```
trigger Email_Account_Subscribers on Account (after
update) {
    for (Account_Subscriber__c[] subs :
                    [select Id, Last_Email_Sent__c
                     from Account_Subscriber__c
                    where account__c in :Trigger.new])
    {
        for (Account_Subscriber__c sub : subs) {
            sub.Last_Email_Sent__c = System.now();
        }
        update subs;
```

```
        }
    }
```

   c. Click **Save**.

3. Create an email template that can be used to notify a user when an account is updated:

   a. Click **Setup ➤ Communication Templates ➤ Email Templates**, and click **New Template**.

   b. Select `Text`, and click **Next**.

   c. Create a template with the following attributes:

- `Available for Use`: Selected
- `Email Template Name`: Email_Account_Subscribers
- `Subject`: One of the accounts you've subscribed to has been updated: {!Account_Subscriber__c.Account__c}!

   d. In the `Email Body` enter the following:

```
{!Account_Subscriber__c.Account__c} has been updated!

Click here to view it: {!Account_Subscriber__c.Link}
```

   e. Click **Save**.

4. Create a workflow rule that sends an email whenever an account subscriber record is updated (as long as `Last Email Sent` is not null):

   a. Click **Setup ➤ Customize ➤ Workflow & Approvals ➤ Workflow Rules**, and click **New Rule**.

   b. Select the Account Subscriber object and click **Next**.

   c. Define the rule as follows:

- `Rule Name`: Account Has Been Updated
- `Trigger Type`: Every time a record is created or updated
- `Rule Criteria`: Account Subscriber: Last Email Sent not equal to <blank value>

   d. Click **Save and Next**.

   e. In the Immediate Workflow Actions area, click **Add Workflow Action ➤ New Email**.

   f. Define the workflow alert as follows:

- `Description`: Account has been updated
- `Email Template`: Email_Account_Subscribers

- `Selected Recipients`: Record Owner (select Owner from the Search drop-down list to view this option)

   g. Click **Save**, then **Done**.

   h. In the Workflow Rule detail page, click **Activate**.

To test out subscriptions, view an account and click **New** in the Account Subscribers related list. Enter any value in the `Account Subscriber Name` field—regardless of what you enter, you'll receive an email update the next time this record is updated because you are the owner of the Account Subscriber record.

Discussion

Although there are numerous ways of expanding and improving this example, this recipe shows just how far you can get leveraging built-in, declarative functionality on the platform. Although we needed to write a simple trigger in Apex to update the `Last Email Update` field on all related account subscriber records, everything else was built using the platform's native point-and-click functionality.

Chapter 9

Integrating with Other Services

Because the apps that run on the Force.com platform are available on demand on the Web, you can take advantage of a wide array of other Web services to create *mash-ups*. From sending outbound messages to an external Web service, to utilizing Salesforce SOA (Service-Oriented Architecture) with Apex, to sending SMS messages to a mobile phone—the platform gives you a variety of integration options to create new types of functionality and new classes of apps.

Sending Outbound Messages with Workflow

Problem

You want to send an outbound message to an external Web service when records are created or updated in Salesforce.

Solution

Set up a workflow rule to send the outbound message, generate the WSDL document for the message, and then set up a listener in your language of choice.

For the following example, we'll revisit our sample Recruiting application. We'll set up a message to a legal services provider if a visa is required before a candidate can start his or her new job:

1. Set up a workflow rule that triggers an outbound message:

   a. Click **Setup ➤ Customize ➤ Workflow & Approvals ➤ Workflow Rules** and create a new workflow rule that fires when a candidate is created, or when a candidate is edited and did not previously meet the rule's criteria. Set the criteria for the rule to be "Visa Required equals True."

   b. Add an outbound message workflow action:

      a. In the Immediate Workflow Actions area, click **Add Workflow Action ➤ New Outbound Message**.

      b. Enter a name and description for the outbound message.

      c. Specify the `Endpoint URL` for the recipient of the message. Salesforce sends a SOAP message to this endpoint, which is the Web service listener that will consume the outbound message.

      d. Select a Salesforce user whose security settings will control the data that's visible for the message.

      e. Select `Include Session ID` if you want the Salesforce `sessionId` included in the message. You should include it if you intend to make API calls and you don't want to include a username and password in the body of your message (which is far less secure than sending the `sessionId`).

      f. Select the field values that you want included in the outbound message.

      g. Click **Save**.

   c. Activate the workflow rule by returning to the Workflow Rule detail page and clicking **Activate**.

"Sending Outbound Messages with Workflow" contributed by Markus Spohn, Director of Product Management, Integration, for salesforce.com

2. Generate the WSDL document for your outbound message: Return to the Outbound Message detail page by clicking **Setup ➤ Customize ➤ Workflow & Approvals ➤ Outbound Messagaes** and selecting the name of the outbound message. Then click **Click for WSDL**. This file is bound to the outbound message and contains the instructions about how to reach the endpoint service and what data is sent to it. Save the file to your local machine.

3. Build a listener for the outbound message. This Web service endpoint has to conform to the definition of the WSDL file. For example, to build a listener using .NET:

   a. Run `wsdl.exe/serverInterfaceleads.wsdl` with .NET 2.0. This generates `NotificationServiceInterfaces.cs`, which defines the notification interface.

   b. Create a class that implements `NotificationServiceInterfaces.cs`.

   While there are a number of ways to do this, one simple way is to compile the interface to a .dll first (.dlls must be in the `bin` directory in ASP.NET):

   ```
   mkdir bin csc /t:library /out:bin\nsi.dll
   NotificationServiceInterfaces.cs
   ```

   Then write an ASMX-based Web service that implements this interface. For example, a very simple implementation in `MyNotificationListener.asmx` might be:

   ```
   <%@WebService class="MyNotificationListener"
                 language="C#"%>
   class MyNotificationListener : INotificationBinding
   {
       public notificationsResponse
             notifications(notifications n)
       {
           notificationsResponse r =
                 new notificationsResponse();
           r.Ack = true;
           return r;
       }
   }
   ```

   c. Deploy the service by creating a new virtual directory in IIS for the directory that contains `MyNotificationListener.asmx`.

   You can test that the service is deployed by viewing the service page with a browser. For example, if you create a virtual directory named `salesforce`, navigate to `http://localhost/salesforce/MyNotificationListener.asmx`.

Discussion

Although this recipe only outlines the procedure for a .NET-based solution using IIS, the process for other Web services-enabled languages and tools is similar. Note that your listener must meet the following requirements:

- It must be reachable from the public Internet.
- If it uses SSL, it must use one of the following ports:

  - 80: this port only accepts HTTP connections
  - 443: this port only accepts HTTPS connections
  - 7000-10000: these ports accept HTTP or HTTPS connections

- If it requires client certificates, you must have the current Salesforce client certificate available at **Setup ➤ Integrate ➤ API**.
- The common name (CN) of the listener's certificate must match the domain name for your endpoint's server, and the certificate must be issued by a Certificate Authority trusted by the Java 2 Platform, Standard Edition 5.0 (JDK 1.5).

See Also

- *Tracking Outbound Messages from Workflow* on page 168
- *Sending Messages from Apex* on page 169
- *Creating an Integration User* on page 180
- "Outbound Messaging" in the *Force.com Web Services API Developer's Guide* at www.salesforce.com/us/developer/docs/api/index_CSH.htm# sforce_api_om_outboundmessaging.htm
- The "Creating an Outbound Messaging Notification Service with CSharp and .Net Framework 2.0" whitepaper at wiki.apexdevnet.com/index.php/ Creating_an_Outbound_Messaging_Notification_Service_with_CSharp_and_.Net_Framework_2.0

Tracking Outbound Messages from Workflow

Problem

You want to track the status of the outbound messages that have been sent to external servers as a result of a workflow rule.

Solution

Click **Setup ➤ Monitoring ➤ View the Outbound Message Queue**.

"Tracking Outbound Messages from Workflow" contributed by Markus Spohn, Director of Product Management, Integration, for salesforce.com

Alternatively, click **Setup ➤ Customize ➤ Workflow & Approvals ➤ Outbound Messages**, and then click **View Message Delivery Status**. From this page you can:

- View the status of your outbound messages, including the total number of attempted deliveries
- View the action that triggered the outbound message by clicking any workflow or approval process action ID
- Click **Retry** next to a message to immediately re-deliver the message
- Click **Del** next to a message to permanently remove the outbound message from the queue

See Also

- *Sending Outbound Messages with Workflow* on page 166
- *Sending Data to a Mobile Phone from an S-Control* on page 173
- *Sending Messages from Apex* on page 169
- "Outbound Messaging" in the *Force.com Web Services API Developer's Guide* at www.salesforce.com/us/developer/docs/api/index_CSH.htm# sforce_api_om_outboundmessaging.htm
- The "Creating an Outbound Messaging Notification Service with CSharp and .Net Framework 2.0" whitepaper at wiki.apexdevnet.com/index.php/ Creating_an_Outbound_Messaging_Notification_Service_with_CSharp_and_.Net_Framework_2.0

Sending Messages from Apex

Problem

You want to send a message to a third-party Web service from an Apex class or trigger because the logic that controls when the message should be sent can't be defined with workflow rules and outbound messaging.

Solution

Use Salesforce SOA (Service-Oriented Architecture) to transform a WSDL into an Apex class, register the external service, and write an Apex trigger or class that makes calls to it.

For example, to invoke the Stock Quote service from www.webservicex.net:

1. Download the Stock Quote WSDL from www.webservicex.net/WCF/ServiceDetails.aspx?SID=19.
2. Consume the Stock Quote WSDL using Salesforce SOA:

"Sending Messages from Apex" contributed by Chris Fry, Senior Director of Platform Development for salesforce.com

a. In the application, click **Setup ➤ Build ➤ Code**.

b. Click **Generate from WSDL**.

c. Click **Browse** to navigate to a WSDL document on your local hard drive or network, or type in the full path. This WSDL document is the basis for the Apex class you are creating and must be 1 MB or less.

Note:

The WSDL document you specify may contain a URL that references an outbound port.

For security reasons, Salesforce restricts the outbound ports you may specify to one of the following:

- 80: This port only accepts HTTP connections.
- 443: This port only accepts HTTPS connections.
- 7000-10000 (inclusive): These ports accept HTTP or HTTPS connections.

d. Click **Parse WSDL** to verify the WSDL document contents. The application generates a default class name for each namespace in the WSDL document and reports any errors.

e. Modify the class names as desired. While you can save more than one WSDL namespace into a single class by using the same class name for each namespace, Apex classes can be no more than 100,000 characters total.

f. Click **Generate Apex**. The final page of the wizard shows which classes were successfully generated, along with any errors from other classes. The page also provides a link to view the generated code if it was successful.

Note: You can't make changes to Apex using the Salesforce user interface in a Salesforce production organization. See *Migrating Apex Between Two Salesforce Organizations* on page 39.

3. Register the www.webservicex.com site with your Salesforce organization:

a. Click **Setup ➤ Security Controls ➤ Remote Site Settings**, and click **New Remote Site**.

b. Enter a descriptive term for the `Remote Site Name`.

c. Enter http://www.webservicex.com as the URL for the remote site.

Note: For security reasons, Salesforce restricts the outbound ports you can specify in this link to one of the following:

- 80: This port only accepts HTTP connections.
- 443: This port only accepts HTTPS connections.

- 7000-10000 (inclusive): These ports accept HTTP or HTTPS connections.

   d. Optionally, enter a description of the site that will help you and others identify it.

   e. Click **Save**.

4. Click **Setup ➤ Build ➤ Code**, click **New**, and define the following Apex class:

```
global class TestCallOut {

   WebService static String quote(String symbol) {
     wwwWebservicexNet.StockQuoteSoap stub =
        new wwwWebservicexNet.StockQuoteSoap();
     return stub.GetQuote(symbol);
   }

}
```

5. Define an s-control that makes a call to `TestCallOut.quote()` for the CRM stock ticker symbol:

   a. Click **Setup ➤ Build ➤ Custom S-Controls**, and click **New Custom S-Control**.

   b. Enter the following values:

   - `Label`: Generate Stock Quote
   - `S-Control Name`: Generate_Stock_Quote
   - `Type`: HTML

   c. Copy the following code into the body of the s-control.

```
<html>
<head>
<script type="text/javascript"
src="/js/functions.js"></script>
<script src="/soap/ajax/10.0/connection.js"></script>
<script src="/soap/ajax/10.0/apex.js"></script>
<script>

   function stockQuote() {
       var result =
sforce.apex.execute("TestCallOut","quote",{symbol:"CRM"});

       document.getElementById('userNameArea').innerHTML
 = 'Today's CRM Stockquote:  '+result;
}
</script>
</head>

<body onload=stockQuote()>
  <div id=userNameArea>
```

```
            </div>
          </body>
        </html>
```

    d. Click **Save**.

To test the s-control, add it to a custom Web tab by clicking **Setup ➤ Build ➤ Custom Tabs**, clicking **New** in the Web Tabs related list, and stepping through the wizard.

Figure 15: A Stock Quote Callout that Uses Salesforce SOA

Discussion

When you need to send a message to an external Web service from Salesforce, there are two ways of doing it:

- With an outbound message from a workflow process
- With an outbound message from Apex using Salesforce SOA

The difference between these two solutions is that outbound messages from workflow are asynchronous, while outbound messages from Apex using Salesforce SOA are not. As a result, it's a better practice to use workflow to send your outbound messages because the solution is more scalable and your process won't consume a synchronous end user request thread to do something that could have used a bulk background process instead.

However, just as workflow has limitations in the ways that it can be used to define business logic, outbound messaging via workflow also has its own restrictions. When you need to send an message to an external Web service according to logic that can't be defined with a workflow rule, use Salesforce SOA instead.

See Also

- *Sending Outbound Messages with Workflow* on page 166

Sending Data to a Mobile Phone from an S-Control

Problem

You want to send data from Salesforce to a mobile phone using an SMS service.

Solution

Use an s-control to gather data and create a request, and then take advantage of the AJAX toolkit's `remoteFunction()` feature to make a callout to Google's free `sendtophone` service.

The following example creates a custom button that sends an account's name and address to the mobile phone of a Salesforce user:

Note: With minor changes, this code can work with any standard or custom object.

1. Enable www.google.com as a remote site for your organization:

   a. Click **Setup ➤ Security Controls ➤ Remote Site Settings**, and click **New Remote Site**.

   b. Enter the following information:

      - `Remote Site Name`: Google
      - `Remote Site URL`: http://www.google.com

   c. Click **Save**.

2. Add a custom `Cell Phone Carrier` text field to the User object (click **Setup ➤ Customize ➤ Users ➤ Fields ➤ New**).

3. For each user who you'll be using for testing, update the `Mobile` phone number and the `Cell Phone Carrier` fields as appropriate (click **Setup ➤ Manage Users ➤ Users**). Use one of the values that the Google service expects:

Cell Phone Carrier	Value for Cell Phone Carrier Field
Alaska Communications Systems	ACS
Alltel	ALLTEL

Cell Phone Carrier	Value for Cell Phone Carrier Field
AT&T/Cingular	ATT
Cellular South	CELL_SOUTH
CellularOne	CELLULARONE
Centennial Wireless	CENTENNIAL
Cincinnati Bell	CINCINNATI_BELL
Helio	HELIO
MetroPCS	METROPCS
Midwest Wireless	MIDWEST_WIRELESS
Nextel	NEXTEL
Omnipoint	OMNIPOINT
Qwest	QWEST
Sprint	SPRINT
SunCom Wireless	SUNCOM
T-Mobile	TMOBILE
Tracfone	TRACFONE_US
Unicel	RCC
US Cellular	USCELLULAR
Verizon	VERIZON
Virgin Mobile	VIRGIN
Western Wireless	WESTERN_WIRELESS

4. Define an s-control to send the appropriate message:

    a. Click **Setup ➤ Build ➤ Custom S-Controls**, and click **New Custom S-Control**.

    b. Enter the following values:

- `Label`: Send Account Location to Phone
- `S-Control Name`: Send_Account_Location_to_Phone
- `Type`: HTML

c. Copy the following code into the body of the s-control.

```
<html>
<head>
<script type="text/javascript"
        src="/js/functions.js"></script>
<script src="/soap/ajax/10.0/connection.js"></script>

<script type="text/javascript">

// Construct a simple message, and send it to a phone
// using the Google sendtophone service.
function init() {

    var l = window.location;
    if ( l.protocol == 'https:' ) {
        // This code replaces the iframe protocol
        // to match google
        l.href = l.href.replace(/https/,'http');
        return;
    }

    /* Send the account address of the current
     * account to the current user's phone,
     * based on the Mobile and Call Carrier
     * fields on the current User record.
     */
    var carrier = "{!User.Cell_Phone_Carrier__c}";
    if ( carrier == "" ) {
        alert( "No cell phone carrier specified" +
                " in your personal information");
        setTimeout("window.close();",100);
        return;
    }

    var cell_number = "{!User.MobilePhone}";
    if ( cell_number == "" ) {
        alert( "No cell phone number specified"+
                " in your personal information");
        setTimeout("window.close();",100);
        return;
    }

    // Send the message to google.
    sforce.connection.remoteFunction( {
        url :'http://www.google.com/sendtophone',
        mimeType: "text/plain",
        requestHeaders:
            {"Content-Type":"application/x-www"
                         + "-form-urlencoded"},
        method: "POST",
        requestData: "gl=US&hl=en"
            + "&client=navclient-ffsms"
            + "&c=1&carrier="
            + carrier
            + "&subject={!Account.Name}"
```

```
                    + "&text={!Account.BillingStreet}\n"
                    + "{!Account.BillingCity}"
                    + "&mobile_user_id="
                    + cell_number,
            async: true,
            onFailure : done,
            onSuccess : done
        });
    }

    function done( response ) {
    document.getElementById('sendtophone').
                        innerHTML = response;
    setTimeout("window.close();",5000);
    }
    </script>
    </head>


    <body onload="init();">
    <div id="sendtophone" >
    </div>
    </body>
    </html>
```

   d. Click **Save**.

5. Add the s-control to a custom button on the Account detail page:

   a. Click **Setup ➤ Customize ➤ Accounts ➤ Buttons and Links**, and click **New**.

   b. Enter the following values:

   - `Label`: Send to My Phone
   - `Name`: Send_to_My_Phone
   - `Display Type`: Detail Page Button
   - `Behavior`: Display in New Window
   - `Content Source`: Custom S-Control
   - `Custom S-Control`: Send Account Location to Phone

   c. Click **Save**.

    Tip: If you define a button that displays in a new window, you can control the properties of that window by clicking **Window Open Properties** in the button's detail page.

   d. Click **Setup ➤ Customize ➤ Accounts ➤ Page Layouts**, and click **Edit** next to the appropriate account layout.

   e. Double-click **Detail Page Buttons** in the Button Section.

   f. Move Send to My Phone to the Selected Buttons list, and click **OK**.

> **g.** Click **Save** on the page layout.

To test the button, visit an account record with a valid name and billing address and click **Send to My Phone**. A text message should arrive shortly.

Discussion

Prior to the introduction of Salesforce SOA, using an external service like `sendtophone` presented problems because the Web page that called the service violated the cross-domain security limitation imposed by modern browsers. With Salesforce SOA, the AJAX `remoteFunction` method makes it possible to call out to other services through the salesforce.com domain, avoiding the security limitation.

See Also

- *Sending Outbound Messages with Workflow* on page 166
- *Sending Messages from Apex* on page 169
- An example of the Google `sendtophone` service at toolbar.google.com/send/sms/index.php

Chapter 10

Writing Web Controls and Client Applications

As you become more experienced developing on the platform, you'll find that there are some types of applications and integrations that can't be handled in an s-control. For situations like these, you can leverage the powerful, SOAP-based API to write Web controls or client applications that execute on an external server.

In this chapter, you'll learn about choosing a development language, selecting a WSDL document, and managing API authentication, sessions, and timeouts. We'll also take a look at what it takes to build a full-fledged client application that demonstrates several API best practices.

Selecting a Development Language

Problem

You want to add composite functionality to your application but you don't know what languages are supported.

Solution

Use HTML or HTML plus JavaScript if you're interested in building an s-control. Alternatively, you can also write Java applets, use Microsoft Silverlight content, or use Adobe Flex to develop s-controls (if you download the Flex Toolkit for Force.com). Only these languages are supported for s-controls because the code in an s-control is always executed within a Web browser.

If you're interested in building a Web control or client application, write your code in any language that supports Web services, including Java, Perl, Python, PHP, Ruby on Rails, C#.NET, Visual Basic.NET, and Cocoa for Mac OS X. You can find toolkits and code samples for several Web-services-enabled languages on the ADN website at wiki.apexdevnet.com/index.php/API.

See Also

- *Deciding When to Use S-Controls, Client Apps, Apex, or Visualforce* on page 30
- *Selecting a WSDL* on page 181
- *Installing the Flex Toolkit for Force.com* on page 21

Creating an Integration User

Problem

You're setting up a Web control or client application that logs into Salesforce through the API, and you need to log in as a Salesforce user for authentication. However, you don't want to choose a user who may end up leaving the company in the future.

Solution

Create a special user in your organization that you use solely for integration purposes. Assign this user a special profile with the following permissions selected:

- **API Only**. This permission specifies that the user can only log in through the API. This prevents the user from being used for any purpose other than integration scenarios.
- **Modify All Data**. This permission specifies that the user can view any data stored in the database and edit any field with the editable flag (some fields, like CreatedDate, do not

have the editable flag set and cannot be edited by any user, regardless of the "Modify All Data" permission). This permission is also required for any user who wants to upsert non-unique external IDs through the API.

Selecting a WSDL

Problem

You want to use the API in a Web control or a client application, but you don't know which WSDL document you should import into your development environment.

Solution

A WSDL document is an XML file that describes the format of messages you send and receive from a Web service. It's the protocol that your development environment's SOAP client uses to communicate with external services like Salesforce.

Salesforce provides two primary WSDL documents for operating on objects and fields in an organization, plus three additional WSDL documents for specific features of workflow rules and the API. Choose the WSDL document you should download and consume based on the type of application you're going to develop:

Enterprise WSDL

The Enterprise WSDL is a strongly-typed WSDL document for customers who want to build an integration with their Salesforce organization only, or for partners who are using tools like Tibco or webMethods to build integrations that require strong typecasting.

Strong typing means that an object in Salesforce has an equivalent object in Java, .NET, or whatever environment is accessing the API. This model generally makes it easier to write code because you don't need to deal with any underlying XML structures. It's also safer because data and schema dependencies are resolved at compile time, not at runtime.

The downside of the Enterprise WSDL, however, is that it only works with the schema of a single Salesforce organization because it's bound to all of the unique objects and fields that exist in that organization's data model. Consequently, if you use the Enterprise WSDL, you must download and re-consume it whenever your organization makes a change to its custom objects or fields. Additionally, you can't use it to create solutions that can work for multiple organizations.

Partner WSDL

The Partner WSDL is a loosely-typed WSDL document for customers, partners, and ISVs who want to build an integration or an AppExchange app that can work across multiple Salesforce organizations.

With this WSDL document, the developer is responsible for marshaling data in the correct object representation, which typically involves editing the XML. However, you're also freed from being dependent on any particular data model or Salesforce organization. Consequently, if you use the Partner WSDL, you only need to download and consume it once, regardless of any changes to custom objects or fields.

Outbound Message WSDL

The Outbound Message WSDL document is for developers who want to send outbound messages from a workflow rule or approval process to an external service.

Apex WSDL

The Apex WSDL document is for developers who want to run or compile Apex scripts in another environment or build a new Apex IDE.

Metadata WSDL

The Metadata WSDL document is for users who want to use the API metadata calls. See "Metadata Calls and Objects (Developer Preview Release)" at www.salesforce.com/us/developer/docs/api/index_CSH.htm#Template/meta_intro.htm.

See Also

- *Generating a WSDL Document* on page 182
- *Using the Partner WSDL* on page 183
- *Sending Outbound Messages with Workflow* on page 166

Generating a WSDL Document

Problem

You want to use the API in a Web control or client application, but first you need to generate the appropriate WSDL document.

Solution

If you want to generate a WSDL document other than an Outbound Message WSDL document, log in to your Salesforce organization and click **Setup ➤ Integrate ➤ API**.

Right-click the WSDL document you want to generate, and select **Save Link As** in Firefox, or **Save Target As** in Internet Explorer.

If you want to view a WSDL document without downloading it, simply click the download link for the WSDL document you want to view.

 Tip: To keep track of the WSDL documents you download, name them with a date/time stamp.

If you want to generate an Outbound Message WSDL document, click **Setup ➤ Customize ➤ Workflow & Approvals ➤ Outbound Messagaes**. Select the name of the outbound message and then click **Click for WSDL**. This file is bound to the outbound message and contains the instructions about how to reach the endpoint service and what data is sent to it.

See Also

- *Selecting a WSDL* on page 181
- *Using the Partner WSDL* on page 183

Using the Partner WSDL

Problem

You've decided that you want to use the Partner WSDL, but you don't know how to work with the loosely-typed SOAP messages.

Solution

The Partner WSDL is based on a generic SObject, which represents a Salesforce record such as a particular account or contact. Every SObject has the following properties:

Name	Type	Description
Type	string	The API name of the object on which this SObject is based. For example, Account, Position__c, and so on.
ID	ID	The unique ID for this SObject. For the create() call, this value is null. For all other API calls, this value must be specified.

"Using the Partner WSDL" contributed by Simon Fell, Principal Member of the Technical Staff at salesforce.com

Name	Type	Description
Any	XMLElement[] (in .NET) MessageElement[] (in Java)	An array of fields for the SObject. Each element of the array consists of an XML tag, where the name of the field is the name of the element, and the value of the field is the body of the tag. For example: `<name>value</name>`
FieldsToNull	string[]	An array of one or more field names whose value you want to explicitly set to null. This array is used only with the update() or upsert() calls. Note that you can only specify fields that you can update and that are nillable. For example, specifying an ID field or required field results in a runtime error.

The Partner WSDL provides methods that allow you to work with these properties so that you can perform the same tasks with the Partner WSDL as you can with the Enterprise WSDL. For example, the following Java code creates a job application record using the Enterprise WSDL:

```
public Job_Application__c createJobApp(String candidateId,
                                       String positionId) {
    Job_Application__c jobApp = new Job_Application__c();
    jobApp.setCandidate__c(new ID(candidateId));
    jobApp.setPosition__c(new ID(positionId));
    jobApp.setStatus__c("New");
    SaveResult [] sr = binding.create(new SObject[] {jobApp});
    if(!sr[0].isSuccess())
        throw new SaveException(sr[0]);
    jobApp.setId(sr[0].getId());
    return jobApp;
}
```

The same createJobApp() method can also be written in Java with the Partner WSDL:

```
public SObject createJobApp(String candidateId,
                            String positionId) {
    SObject jobApp = new SObject();
    // Submit four fields as part of the Any array on the 184
    // Chapter 11:Writing Web Controls and Client Applications
    // Job_Application__c record
    MessageElement[] fields = new MessageElement[3];
    // Candidate id
    field[0] = util.createNewXmlElement("Candidate__c", candidateId);

    // Position id
```

```
        field[1] = util.createNewXmlElement("Position__c", positionId);
        // Status
        field[2] = util.createNewXmlElement("Status__c", "New");
        jobApp.set_any(fields);
        jobApp.setType("Job_Application__c");
        SaveResult [] sr = binding.update(new SObject[] {jobApp});
        if(!sr[0].isSuccess())
            throw new SaveException(sr[0]);
        jobApp.setId(sr[0].getId());
        return jobApp;
}
```

The following VB.NET code creates a position record using the Enterprise WSDL:

```
Dim p as New Position__c
p.Id = "a00D0000005iYiq"
p.Name = "Analyst"
p.Status__c = "Open"
binding.create(New sObject() {p})
```

This code can be written using the Partner WSDL as follows:

```
Dim p as New SObject
  p.Type = "Position__c"
  p.Id = "a00D0000005iYiq"
  Dim doc as New XmlDocument
  Dim e1, e2 as XmlElement
  e1 = doc.CreateNewElement("Name")
  e2 = doc.CreateNewElement("Status")
  e1.InnerText = "Analyst"
  e2.InnerText = "Open"
  p.Any = new XmlElement() {e1,e2}
  binding.update(New sObject() {p})
```

 Note: In these examples, notice that Java and .NET use different elements to represent field name/value pairs. For example, given the following name/value pair:

```
<City__c>Chicago</City__c>
```

- Java uses a `MessageElement` where:

    - City__c is the `Name`
    - Chicago is the `Value`

- .NET uses an `XMLElement` where:

    - City__c is the `LocalName`
    - Chicago is the `InnerText`

Use the Partner WSDL in conjunction with the `describeGlobal()` and `describeSObject()` metadata API calls. For example, a particular object's type is defined in the `name` field in the returned `DescribeSObjectResult`. Likewise, the name of an object's field is defined in the name field of the Field type in the returned `DescribeSObjectResult`.

See Also

- *Selecting a WSDL* on page 181
- *Generating a WSDL Document* on page 182
- *Building a Web Portal with Salesforce Data* on page 208

Logging In to the API

Problem

You need to log in to the API because you're writing a Web control or client application that originates from outside the Salesforce user interface.

Solution

Acquire a Salesforce session ID and the appropriate host for your organization by using the `login()` call.

For example, the following Java code from the wrapper class described in *Using a Wrapper Class for Common API Functions* on page 195:

- Logs in to Salesforce
- Sets the login time
- Resets the URL for the SOAP binding stub to the returned server URL
- Creates a new session header for the binding class variable
- Updates the wrapper class' `sessionID` and `serverURL` variables

```
/**
 * This method is used to log in to salesforce and set the
 * private class variables for the wrapper, including the
 * session ID.
 */
public void login() throws UnexpectedErrorFault, InvalidIdFault,
                           LoginFault, RemoteException,
                           ServiceException {

        resetBindingStub();
```

"Logging In to the API" contributed by Simon Fell, Principal Member of the Technical Staff at salesforce.com

```
        LoginResult loginResult = binding.login(username, password);
        this.nextLoginTime = System.currentTimeMillis() +
                             (this.sessionlength * 60000);

        this.binding._setProperty(SoapBindingStub.
                             ENDPOINT_ADDRESS_PROPERTY,
                             loginResult.getServerUrl());
        this.sessionId = loginResult.getSessionId();
        this.serverUrl = loginResult.getServerUrl();

        // Create a new session header object and set the
        // session id to that returned by the login
        SessionHeader sh = new SessionHeader();
        sh.setSessionId(loginResult.getSessionId());
        this.binding.setHeader(new
           SforceServiceLocator().getServiceName().getNamespaceURI(),

           "SessionHeader", sh);
    }
```

This VB.NET code performs the same logic as for the VB.NET version of the wrapper class (see *Using a Wrapper Class for Common API Functions* on page 195):

```
    Public Sub Login()
        Dim lr As sforce.LoginResult
        Me._binding.Url = Me._host
        lr = Me._binding.login(username, password)
        Me._nextLoginTime = Now().AddMinutes(Me.sessionlength)
        'Reset the SOAP endpoint to the returned server URL
        Me._binding.Url = lr.serverUrl
        Me._binding.SessionHeaderValue = New sforce.SessionHeader
        Me._binding.SessionHeaderValue.sessionId = lr.sessionId
        Me._sessionId = lr.sessionId
        Me._serverURL = lr.serverUrl
    End Sub
```

Discussion

Similar to the way the login page works in the Salesforce user interface, the `login()` call takes a username and password and executes a login sequence on `https://www.salesforce.com/`. If the login is successful, the `login()` call returns a session ID and URL. The session ID represents the user's authentication token and the URL points to the host that contains data for the user's organization.

 Note: For performance and reliability, the platform runs on multiple instances (for example, na1.salesforce.com, na2.salesforce.com, and so on), but data for any single organization is always consolidated on a single instance. As long as you use the URL that is returned from the `login()` call, you should never need to know the actual instance that hosts an organization's data.

Figure 16: Authenticating with the login() Call

Once you've obtained a session ID and server URL, you'll generally include the session ID in every API call, and you'll direct your client to make the API request to the host that you obtained.

Tip: It's not necessary to use `login()` when writing an s-control that executes within the Salesforce user interface because the user accessing the s-control has already logged in and acquired a session ID.

See Also

- *Using a Wrapper Class for Common API Functions* on page 195
- *Managing Sessions* on page 188
- *Changing the Session Timeout Value* on page 190
- *Batching Records for API Calls* on page 192

Managing Sessions

Problem

You've written an integration that will last longer than your session timeout value, but logging in to Salesforce every time you need to make an API call is inefficient.

Solution

Write a method that checks to see whether your session ID is about to expire by comparing your last login time with the current session length. When this method returns true, log in again.

"Managing Sessions" contributed by Simon Fell, Principal Member of the Technical Staff at salesforce.com

For example, the following Java code from the wrapper class discussed in *Using a Wrapper Class for Common API Functions* on page 195 implements a `loginRequired()` method:

```java
/**
 * This method returns true if a login to Salesforce is
 * necessary, otherwise false. It should be used to check the
 * session length before performing any API calls.
 */
private boolean loginRequired() {
    if (sessionId == null || sessionId.length() == 0)
        return true;
    return !isConnected();
}

/**
 * This method checks whether the session is active or not
 * @return boolean
 */
public boolean isConnected() {
    return System.currentTimeMillis() < nextLoginTime;
}
```

This VB.NET function implements the same logic:

```vbnet
Private Function loginRequired() As Boolean
    loginRequired = Not (isConnected())
End Function

Public Function isConnected() As Boolean
    If _sessionId <> "" And _sessionId <> Nothing Then
        If Now() > Me._nextLoginTime Then
            isConnected = False
        End If
        isConnected = True
    Else
        isConnected = False
    End If
End Function
```

 Tip: Be sure that the value you use for session length is no more than the configured session timeout value. Because the session timeout value for an organization is not accessible through the API, it's a good idea to build applications that assume a thirty-minute session timeout so that administrators don't inadvertently break your integrations.

Discussion

The session timeout value is the amount of time a single session ID remains valid before expiring. While a session is always valid for a user while he or she is working in the Web interface, sessions instantiated via the API expire after the duration of the session timeout, regardless of how many transactions are still taking place.

The example provided in this recipe is very simple. Another, more robust option is to catch the session expiration remove exception (Exception Code - INVALID_SESSION_ID) and only then log in again. This ensures that you only log in when absolutely necessary and that you'll get a new session ID if your current session ever becomes invalid. This method is usually coupled with implementing retry logic.

See Also

- *Changing the Session Timeout Value* on page 190
- *Logging In to the API* on page 186
- *Implementing the Query/Query More Pattern* on page 191
- *Using a Wrapper Class for Common API Functions* on page 195
- *Batching Records for API Calls* on page 192

Changing the Session Timeout Value

Problem

You want to change the session timeout value from the two hour default so that your integrations can work longer without having to get a new session ID.

Solution

Log in to the application as an administrator and click **Setup ➤ Security Controls ➤ Session Settings**. Change the Timeout value to one of the few preset values. They range from as little as 30 minutes to as long as 8 hours.

 Note:

- Make sure you update any integration code so that it uses the new timeout value! Otherwise your integrations might break.
- Changing the session timeout value affects all users equally in an organization.

See Also

- *Logging In to the API* on page 186
- *Managing Sessions* on page 188

Implementing the Query/Query More Pattern

Problem

You need to issue queries that return more than 2000 records, but the `query()` call can only return up to 2000 at a time.

Solution

Use `queryMore()` to retrieve any additional records in batches of up to 2000 at a time. The `queryMore()` call takes a single `queryLocator` parameter that specifies the index of the last result record that was returned. This `queryLocator` is created and returned by the previous `query()` or `queryMore()` call.

When the `query()` or `queryMore()` calls return a result with the `isDone` flag set to true, there are no more records to process.

For example, the following Java code implements the `query()`/`queryMore()` pattern when querying leads:

```
QueryResult queryResult = this.stub.query("Select name From lead");
do {
    for(sObject lead : queryResult.getRecords()) {
        System.out.println(lead.get_any()[0].getValue());
    }
    if(queryResult.isDone())
        break;
    queryResult = this.stub.queryMore(queryResult.
                                        getQueryLocator());
} while(true);
```

This code implements `query()`/`queryMore()` in VB.NET:

```
Dim lead As sforce.sObject
Dim i As Integer
Dim qr As sforce.QueryResult = binding.query("select name from lead")
Do
    For i = 0 To qr.records.Length
        lead = qr.records(i)
        Console.WriteLine(lead.Any(0).InnerText)
    Next
        If qr.done Then Exit Do
        qr = binding.queryMore(qr.queryLocator)
Loop
```

"Implementing the Query/Query More Pattern" contributed by Simon Fell, Principal Member of the Technical Staff at salesforce.com and Nick Tran, Developer Relations Manager for salesforce.com

The `query()`/`queryMore()` batch size defaults to 500 records, but can be as small as 200 or as large as 2000. To change the batch size, use the `QueryOptions` header.

Note:

- If you use `query()`/`queryMore()` during a long-running integration scenario where you need to log in again to get new session IDs, the `queryLocator` cursor remains valid after you log in, as long as you get the next batch of records within fifteen minutes of idle time.
- Only five `queryLocator` cursors can be active for an organization at any one time.

See Also

- *Managing Sessions* on page 188
- *Using a Wrapper Class for Common API Functions* on page 195
- *Logging In to the API* on page 186
- *Batching Records for API Calls* on page 192

Batching Records for API Calls

Problem

You want to create, update, or delete records in the Salesforce database, but you have more than 200 records you want to process, which exceeds the maximum allowed per call.

Solution

Write a method that batches the records into multiple API calls.

For example, the following Java code from the wrapper class described in *Using a Wrapper Class for Common API Functions* on page 195 implements a `create()` method that takes an array of SObjects and a batch size as parameters. Any method that calls `create()` can pass in any number of records and dynamically vary the batch size to improve performance:

```
/**
 * This method creates an array of sObjects with a specified
 * batchSize.
 * @param records
 * @param batchSize
 * @return SaveResult[]
 */
```

Code for "Batching Records for API Calls" contributed by Simon Fell, Principal Member of the Technical Staff at salesforce.com

```
public SaveResult[] create(SObject[] records, int batchSize)
      throws InvalidSObjectFault, UnexpectedErrorFault,
            InvalidIdFault, RemoteException,
            ServiceException {
    if (batchSize > 200 || batchSize < 1)
        throw new IllegalArgumentException(
                    "batchSize must be between 1 and 200");
    return batch(records, batchSize, new CreateBatcher());
}


private SaveResult[] batch(SObject[] records, int batchSize,
                        Batcher batchOperation)
        throws UnexpectedErrorFault, InvalidIdFault,
            LoginFault, RemoteException, ServiceException {
    if (records.length <= batchSize) {
        checkLogin();
        return batchOperation.perform(records);
    }
    SaveResult[] saveResults = new SaveResult[records.length];
    SObject[] thisBatch = null;
    int pos = 0;
    while (pos < records.length) {
        int thisBatchSize = Math.min(batchSize,
                                    records.length - pos);
        if (thisBatch == null ||
                thisBatch.length != thisBatchSize)
            thisBatch = new SObject[thisBatchSize];

        System.arraycopy(records, pos, thisBatch, 0,
                        thisBatchSize);
        SaveResult [] batchResults = batch(thisBatch,
                                            thisBatchSize,
                                            batchOperation);
        System.arraycopy(batchResults, 0, saveResults,
                        pos, thisBatchSize);
        pos += thisBatchSize;
    }
    return saveResults;
}


private abstract class Batcher {
    abstract SaveResult[] perform(SObject [] records)
            throws UnexpectedErrorFault, InvalidIdFault,
                LoginFault, RemoteException,
                ServiceException;
}


private class CreateBatcher extends Batcher {
    SaveResult [] perform(SObject [] records)
        throws UnexpectedErrorFault, InvalidIdFault,
            LoginFault, RemoteException, ServiceException {
        checkLogin();
        return binding.create(records);
```

```
        }
    }

    private class UpdateBatcher extends Batcher {
        SaveResult [] perform(SObject [] records)
            throws UnexpectedErrorFault, InvalidIdFault, LoginFault,
                    RemoteException, ServiceException {
            checkLogin();
            return binding.update(records);
        }
    }
```

This VB.NET function implements the same logic:

```
    Public Function create(ByVal records() As sObject,
                            Optional ByVal batchSize As Integer = 200)

                    As sforce.SaveResult()
        Return batch(records, batchSize, New CreateBatcher)
    End Function


    Private Function batch(ByVal records() As sObject,
                            ByVal batchSize As Integer,
                            ByVal oper As Batcher)
                    As sforce.SaveResult()
        If (records.Length <= batchSize) Then
            batch = oper.perform(Binding, records)
            Exit Function
        End If

        Dim saveResults(records.Length - 1) As sforce.SaveResult
        Dim thisBatch As sforce.sObject()
        Dim pos As Integer = 0
        Dim thisBatchSize As Integer

        While (pos < records.Length)
            thisBatchSize = Math.Min(batchSize,
                                    records.Length - pos)
            ReDim thisBatch(thisBatchSize)
            System.Array.Copy(records, pos, thisBatch,
                            0, thisBatchSize)
            Dim sr As sforce.SaveResult() =
                            oper.perform(Binding, thisBatch)
            System.Array.Copy(sr, 0, saveResults, pos, thisBatchSize)

            pos += sr.Length
        End While
        batch = saveResults
    End Function

    Private Class Batcher
        Public Function perform(ByVal binding As sforce.SforceService,

                                ByVal records As sforce.sObject())
```

```
                            As sforce.SaveResult()
            perform = Nothing
        End Function
    End Class

    Private Class CreateBatcher
        Inherits Batcher
        Public Overloads Function perform(
                        ByVal binding As sforce.SforceService,
                        ByVal records As sforce.sObject())
            As sforce.SaveResult()
            perform = binding.create(records)
        End Function
    End Class

    Private Class UpdateBatcher
        Inherits Batcher
        Public Overloads Function perform(
                        ByVal binding As sforce.SforceService,
                        ByVal records As sforce.sObject())
            As sforce.SaveResult()
            perform = binding.update(records)
        End Function
    End Class
```

See Also

- *Managing Sessions* on page 188
- *Using a Wrapper Class for Common API Functions* on page 195
- *Logging In to the API* on page 186

Using a Wrapper Class for Common API Functions

Problem

You find yourself writing similar sections of code wherever you need to make calls to the API in a client application.

Solution

Use an API wrapper class to abstract common functions whenever you write client applications and integrations. A wrapper class makes your integration more straightforward to develop and maintain, keeps the logic necessary to make API calls in one place, and affords easy reuse across all components that require API access.

"Using a Wrapper Class for Common API Functions" contributed by Simon Fell, Principal Member of the Technical Staff at salesforce.com

Wrapper classes typically include methods for the following types of actions:

* Logging in
* Managing sessions
* Querying with the `query()`/`queryMore()` pattern
* Batching records for create, update, delete, and so on

For example, the following Java code is a complete implementation of the wrapper class used in *Building a Web Portal with Salesforce Data* on page 208:

```java
package com.sforce.client;

import java.net.MalformedURLException;
import java.net.URL;
import java.rmi.RemoteException;

import javax.xml.rpc.ServiceException;

import org.apache.axis.transport.http.HTTPConstants;

import com.sforce.soap.partner.AssignmentRuleHeader;
import com.sforce.soap.partner.LoginResult;
import com.sforce.soap.partner.QueryOptions;
import com.sforce.soap.partner.QueryResult;
import com.sforce.soap.partner.SaveResult;
import com.sforce.soap.partner.SessionHeader;
import com.sforce.soap.partner.SforceServiceLocator;
import com.sforce.soap.partner.SoapBindingStub;
import com.sforce.soap.partner.fault.InvalidIdFault;
import com.sforce.soap.partner.fault.InvalidSObjectFault;
import com.sforce.soap.partner.fault.LoginFault;
import com.sforce.soap.partner.fault.UnexpectedErrorFault;
import com.sforce.soap.partner.sobject.SObject;


public class Client {

    // Private wrapper class variables
    private String username;
    private String password;
    private URL host;
    private int querySize;
    private int sessionlength;
    private String sessionId;
    private String serverUrl;
    private long nextLoginTime;
    private SoapBindingStub binding;
    private boolean useCompression;

    private QueryOptions queryOptions;
    private AssignmentRuleHeader assignmentRules;


    /**
```

```
   * This method initializes the private class variables
   */
  public Client() throws MalformedURLException {
      this.querySize = 500;
      this.sessionlength = 29;
      this.useCompression = true;
      this.host = new URL(
              "https://www.salesforce.com/services/Soap/u/10.0");
  }

/**
  * These methods get and set the private class variables
  */
  public String getUsername() {
      return this.username;
  }

  public void setUsername(String value) {
      this.username = value;
  }

  public String getPassword() {
      return this.password;
  }

  public void setPassword(String value) {
      this.password = value;
  }

  public URL getHost() {
      return this.host;
  }

  public void setHost(URL value) {
      this.host = value;
  }

  public void setHost(String url) throws MalformedURLException {
      this.host = new URL(url);
  }

  public String getServerURL() {
      return this.serverUrl;
  }

  public int getQuerySize() {
      return this.querySize;
  }

  public void setQuerySize(int value) {
      this.querySize = value;
  }

  public int getSessionlength() {
      return this.sessionlength;
  }
```

```
public void setSessionlength(int value) {
    this.sessionlength = value;
}

public boolean getUseCompression() {
    return this.useCompression;
}

public void setUseCompression(boolean value) {
    this.useCompression = value;
    setCompressionOnBinding();
}


/**
 * This method is used to log in to salesforce and set the
 * private class variables for the wrapper, including the
 * session ID.
 */
public void login() throws UnexpectedErrorFault, InvalidIdFault,
                           LoginFault, RemoteException,
                           ServiceException {

    resetBindingStub();
    LoginResult loginResult = binding.login(username, password);
    this.nextLoginTime = System.currentTimeMillis() +
                         (this.sessionlength * 60000);

    this.binding._setProperty(SoapBindingStub.
                              ENDPOINT_ADDRESS_PROPERTY,
                              loginResult.getServerUrl());
    this.sessionId = loginResult.getSessionId();
    this.serverUrl = loginResult.getServerUrl();

    // Create a new session header object and set the
    // session id to that returned by the login
    SessionHeader sh = new SessionHeader();
    sh.setSessionId(loginResult.getSessionId());
    this.binding.setHeader(new SforceServiceLocator().
        getServiceName().getNamespaceURI(),
        "SessionHeader", sh);
}


private void checkLogin() throws UnexpectedErrorFault,
                InvalidIdFault, LoginFault, RemoteException,
                ServiceException {
    if (this.loginRequired())
        login();
}


/**
 * This method is used to log in with an existing sessionId
 * @param String sid sessionId
```

```
     * @param String sURL serverUrl
     */
    public void loginBySessionId(String sid, String sURL)
                              throws ServiceException {
        this.nextLoginTime = System.currentTimeMillis() +
                            (this.sessionlength * 60000);
        resetBindingStub();
        binding._setProperty(
                SoapBindingStub.ENDPOINT_ADDRESS_PROPERTY, sURL);
        this.sessionId = sid;
        this.serverUrl = sURL;
        SessionHeader sh = new SessionHeader();
        sh.setSessionId(sid);
        binding.setHeader(new SforceServiceLocator().
                getServiceName().getNamespaceURI(),
                "SessionHeader", sh);
    }


    /** This method resets the binding object back to its
      * initial state.
      */
    private void resetBindingStub() throws ServiceException {
        this.binding = (SoapBindingStub) new
                SforceServiceLocator().getSoap(this.host);
        this.binding.setTimeout(60000);
        setCompressionOnBinding();
        this.assignmentRules = null;
        this.queryOptions = null;
    }


    private void setCompressionOnBinding() {
        binding._setProperty(HTTPConstants.MC_ACCEPT_GZIP,
                            useCompression);
        binding._setProperty(HTTPConstants.MC_GZIP_REQUEST,
                            useCompression);
    }


  /**
   * This method checks whether the session is active or not
   * @return boolean
   */
  public boolean isConnected() {
      return System.currentTimeMillis() < nextLoginTime;
  }


/**
 * This method returns true if a login to Salesforce is
 * necessary, otherwise false. It should be used to check the
 * session length before performing any API calls.
 */
private boolean loginRequired() {
    if (sessionId == null || sessionId.length() == 0)
        return true;
```

```
            return !isConnected();
    }

    private void setBatchSizeHeader(int batchSize) {
        if (queryOptions == null) {
            this.queryOptions = new QueryOptions();
            binding.setHeader(new SforceServiceLocator().
                    getServiceName().getNamespaceURI(),
                    "QueryOptions", queryOptions);
        }
        queryOptions.setBatchSize(batchSize);
    }


/**
 * This method queries the database and returns the results.
 * @param String strSOQLStmt
 * @return SObject[]
 */
public QueryResult executeQuery(String strSOQLStmt,
        Integer queryBatchSize)
        throws UnexpectedErrorFault, InvalidIdFault, LoginFault,
                RemoteException, ServiceException {

        checkLogin();
        setBatchSizeHeader(queryBatchSize ==
                null ? querySize : queryBatchSize);
        return binding.query(strSOQLStmt);
    }


public QueryResult executeSOQL(String strSOQLStmt)
        throws UnexpectedErrorFault, InvalidIdFault, LoginFault,
                RemoteException, ServiceException {
        return executeQuery(strSOQLStmt, null);
    }


public QueryResult executeQueryMore(String queryLocator)
        throws UnexpectedErrorFault, InvalidIdFault, LoginFault,
                RemoteException, ServiceException {
        checkLogin();
        return binding.queryMore(queryLocator);
    }

/**
 * This method sets the assignment rule header.
 * @param ruleId
 */
public void setAssignmentRuleHeaderId(String ruleId) {
        setAssignmentRuleHeader(ruleId, false);
    }

/**
 * This method sets the assignment rule header with a
 * default ruleId.
```

```
 * @param ruleId
 */
public void setAssignmentRuleHeaderToDefault
                                (boolean runDefaultRule) {
    setAssignmentRuleHeader(null, runDefaultRule);
}

private void setAssignmentRuleHeader(String ruleId,
                                boolean useDefault) {
    if (this.assignmentRules == null) {
        this.assignmentRules = new AssignmentRuleHeader();
        binding.setHeader(new SforceServiceLocator().
                getServiceName().getNamespaceURI(),
                "AssignmentRuleHeader", this.assignmentRules);
    }
    this.assignmentRules.setUseDefaultRule(useDefault);
    this.assignmentRules.setAssignmentRuleId(ruleId);
}

public SoapBindingStub getBinding()
        throws UnexpectedErrorFault, InvalidIdFault, LoginFault,
            RemoteException, ServiceException {
    checkLogin();
    return this.binding;
}

/**
 * This method creates an array of sObjects with a specified
 * batchSize.
 * @param records
 * @param batchSize
 * @return SaveResult[]
 */
public SaveResult[] create(SObject[] records, int batchSize)
        throws InvalidSObjectFault, UnexpectedErrorFault,
            InvalidIdFault, RemoteException,
            ServiceException {
    if (batchSize > 200 || batchSize < 1)
        throw new IllegalArgumentException(
                    "batchSize must be between 1 and 200");
    return batch(records, batchSize, new CreateBatcher());
}

public SaveResult[] create(SObject[] records)
        throws InvalidSObjectFault, UnexpectedErrorFault,
            InvalidIdFault, RemoteException, ServiceException {

    return create(records, 200);
}

public SaveResult[] update(SObject[] records, int batchSize)
        throws UnexpectedErrorFault, InvalidIdFault, LoginFault,
            RemoteException, ServiceException {
    if (batchSize > 200 || batchSize < 1)
```

```java
                throw new IllegalArgumentException(
                            "batchSize must be between 1 and 200");

        return batch(records, batchSize, new UpdateBatcher());
    }

    /**
     * This method updates an array of sObjects with a specified
     * batchSize.
     * @param records
     * @param batchSize
     * @return SaveResult[]
     */
    public SaveResult[] update(SObject[] records)
            throws UnexpectedErrorFault, InvalidIdFault, LoginFault,
                    RemoteException, ServiceException {
        return update(records, 200);
    }

    private SaveResult[] batch(SObject[] records, int batchSize,
                                Batcher batchOperation)
            throws UnexpectedErrorFault, InvalidIdFault,
                    LoginFault, RemoteException, ServiceException {
        if (records.length <= batchSize) {
            checkLogin();
            return batchOperation.perform(records);
        }
        SaveResult[] saveResults = new SaveResult[records.length];
        SObject[] thisBatch = null;
        int pos = 0;
        while (pos < records.length) {
            int thisBatchSize = Math.min(batchSize,
                                        records.length - pos);
            if (thisBatch == null ||
                    thisBatch.length != thisBatchSize)
                thisBatch = new SObject[thisBatchSize];

            System.arraycopy(records, pos, thisBatch, 0,
                            thisBatchSize);
            SaveResult [] batchResults = batch(thisBatch,
                                                thisBatchSize,
                                                batchOperation);
            System.arraycopy(batchResults, 0, saveResults,
                            pos, thisBatchSize);
            pos += thisBatchSize;
        }
        return saveResults;
    }


    private abstract class Batcher {
        abstract SaveResult[] perform(SObject [] records)
                throws UnexpectedErrorFault, InvalidIdFault,
                        LoginFault, RemoteException,
                        ServiceException;
    }
```

```
    private class CreateBatcher extends Batcher {
        SaveResult [] perform(SObject [] records)
            throws UnexpectedErrorFault, InvalidIdFault,
                LoginFault, RemoteException, ServiceException {
            checkLogin();
            return binding.create(records);
        }
    }

    private class UpdateBatcher extends Batcher {
        SaveResult [] perform(SObject [] records)
            throws UnexpectedErrorFault, InvalidIdFault, LoginFault,
                RemoteException, ServiceException {
            checkLogin();
            return binding.update(records);
        }
    }
}
```

This code implements the VB.NET version of the wrapper class used in *Building a Web Portal with Salesforce Data* on page 208:

```
Imports Microsoft.VisualBasic
Imports System
Imports System.Collections
Imports sforce

Public Class Client

    Private _binding As SforceServiceCompressed
    Private _username As String
    Private _password As String
    Private _host As String
    Private _querySize As Integer
    Private _sessionlength As Integer
    Private _sessionId As String
    Private _serverURL As String
    Private _nextLoginTime As DateTime

    'Initialize private variables for the class
    Sub New()
        Me._binding = New SforceServiceCompressed
        Me._querySize = 500
        Me._sessionlength = 29
        Me._host = "https://www.salesforce.com/services/Soap/u/10.0"
    End Sub


    'Expose variables to calling function
    Public Property username() As String
        'Allows calling class to get values
        Get
            Return Me._username
```

```vbnet
        End Get
        'Allows calling class to set value
        Set(ByVal Value As String)
            Me._username = Value
        End Set
    End Property

    Public Property password() As String
        Get
            Return Me._password
        End Get
        Set(ByVal Value As String)
            Me._password = Value
        End Set
    End Property

    Public Property host() As String
        Get
            Return Me._host
        End Get
        Set(ByVal Value As String)
            Me._host = Value
        End Set
    End Property

    Public ReadOnly Property serverURL() As String
        Get
            Return Me._serverURL
        End Get
    End Property

    Public Property querySize() As Integer
        Get
            Return Me._querySize
        End Get
        Set(ByVal Value As Integer)
            Me._querySize = Value
        End Set
    End Property

    Public Property sessionlength() As Integer
        Get
            Return Me._sessionlength
        End Get
        Set(ByVal Value As Integer)
            Me._sessionlength = Value
        End Set
    End Property

    'In case of proxy server...
    Public Property proxy() As System.Net.WebProxy
        Get
            Return Me._binding.Proxy
        End Get
        Set(ByVal Value As System.Net.WebProxy)
            Me._binding.Proxy = Value
```

```vb
        End Set
End Property

' Compress SOAP messages
Public Property useCompression() As Boolean
    Get
        Return Me._binding.AcceptCompressedResponse()
    End Get

    Set(ByVal Value As Boolean)
        Me._binding.AcceptCompressedResponse = Value
        Me._binding.SendCompressedRequest = Value
    End Set
End Property


Public Sub Login()
    Dim lr As sforce.LoginResult
    Me._binding.Url = Me._host
    lr = Me._binding.login(username, password)
    Me._nextLoginTime = Now().AddMinutes(Me.sessionlength)
    'Reset the SOAP endpoint to the returned server URL
    Me._binding.Url = lr.serverUrl
    Me._binding.SessionHeaderValue = New sforce.SessionHeader
    Me._binding.SessionHeaderValue.sessionId = lr.sessionId
    Me._sessionId = lr.sessionId
    Me._serverURL = lr.serverUrl
End Sub


Public Sub loginBySessionId(ByVal sid As String, _
                            ByVal sURL As String)
    Me._nextLoginTime = Now().AddMinutes(Me.sessionlength)
    Me._binding.Url = sURL
    Me._binding.SessionHeaderValue = New sforce.SessionHeader
    Me._binding.SessionHeaderValue.sessionId = sid
    Me._sessionId = sid
    Me._serverURL = sURL
End Sub


Public Function isConnected() As Boolean
    If _sessionId <> "" And _sessionId <> Nothing Then
        If Now() > Me._nextLoginTime Then
            isConnected = False
        End If
        isConnected = True
    Else
        isConnected = False
    End If
End Function


Private Function loginRequired() As Boolean
    loginRequired = Not (isConnected())
End Function
```

```
Public Function executeQuery(ByVal strSOQLStmt As String,
                Optional ByVal queryBatchSize As Integer = -1)
            As sforce.QueryResult
    If queryBatchSize = -1 Then
        queryBatchSize = _querySize
    End If
    If (Me.loginRequired()) Then
        Login()
    End If
    _binding.QueryOptionsValue = New sforce.QueryOptions
    _binding.QueryOptionsValue.batchSizeSpecified = True
    _binding.QueryOptionsValue.batchSize = queryBatchSize
    executeQuery = _binding.query(strSOQLStmt)
End Function


Public Function executeQueryMore(ByVal queryLocator As String)
            As sforce.QueryResult
    If loginRequired() Then Login()
    Return _binding.queryMore(queryLocator)
End Function


Public Sub setAssignmentRuleHeaderId(ByVal ruleId As String)
    _binding.AssignmentRuleHeaderValue =
                        New AssignmentRuleHeader
    _binding.AssignmentRuleHeaderValue.assignmentRuleId = ruleId
End Sub


Public Sub setAssignmentRuleHeaderToDefault(
                            ByVal runDefaultRule As Boolean)

    _binding.AssignmentRuleHeaderValue = New AssignmentRuleHeader

    _binding.AssignmentRuleHeaderValue.useDefaultRule =
                                        runDefaultRule

End Sub

Public ReadOnly Property Binding() As sforce.SforceService
    Get
        Return _binding
    End Get
End Property


Public Function create(ByVal records() As sObject,
                Optional ByVal batchSize As Integer = 200)

            As sforce.SaveResult()
    Return batch(records, batchSize, New CreateBatcher)
End Function
```

```
Public Function update(ByVal records() As sObject,
                    Optional ByVal batchSize As Integer = 200)
                As sforce.SaveResult()
    Return batch(records, batchSize, New UpdateBatcher)
End Function


Private Function batch(ByVal records() As sObject,
                    ByVal batchSize As Integer,
                    ByVal oper As Batcher)
                As sforce.SaveResult()
    If (records.Length <= batchSize) Then
        batch = oper.perform(Binding, records)
        Exit Function
    End If

    Dim saveResults(records.Length - 1) As sforce.SaveResult
    Dim thisBatch As sforce.sObject()
    Dim pos As Integer = 0
    Dim thisBatchSize As Integer

    While (pos < records.Length)
        thisBatchSize = Math.Min(batchSize,
                            records.Length - pos)
        ReDim thisBatch(thisBatchSize)
        System.Array.Copy(records, pos, thisBatch,
                        0, thisBatchSize)
        Dim sr As sforce.SaveResult() =
                        oper.perform(Binding, thisBatch)
        System.Array.Copy(sr, 0, saveResults, pos, thisBatchSize)

        pos += sr.Length
    End While
    batch = saveResults
End Function

Private Class Batcher
    Public Function perform(ByVal binding
                        As sforce.SforceService,
                    ByVal records
                        As sforce.sObject())
                As sforce.SaveResult()
        perform = Nothing
    End Function
End Class

Private Class CreateBatcher
    Inherits Batcher
    Public Overloads Function perform(
                    ByVal binding As sforce.SforceService,
                    ByVal records As sforce.sObject())
            As sforce.SaveResult()
        perform = binding.create(records)
    End Function
```

```
    End Class

    Private Class UpdateBatcher
        Inherits Batcher
        Public Overloads Function perform(
                      ByVal binding As sforce.SforceService,
                      ByVal records As sforce.sObject())
            As sforce.SaveResult()
            perform = binding.update(records)
        End Function
    End Class
End Class
```

See Also

- *Building a Web Portal with Salesforce Data* on page 208
- *Logging In to the API* on page 186
- *Managing Sessions* on page 188
- *Implementing the Query/Query More Pattern* on page 191
- *Batching Records for API Calls* on page 192

Building a Web Portal with Salesforce Data

Problem

You want to build a Web portal for the Recruiting app that allows visitors to apply online for open positions. The portal needs to include the following Web pages:

- A list view of all currently open positions, with data from the position records that are stored in Salesforce
- Detail views of all currently open positions, also with data from the position records that are stored in Salesforce
- An online application form that allows a visitor to apply for an open position. When the user clicks **Submit**, the data is sent back to Salesforce as a new job application and candidate record.

Most importantly, your Web portal visitors shouldn't have to log in to view the open positions in your organization.

Code for "Building a Web Portal with Salesforce Data" contributed by Sarah Whitlock, Senior Program Manager for Education Services at salesforce.com and Simon Fell, Principal Member of the Technical Staff at salesforce.com

Note: This Web portal is part of the Application Laboratory class offered by salesforce.com's Education Services department. For more information, see *Finding Training Courses* on page 14.

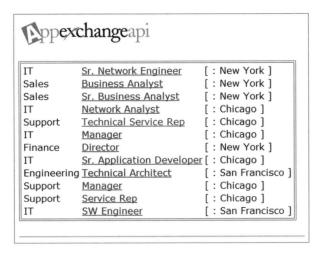

Figure 17: The Web Portal's Job Listings Page

Figure 18: The Web Portal's Position Detail Page

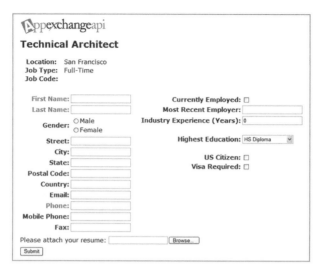

Figure 19: The Web Portal's Application Page

Solution

Write a client application that runs on an external server and uses the Force.com API to access Salesforce data.

 Note: Because there's a lot of code involved with this solution, this recipe discusses how such a client can be designed, and some of the features that can be implemented. To download the complete Java, C#.NET, or VB.NET code that implements this client application, visit wiki.apexdevnet.com/index.php/Platform_Cookbook.

The following diagram shows the key components of such an application. While there can be some overlap, each component represents a different aspect of the MVC (Model-View-Controller) design paradigm:

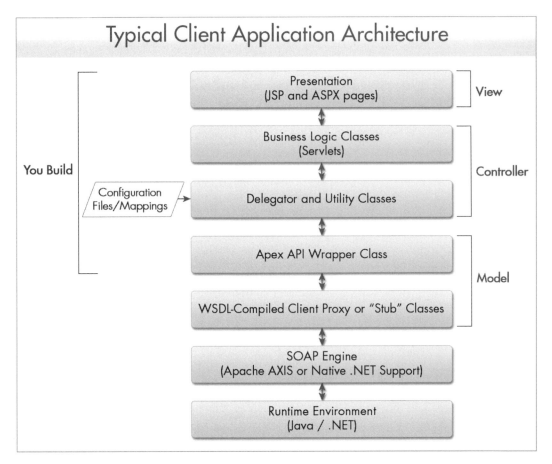

Figure 20: Typical Client Application Architecture

Model

The API wrapper class and the WSDL-compiled proxy classes provide non-application-specific access to the data in Salesforce. See *Using a Wrapper Class for Common API Functions* on page 195 for the wrapper class used to implement the Web portal application.

View

The JSP or ASPX pages contain the user interface of the application, including how the data is displayed for and captured from the user.

Controller

The delegator, utility, and business logic classes define the application-specific logic, including the logic that controls how captured data is returned to Salesforce as new or updated records.

Of particular note is the delegator class that the Web portal application uses to provide common, reusable code for creating and updating the key objects related to the application, such as Job Application and Candidate. Unlike the API wrapper class, which can be reused by many different client applications, the delegator is application-specific, providing an additional layer of abstraction between the API and the logic required to display the application's pages.

For example, the following Java-based delegator method provides the logic for creating a job application record. Based on the Partner WSDL, it prepares a single record and passes it to the wrapper class for creation via the API:

```
public SObject createJobApp(String candidateId,
                            String positionId) {

  SObject application = new SObject();

  try {
    MessageElement[] fields = new MessageElement[3];
    MessageElement field;

    //Candidate id
    field = util.createNewXmlElement("Candidate__c",
                                     candidateId);
    fields[0] = field;

    //Positionid
    field = util.createNewXmlElement("Position__c",
                                     positionId);
    fields[1] = field;

    //Status
    field = util.createNewXmlElement("Status__c",
                                     "New");
    fields[2] = field;

    application.set_any(fields);
    application.setType("Job_Application__c");
    application = createOneRecord(application);

  } catch (Exception e) {
    System.out.println(e.getMessage());
  }

  return application;
}
```

This same logic can be implemented in VB.NET as follows:

```
Public Function createJobApp(ByVal candidateId As String,
      ByVal positionId As String) As sforce.sObject
   Dim application As New sforce.sObject

   Dim fields(2) As System.Xml.XmlElement
   Dim field As System.Xml.XmlElement
```

```
    ' Candidate id
    field = util.createNewXmlElement("Candidate__c",
                                 candidateId)
    fields(0) = field

    ' Position id
    field = util.createNewXmlElement("Position__c",
                                 positionId)
    fields(1) = field

    ' Status
    field = util.createNewXmlElement("Status__c",
                                 "New")
    fields(2) = field

    application.Any = fields
    application.type = "Job_Application__c"

    application = createOneRecord(application)

    Return application
End Function
```

Discussion

The code that implements this Web portal client application also uses a configuration file and SOAP message compression, two best practices for client application development:

- Using a configuration file to control dynamic aspects of a client application is highly recommended because it reduces code maintenance time. It can include properties such as the API URL, username, password, and any SOQL or SOSL queries that drive business logic. For example, by storing the URL of the targeted Salesforce host in a configuration file, changing an integration target from sandbox to production only requires a simple configuration file edit.

  The Java-based solution uses a configuration file named `config.properties`, while the VB.NET and C#.NET solutions use configuration files named `web.config`.

- SOAP messages generated by both an API client and the API service can become very large, especially when they include large clobs of data, such as the resume attachment in the Web portal client application. To avoid lengthy transmission times across the Internet, you can configure your SOAP binding to use GZIP compression to reduce the size of SOAP messages by up to 90%. When the API server receives a compressed message, it decompresses the message, processes it, and then recompresses the response before returning it.

  The Java-based solution uses the following classes to compress and decompress SOAP messages:

  - GZipWebRequest.java

- GZipWebResponse.java
- GZIP2WayRequestStream.java
- GZIP2WayRequestWrapper.java
- GZIP2WayResponseStream.java
- GZIP2WayResponseWrapper.java

The VB.NET and C#.NET solutions use these classes:

- GZipWebRequest.vb/GZipWebRequest.cs
- GZipWebResponse.vb/GZipWebResponse.cs
- SforceServiceCompressed.vb/SforceServiceCompressed.cs

For information about SOAP compression in Java, see
wiki.apexdevnet.com/index.php/Compression_with_Axis_1.3. For information about
SOAP compression in VB.NET and C#.NET, see
wiki.apexdevnet.com/index.php/SOAP_Compression.

See Also

- *Logging In to the API* on page 186
- *Managing Sessions* on page 188
- *Implementing the Query/Query More Pattern* on page 191
- *Batching Records for API Calls* on page 192

Chapter 11

Debugging S-Controls and Apex

On-demand development is no different than any other type of development in one regard—no matter how good of a developer you are, you're bound to get some bugs!

In this chapter, we'll explore some tools and best practices for debugging s-controls, HTTP requests, and Apex. You'll learn how to use Fiddler to debug HTTP requests, and Firebug and the IE DOM Explorer to debug s-controls. Finally, we'll show you some different tools you can use to debug Apex. Bugs are a fact of life with any kind of development, but with a little bit of knowledge and the right tools, you can debug your code in no time.

Best Practices for Debugging S-Controls

Problem

You've developed an s-control that doesn't work exactly the way you'd envisioned, but you're not sure what the best way is to debug it.

Solution

Depending on your problem, install the appropriate tools to help you track down the issue.

 Tip: Because Firefox has the most robust set of free tools, it's generally easier to use for development and debugging. However, because a majority of users run Salesforce on Internet Explorer, you should periodically check your work on that browser as well.

While there are many tools available, developers at salesforce.com have found it best to have at least one of each of the following types of tools:

An HTTP Debugger

HTTP debuggers are used to identify and inspect SOAP requests that are sent from the AJAX Toolkit. They behave as proxy servers running on your local machine and allow you to inspect and author individual requests.

Examples of HTTP debuggers include Fiddler, TCPMon, and TCPTrace.

Web Developer Plug-ins

Web developer plug-ins for Firefox and Internet Explorer can give you increased insight into your s-control by helping you to debug CSS styles and complex JavaScript.

Firebug, a Web developer plug-in for Firefox, allows you to:

- Set breakpoints and examine variables through a watch window
- Inspect DOM elements and the CSS style rules that are applied to a particular node

Microsoft Script Debugger, a Web developer plug-in for Internet Explorer, allows you to:

- Set breakpoints and examine variables through a watch window

Internet Explorer DOM Inspector, a Web developer plug-in for Internet Explorer, allows you to:

- Inspect DOM elements and the CSS style rules that are applied to a particular node (though with less functionality than Firebug)

See Also

- *Debugging HTTP Requests with Fiddler* on page 217
- *Debugging S-Controls with Firebug* on page 219
- *Debugging S-Controls with IE DOM Explorer* on page 224
- *Understanding Browser Differences* on page 226

Debugging HTTP Requests with Fiddler

Problem

You've written an s-control that takes advantage of the AJAX Toolkit, but Salesforce isn't returning the data you expect and you need help debugging.

Solution

Use an HTTP debugging proxy such as Fiddler2, a free tool from Microsoft that allows you to view and edit HTTP and HTTPS traffic.

Discussion

To begin you'll need to install Fiddler2 from the Fiddler website (www.fiddlertool.com/fiddler2).

After you install the tool, you can access it in Internet Explorer by clicking **Tools ➤ Fiddler**, or in Windows by clicking **Start ➤ Programs ➤ Fiddler2**.

Fiddler works by setting up a proxy server on your local machine. This means that when you start Fiddler, it automatically instructs Internet Explorer to send HTTP requests to `localhost:8081`, and then forwards the requests on to Salesforce. When Salesforce replies, Fiddler gets the response and then forwards it on to your browser. Fiddler is the intermediary for all requests that your browser makes, including XMLHTTP requests.

 Note: Fiddler can intercept requests from Firefox as well. Simply configure Firefox to use a proxy server on `localhost:8081`. However, note that once Firefox is set to use a proxy, it won't work without one.

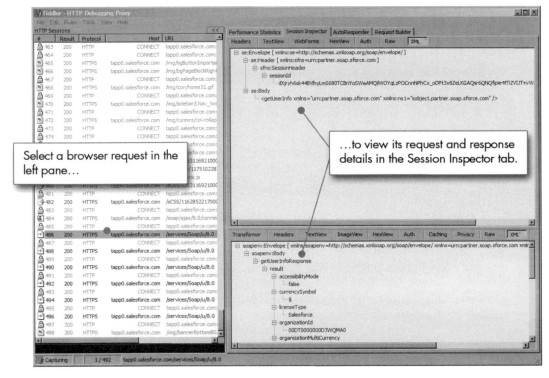

Figure 21: The Fiddler HTTP Debugging Proxy

Each request that your browser makes is displayed in the left pane with information about its result, URL, size, and so on. To drill down on a request for more detail, select the request and then click the Session Inspector tab. The top area shows information about the request, while the bottom area shows information about the response. To inspect a SOAP response more closely, click the **XML** button to see the actual message.

See Also

Debugging S-Controls with Firebug

Problem

Your s-controls include a large amount of JavaScript code, making it hard to find any errors in the code.

Solution

Firebug is an extension for Firefox that detects JavaScript syntax errors and helps you to fix them. Firebug can also help you spot logical errors by letting you examine the runtime state of the code and its variables.

Discussion

To begin you'll need to install the Firebug extension for the Firefox browser. You can get this plug-in at the Firebug website at www.getfirebug.com.

After you install the plug-in, you'll be prompted to restart your browser. When the browser restarts, click the gray circle at the lower right corner of the browser to enable Firebug.

Figure 22: Enabling Firebug

There are many powerful features in Firebug, but we'll just concentrate on the portions of the plug-in that can help you with debugging s-controls. As an example, let's take a look at the following code sample. It includes two bugs—one syntactical and one logical. Firebug will help us find both problems:

```
function initPage() {
    main = document.getElementById('main');
    main.innerHTML = "Hello World!";
    var Events = sforce.connection.query(
        "Select Id, Subject, Location, ActivityDateTime,
        ActivityDate " + " from Event limit 10" eventCallback );
}

function eventCallback( query ) {
    var qr = query;
    var records = qr.record;

    main.innerHTML += '<br>';
    for (var i=0;i<records.length;i++) {
        main.innerHTML += records[i].Subject + ' ' +
```

```
                    records[i].ActivityDateTime + '<br>';

    }

}
```

When your browser displays a page that uses this code in an s-control, the first thing you'll see is a small red message in the lower right corner of the browser. You can get details for this error by clicking on that red circle, and selecting the Console tab in the Firebug window, as shown in the following screenshot:

Figure 23: The Firebug Console Tab

The error message, in this case, is not really definitive. It states that there's a missing parenthesis in the argument list. To see more, you can click on the green text of

```
eventCallback ); \n
```

which takes you to the specific location in the code where the error occurred.

Once you get to the specific line of code, you can see that the problem is not a missing parenthesis, but a missing comma between the query string and the `eventCallback()` parameter. Although the Firebug message was a little misleading, once you get to the location of the error, finding the root cause is fairly easy—much simpler than if you were left to comb your code for this type of small error.

 Tip: If the console error message has a "\n" at the end, the cause of the error is probably due to a run-on string or some missing punctuation in your JavaScript.

The preceding error was in the JavaScript syntax, but you can also use Firebug to help you find logical errors. For example, after fixing the syntax error and running the code, the following dialog box lets you know that one of the variables in your code has no properties.

Figure 24: A Firefox Error Message

These types of errors are frequently caused by the incorrect spelling of an object, so you would start your investigation by trying to track down exactly where the assignment of a value went wrong.

To find out exactly how your code works, you can add a `debugger` statement directly into your code. When Firefox with Firebug hits the `debugger` statement, control of code execution passes to you.

The revised code now looks like this:

```
function initPage() {
    main = document.getElementById('main');
    main.innerHTML = "Hello World!";
    var Events = sforce.connection.query(
        "Select Id, Subject, Location, ActivityDateTime,
         ActivityDate " + " from Event limit 10", eventCallback );
}

function eventCallback( query ) {
    debugger;

    var qr = query;
    var records = qr.record;

    main.innerHTML += '<br>';
    for (var i=0;i<records.length;i++) {
        main.innerHTML += records[i].Subject + ' ' +
                          records[i].ActivityDateTime + '<br>';

    }
}
```

When Firefox with Firebug runs and hits this `debugger` statement, you are taken directly to the statement in your code:

Figure 25: Stepping Through Code with Firebug

The control bar shown in the following screenshot allows you to step through your code one line at a time or perform other options, such as skipping over a line of code.

Figure 26: Firebug Step-Through Controls

You already know that the `records` variable is the source of the confusion, so when you get to the line of code where a value is assigned to the variable, you can look at the right-hand pane of Firebug and see that the `records` variable remains undefined, even after you have ostensibly given it a value.

Figure 27: Firebug Variable Values

When you examine the variables and their values in the pane, you can see that you probably should have assigned the value of the `query.records` array to the records variable.

Figure 28: Firebug Variable Values

If you modify the assignment statement, the following code should take care of the problem:

```
var records = qr.getArray('records');
```

If you make the change in your s-control, you'll see that the object now produces the results you want. Remove the `debugger` statement and you'll have the correct code:

```
function initPage() {
    main = document.getElementById('main');
    main.innerHTML = "Hello World!";
    var Events = sforce.connection.query(
        "Select Id, Subject, Location, ActivityDateTime,
        ActivityDate " + " from Event limit 10", eventCallback );
}

function eventCallback( query ) {

    var qr = query;
    var records = qr.getArray('records');

    main.innerHTML += '<br>';
```

```
    for (var i=0;i<records.length;i++) {
        main.innerHTML += records[i].Subject + ' ' +
                          records[i].ActivityDateTime + '<br>';

    }
}
```

See Also

- *Best Practices for Debugging S-Controls* on page 216
- *Debugging HTTP Requests with Fiddler* on page 217
- *Debugging S-Controls with IE DOM Explorer* on page 224
- *Understanding Browser Differences* on page 226
- *Mimicking the Salesforce Look-and-Feel in an S-Control* on page 146

Debugging S-Controls with IE DOM Explorer

Problem

You need to debug an s-control that has an issue that only appears in Internet Explorer.

Solution

Use the Internet Explorer DOM (Document Object Model) Explorer, available in the Internet Explorer Developer Toolbar. While the DOM Explorer doesn't support JavaScript debugging, it's a very useful tool for tracking down rendering issues specific to Internet Explorer.

Discussion

To begin, you'll need to download and install the Developer Toolbar from www.microsoft.com/downloads/details.aspx?FamilyID= E59C3964-672D-4511-BB3E-2D5E1DB91038&displaylang=en.

 Caution: There are a number of similarly named plug-ins made by third parties—don't be fooled and install the wrong one!

After you restart Internet Explorer, you can view the toolbar by clicking **View ➤ Explorer Bar ➤ IE Developer Toolbar**.

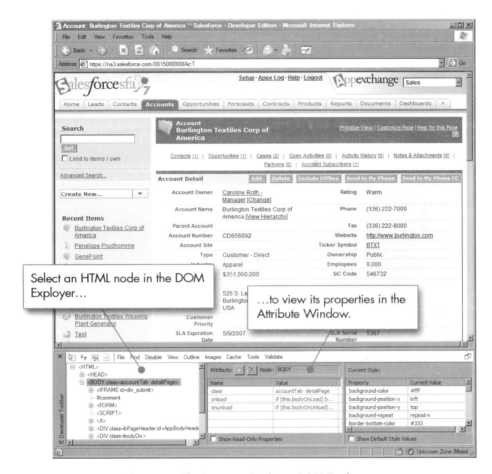

Figure 29: The Internet Explorer DOM Explorer

The left pane of the toolbar shows the DOM Explorer tree, which includes a representation of every node of the HTML document. You can browse through the tree one node at a time, or use the **Select Element By Click** button at the far left of the toolbar to jump directly to a particular node in the tree, based on where you click in the browser window.

When you select a node in the DOM Explorer, the properties that apply to that node appear in the Attribute and Current Styles panes:

- In the Attribute pane, you can modify any attribute to see the changes to the page in real time.

 Tip: Of particular interest in Salesforce pages is the `class` attribute for any given node.

- In the Current Styles pane, you can see the properties applied to this node as a result of CSS rules. To see which rule is responsible for a particular style, right-click the style and select **Trace Style**. While this functionality isn't as robust as Firebug (which shows all matching CSS rules and the order in which they were applied), it can certainly help.

See Also

- *Best Practices for Debugging S-Controls* on page 216
- *Debugging S-Controls with Firebug* on page 219
- *Debugging HTTP Requests with Fiddler* on page 217
- *Understanding Browser Differences* on page 226
- *Mimicking the Salesforce Look-and-Feel in an S-Control* on page 146

Understanding Browser Differences

Problem

You've written code that works one way in Internet Explorer and another way in Firefox. You need a strategy to cope with these differences.

Solution

While we could dedicate an entire book to the subtle nuances and differences between Firefox and Internet Explorer, the best strategy for coping with them is to use sound development techniques from the beginning:

- *Frequently* test your code in all supported browsers.

  It's a bad practice to develop solely in one browser and then wait until the end of the development cycle to check your code in the other. Instead, verify that the functionality you're developing works as expected in both browsers every time you finish a testable piece of code.

- Specify the correct DOCTYPE parameter as the very first line on all of your pages:

  ```
  <!DOCTYPE HTML PUBLIC "-//W3C//DTD HTML 4.01 Transitional//EN"
   "http://www.w3.org/TR/html4/loose.dtd">
  ```

  It's important to set the DOCTYPE properly because modern browsers have two modes for rendering content and executing JavaScript: quirks mode and standards mode. Quirks mode exists in all browser implementations as a way of supporting legacy Web pages that rely on Web browsers' incomplete or incorrect implementations of HTML and CSS to display properly. In standards mode, browsers respect all parts of the HTML and CSS language specifications.

While there are still differences between Firefox and Internet Explorer when operating in standards mode, there is much less deviation in behavior than when these browsers default to quirks mode. To avoid quirks mode, specify the DOCTYPE exactly as indicated previously, as the very first line of your Web page.

- Detect objects rather than browsers.

  For example, when trying to cope with browser differences, it's often tempting to write JavaScript code that examines the browser's type:

```
// A bad approach...
var isIE = navigator.appName.indexOf("Microsoft") != -1;
var images;

if (isIe) {
    images = document.images;
} else {
    images = document.getElementsByTagName('IMG');
}
```

  However, such an approach makes the assumption that other (and future) versions of the browser in question will behave in the same way as the one you're testing.

  Instead, you should isolate the non-standard behaviors and test for individual properties. For example:

```
// A better approach...
function getImages() {
    if (document.images) return document.images;

    return document.getElementsByTagName('img');
}
```

- Be sure that your users have set the appropriate security options on their browsers.

  For example, Internet Explorer 7 users sometimes have to specifically allow websites to make XMLHTTP requests. To set this option:

  1. Click **Tools ➤ Internet Options**.
  2. In the Advanced tab, select Enable native XMLHTTP support and click **OK**.

See Also

- www.quirksmode.org
- www.alistapart.com
- *Best Practices for Debugging S-Controls* on page 216
- *Debugging S-Controls with Firebug* on page 219

Best Practices for Debugging Apex

Problem

You're authoring Apex, but it's difficult to debug because you can't step through the code like you can in a normal debugging environment.

Solution

Use the following techniques to easily determine what's happening throughout your Apex scripts:

- Add `System.debug()` statements to your code to identify the state of variables in your code by writing messages to the Apex debug log.

  For example, the following code prints the value of the String variable `s` to the log:

  ```
  String s = 'Hello Caroline';
  System.debug('Variable s = ' + s);
  ```

   Tip: Although `System.debug()` statements harken back to the days of using `printf()` in your code, once your code works the way you expect, you can convert them into `System.assert()` statements that verify what you saw in the debug log output. For example,

  ```
  String s = 'Hello Caroline';
  System.assert(s.equals('Hello Caroline'));
  ```

  Replacing `System.debug()` statements with `System.assert()` leaves you with a more robust final product.

- Write unit test methods for your Apex triggers and classes that exercise your code with different data. See *Writing Unit Tests for Apex* on page 80.

See Also

Debugging Apex in Salesforce

Problem

You want to debug your Apex triggers from within Salesforce.

Solution

Click **Apex Log** at the top of any Salesforce page to access the Apex debug console. This console displays the debug log for any Apex that executes in your organization while the console is open as the result of a trigger.

The debug console also includes a text area at the bottom of the window that allows you to enter and execute anonymous statements. Anonymous statements allow you to execute Apex class methods, generate test data, or perform bulk operations on data in your organization without wrapping the code you execute in a trigger or class.

See Also

- *Best Practices for Debugging Apex* on page 228
- *Debugging Apex in Eclipse* on page 229
- *Writing Unit Tests for Apex* on page 80

Debugging Apex in Eclipse

Problem

You want to debug your Apex classes and triggers from within the Force.com Toolkit for Eclipse.

Solution

Open the Apex debug log from within Eclipse:

1. In Eclipse, click **Window ➤ Show View ➤ Other**.
2. Select **Apex ➤ Apex Debug Log** and click **OK**.

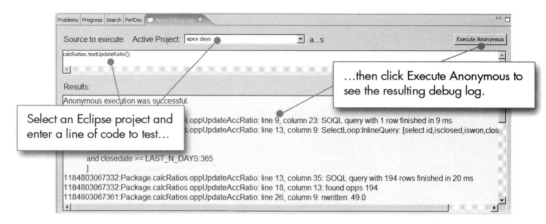

Figure 30: The Apex Debug Log in Eclipse

The debug log displays the results of any Apex that you enter in the anonymous statement text area. The context of the anonymous statements you enter depends on the Eclipse project that you select in the `Active Project` drop-down list.

For example, in the previous screenshot, the "apex day" project is selected, and the anonymous statement text area includes a call to the `testUpdateRatio()` method in the `calcRatios` class. If this class is not accessible from the "apex day" project, clicking **Execute Anonymous** will do nothing. However, if it does evaluate, the debug log that results from the call is displayed in the Results window.

The amount of information that appears in the debug log is controlled by the specified log level. You can adjust this setting by moving the **Adjust Logging Level** slider to the right or left. For example, in the previous screenshot, the logging level is set to Debug and Database stats. At this level, the debug log includes all of the `System.debug()` statements in your code, plus statistics about all calls to the database. If you increase the log level even more, you can also view the complete profile of the call, as shown in the following screenshot:

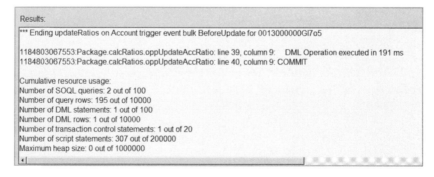

Figure 31: A Portion of a Debug Log at the Maximum Verbosity Setting

See Also

- *Best Practices for Debugging Apex* on page 228
- *Writing Unit Tests for Apex* on page 80
- *Debugging Apex in Salesforce* on page 229

Chapter 12

Packaging an App for the AppExchange

You've studied the recipes, learned to cook "à la Force.com," and now have a fully baked application. Now you might be wondering, "How do I get it out to the marketplace?"

The AppExchange is the world's first online service for browsing, sharing, and installing on-demand business applications. Once published on the AppExchange, your app is available to the entire Salesforce community to review, test drive, comment on, and install. However, in order to publish your app to the AppExchange, you first need to create a package.

A package is like a suitcase that can contain your apps and components. You use packages to bundle one or more application components so that you can upload them to the AppExchange together. Creating, managing, and upgrading packages is what this chapter is all about.

Deciding Whether to Make a Package Managed or Unmanaged

Problem

You want to create a package, but you don't know whether to make it managed or unmanaged.

Solution

Packages come in two flavors—*managed* and *unmanaged*:

- Use a managed package if you want to support package upgrades, or if you want to distribute your application commercially and keep track of which organizations have downloaded and installed your app. Also use managed packages if you want to lock down certain application components to prevent installers from editing them.
- Use an unmanaged package if you want to move application components between organizations for a one-time transfer, or if you don't need to support package upgrades or prevent administrators from editing package components.

By default, all packages are unmanaged when you create them. To specify a package as managed, choose the package in the Developer Settings configuration page by clicking **Setup ➤ Exchange ➤ Shared Apps**, and then clicking **Edit**.

Discussion

Unmanaged packages allow you to take any app components and move them "as is" to the AppExchange without going through a lengthy publishing process. They're ideal for moving components between organizations for a one-time transfer. However, unmanaged packages have the following drawbacks, which prevent them from being good solutions for commercial applications:

- Installers can edit—and break—anything installed as an unmanaged package
- Unmanaged packages don't support versioning, and therefore must be manually upgraded by each installer
- Developers of unmanaged packages have no visibility into who has downloaded or installed their apps

Managed packages circumvent those issues, primarily because they allow package developers to lock one or more components to preserve their existence and behavior. Just as Salesforce has standard fields that can't be deleted or altered, a managed package guarantees that the critical components and functionality delivered with your package will be there for future upgrades to build upon. This allows seamless and easy upgrades for both developers and customers.

Managed packages differ from unmanaged packages in the following ways:

- You must use a Developer Edition organization to create and work with a managed package. A Developer Edition organization can contain a single managed package and many unmanaged packages.
- When you release a managed package (that is, when it's uploaded to the AppExchange with the `Managed - Released` option selected), the properties of some of its components change to prevent publishers and subscribers from making harmful changes.
- You must configure Developer Settings in your Developer Edition organization to set a namespace and identify a License Management Organization (LMO) for your managed package.
- You can track user licenses and installed versions of your managed packages with an LMO.
- Managed packages require registering a namespace prefix, choosing a managed package, installing the License Management App (LMA), and selecting a License Management Organization (LMO).

See Also

- *Registering a Namespace Prefix* on page 235
- *Tracking Package Users* on page 240
- *Posting a Package on the AppExchange* on page 242
- *Converting an Unmanaged Package into a Managed Package* on page 246
- "Properties of Managed Components" and "List of Locked Components" in the Salesforce online help

Registering a Namespace Prefix

Problem

You want to create a managed package, but you don't have a namespace prefix that can be used to prevent naming conflicts between your application components and those of other developers who have posted on the AppExchange.

Solution

Register for a namespace prefix in the Developer Edition organization that you want to use for your managed package. Each managed package that you create must have its own unique namespace:

1. In Salesforce, click **Setup ➤ Exchange ➤ Shared Apps**, and then click **Edit**.

    Note: The **Edit** button no longer appears after you've configured your developer settings. Once saved, developer settings can't be modified.

2. Click **Continue** to open the Developer Settings configuration page.

3. Enter the namespace prefix you want to use, and click **Check Availability** to determine if it's already in use. Your namespace prefix must:

   - Begin with a letter
   - Contain one to 15 alphanumeric characters. We recommend a shorter length for convenience.
   - Not contain two consecutive underscores
   - Be globally unique across all Salesforce organizations

   Repeat the process until you've found a namespace that satisfies these requirements.

    Tip:

   - There are several places where you'll need to enter your namespace manually, so it's preferable to keep it as short and concise as possible.
   - Namespace prefixes can be helpful in identifying the developer and app for a component—for example, gc_app1. Likewise, if you're developing multiple managed apps in multiple Developer Edition organizations, use a namespace naming convention such as dev_app1, dev_app2, and dev_app3 to keep them straight. Or, if you're developing a base package with extensions, use a naming convention like dev_app_base, dev_app_ext1, dev_app_ext2, and so on.

4. Complete the remaining developer settings as desired, then click **Review My Selections** and **Save**.

    Tip: If you're not ready to select a License Management Organization (LMO), select `Do this later`. However, choosing to do this later prevents you from uploading apps to the AppExchange.

Discussion

A namespace prefix is similar to a domain name. It consists of a one- to 15-character alphanumeric identifier that distinguishes your package and its contents from packages of other developers on the AppExchange.

Salesforce automatically prepends your namespace prefix, followed by two underscores ("__"), to all unique component names in your Salesforce organization. A unique component is one that requires a name that no other component has within Salesforce, such as custom objects, custom fields, custom links, s-controls, and validation rules.

For example, if your namespace prefix is abc and your managed package contains a custom object with the API name, Expense__c, you'd use the API name abc__Expense__c to access this object using the API.

Caution: S-controls that are stored in the s-control library or the Documents tab that do not use the Force.com API will still function properly after you register a namespace prefix. However, s-controls stored outside of your organization or s-controls that use the Force.com API to call Salesforce may require some fine-tuning.

Note: If you requested a unique four-character ID from salesforce.com prior to Winter '07, you still need to register a namespace prefix. Existing components that include your unique four-character ID will have the namespace prefix automatically appended to their API name. For example, if you previously used the API name abcd.Expense__c to access the Expense object from the API and you register the same prefix using the new process, use abcd__abcd.Expense__c to access this object from the API going forward.

If your API transactions use components that reference merge fields without their namespace prefix, Salesforce automatically prepends them with your namespace prefix.

See Also

- *Deciding Whether to Make a Package Managed or Unmanaged* on page 234
- *Using Namespaces in S-Controls and Apex* on page 237
- *Using Namespaces in a Client Application* on page 238
- *Posting a Package on the AppExchange* on page 242
- *Creating an Unmanaged Package from a Namespaced Organization* on page 239

Using Namespaces in S-Controls and Apex

Problem

You've registered for a namespace and now you need to use it to reference custom objects and fields in your s-controls and Apex.

Solution

Once a namespace has been associated with an organization, the namespace and two underscore characters ("__") are prepended to all custom object and field names. For example, if your namespace prefix is abc and your managed package contains a custom object with the API name, Expense__c, you'd use the API name abc__Expense__c to access this object using the API

While this namespace prefix is required on all references to your custom objects and fields, you don't always need to explicitly reference the namespace when creating components such as s-controls, formulas, or email templates. The platform's declarative editors for these components support implicit namespacing. For example, if your organization's namespace is battle and you reference a field called botId__c, clicking the **Check Syntax** button doesn't generate an error because the editor automatically prepends the namespace before checking. When your code is saved, battle_botId__c is the value saved in your code. Likewise, inserting field references using the **Insert Merge Field** button always inserts the field with the namespace automatically added, so you don't have to worry about it.

The Eclipse Toolkit also supports implicit namespacing while editing s-controls or Apex.

 Note: If you're developing an extension to a base package, you still have to explicitly reference any namespaced objects and fields in the base package.

See Also

- *Registering a Namespace Prefix* on page 235
- *Using Namespaces in a Client Application* on page 238
- *Posting a Package on the AppExchange* on page 242
- *Creating an Unmanaged Package from a Namespaced Organization* on page 239

Using Namespaces in a Client Application

Problem

You've registered for a namespace and now you need to use it to reference custom objects and fields when making calls to the API through a client application.

Solution

Set the namespace in your `CallOptions` SOAP header to eliminate the need to explicitly reference the namespace prefix when referring to custom objects and fields. In the header, use the `defaultNamespace` parameter to identify a developer namespace prefix. This field can then be used to resolve field names in managed packages.

 Note: The `CallOptions` header is only available for use with the Partner WSDL.

For example, to set the `defaultNamespace` parameter to "battle" in an s-control that uses the AJAX Toolkit, include the following line of code before you issue your first toolkit command:

```
sforce.connection.defaultNamespace="battle";
```

Once `defaultNamespace` is set, queries such as the following will succeed:

```
sforce.connection.query("SELECT id, botId__c from Account");
```

Without this field specified, the full name of the field (`battle__botId__c`) has to be used instead.

To set the `CallOptions` header in Java:

```
// Make a SOAP Call Options header to be sent on subsequent API calls
_CallOptions callOpts = new _CallOptions();

// If we have a namespace
String nameSpaceV = "test_ns1";
callOpts.setDefaultNamespace(nameSpaceV);
```

Note that if the `defaultNamespace` parameter is set, and the query specifies the namespace as well, the response doesn't include the prefix. For example, if you set the namespace to "battle" and issue a query like the following:

```
query("SELECT id, battle__botId__c from Account");
```

The response specifies `botId__c`, not `battle__botId__c`. Describe calls ignore this field, so there's no ambiguity between fields with namespace prefixes and customer fields of the same name without the prefix.

See Also

- *Registering a Namespace Prefix* on page 235
- *Using Namespaces in S-Controls and Apex* on page 237
- *Creating an Unmanaged Package from a Namespaced Organization* on page 239
- *Posting a Package on the AppExchange* on page 242

Creating an Unmanaged Package from a Namespaced Organization

Problem

You want to create an unmanaged package in an organization that has a registered namespace.

Solution

Define the package components using namespace references to custom fields and objects. However, understand that once the unmanaged package is uploaded to the AppExchange, all namespace prefixes are stripped from these components so that other users can download the package without any namespace references. Consequently, if you've built a client application that works against the namespaced organization, the only way to make it work with a subscriber's organization is by modifying the code to remove the namespace, for example, by removing the reference to the `defaultNamespace` in the `CallOptions` header.

See Also

- *Registering a Namespace Prefix* on page 235
- *Using Namespaces in S-Controls and Apex* on page 237
- *Using Namespaces in a Client Application* on page 238
- *Posting a Package on the AppExchange* on page 242

Tracking Package Users

Problem

You want to track the subscribers who install or uninstall your managed package from the AppExchange, including the current version of each installed package.

Solution

Download the free License Management App (LMA) from the AppExchange at www.salesforce.com/appexchange/, and install it in the Enterprise Edition, Unlimited Edition, or Developer Edition organization you use to track sales leads and accounts for your business. This organization is then called your License Management Organization (LMO).

Tip: It's a best practice to install the LMA in an Enterprise Edition or Unlimited Edition organization to avoid storage limit errors. If you choose to use a Developer Edition organization as your LMO, use it only for the LMO and not for developing apps. You can't install the LMA in any other Salesforce editions because the LMA uses record types.

Once your LMO is set up, log in to the Developer Edition organization where you're building your managed app and set the LMO in the Developer Settings configuration page:

1. In Salesforce, click **Setup ➤ Exchange ➤ Shared Apps**, and then click **Edit**.

    Note: The **Edit** button no longer appears after you've configured your developer settings. Once saved, developer settings can't be modified.

2. Click **Continue** to open the Developer Settings configuration page.
3. Decide how you want to set up your LMO:

- Select `Make a different Salesforce organization my license management organization` if you have the username and password for your LMO.
- Select `Make a third-party Salesforce organization my license management organization` if you don't have a username and password for the organization that should be your LMO, but you do have the email address of a user to whom you can send your request. If that user accepts your invitation, the third-party LMO can be used to track your managed package.

4. Complete the remaining developer settings as desired, then click **Review My Selections** and **Save**.

 Caution: Once you specify an LMO for a Developer Edition organization, you can't change it.

Discussion

Once you've specified the LMO for a Developer Edition organization, the LMO receives notification in the form of a new lead record whenever a subscriber installs or uninstalls your managed package, and it tracks each package upload on the AppExchange directory. When a customer purchases your application, you can convert this lead to an account, and you can also track installed packages and version history.

There are a number of ways you can configure your LMO to make it more useful for your business:

- If you want to be notified each time your package is downloaded, set up a workflow rule that sends an email every time a new lead is created.
- If you want to track additional information about your customers, add custom fields to the License object. The only constraint is that these fields must not be required—if they are, the LMA will not be able to create new license records. Note that the same constraint applies to custom fields that you add to the Package and Package Version custom objects as well.
- Each LMO should have a lead manager who is responsible for following up on all leads associated with licenses. When a new lead is created as a result of someone installing the package from the AppExchange, the `Lead Owner` field defaults to the Lead Manager specified for the package. If there is no Lead Manager specified for a package, the lead owner is the License Manager.

To change the Lead Manager for a package:

1. In the Packages tab, click **Edit** next to the package that you want to modify.
2. Next to the `Lead Manager` field, select a user.
3. Click **Save**.

See Also

- *Registering a Namespace Prefix* on page 235
- *Deciding Whether to Make a Package Managed or Unmanaged* on page 234
- *Posting a Package on the AppExchange* on page 242
- The Breeze presentation, "A Developer and Publisher's Guide to the License Management Application" at admin.acrobat.com/_a13852757/lma

Posting a Package on the AppExchange

Problem

You want to create and upload a package onto the AppExchange.

Solution

Before creating a package:

- Decide whether you want to create a managed or an unmanaged package
- If creating a managed package, register a namespace and specify a License Management Organization (LMO)
- If you want to provide instructions for configuring your package once it's installed in another organization, define a custom link on the Home tab that links to an external Web page that you host, or to an HTML-based custom s-control that you've already defined. The Web page or s-control should display configuration information such as:

  - The custom fields and custom links that should be added to standard objects for your app to work properly
  - Instructions on how to provision the external service portion of a composite app
  - An end user license agreement

     Tip: Using a custom link for configuration information is preferable to posting this information on a custom About tab because tabs can't be deleted from managed packages and many Salesforce customers have restrictions on the number of tabs they can use at any time.

Once you're ready:

1. In the Developer Edition organization where your application components are saved, click **Setup ➤ Exchange ➤ Shared Apps** and then click **New**.
2. Enter a name for your package. Note that this doesn't have to be the same name that will appear publicly on the AppExchange.

3. Optionally, choose the custom link that was defined on the Home tab from the `Configure Custom Link` field. If you choose a custom link from this drop-down list, it displays as a **Configure** link within Salesforce on the AppExchange Downloads page and on the app detail page in the installer's organization.

4. Optionally, enter a description that defines the package. Note that you'll have a chance to change this description before you upload it to the AppExchange.

5. Select the `Managed` checkbox if this is a managed package. If the managed checkbox isn't available, then you either already have a managed package in your organization, or you haven't created a namespace prefix yet.

 Note: This checkbox is already selected if you specified the package in your developer settings.

6. Click **Save**.

7. On the Package Items related list, click **Add**, and use the `Item Type` drop-down list to see the application components that you've defined in your organization, organized by component type. Select the checkbox next to each component that you want to include in your package, and click **Add to Package**.

 Tip: When you add some components to a package, additional items are also included. For example, when you add a custom object to a package, its custom fields, page layouts, relationships with standard objects, and other items are automatically included too. Consequently, it's often easier to include high level items such as an app or an object, before including lower-level components.

Once you've selected all the components that you want to include in the package, verify that:

- You've included all the components that are required to make the package work properly
- Nothing has been automatically added to the package that you didn't intend to add.

For a list of items Salesforce automatically includes with each component, see "What is automatically included in a package?" in the Salesforce online help.

8. Click **Upload to AppExchange** in the Package detail page and specify information about your package:

    a. Enter the `Version Number` for your package (for example, 1.0a). This number is how you can identify the specific upload of the package.

    b. If you're uploading a managed package, choose the `Package Status`:

- If you select Managed - Beta, users can only install your package in Developer Edition or sandbox organizations. Additionally, installers won't be able to upgrade your package without first uninstalling it, and all data they create will be deleted.
- If you select Managed - Released, you'll no longer be able to edit certain package components after the release. Only select this option if you have thoroughly tested your app and know that you won't need to make any additional changes.

 Tip: Salesforce strongly recommends that you go through a thorough beta test cycle to ensure that your package is functioning as your desire and you're comfortable no changes will need to be made to the package after it has been changed to Managed - Released.

   c. Set the `Security`:

- Choose No Password to make your app publicly available to anyone on the AppExchange.
- Choose Password Required to share your app privately with anyone who has the password.

 Caution: If you forget this password, you'll have to create another version of the package with a new password and upload it again.

   d. Click **Upload to AppExchange**.

Wait to receive an email instructing you to register your package, or click the indicated link and proceed to a waiting page where you can monitor the status of your package upload and "refresh" until the **Register** button is live.

9. Once the package is uploaded, register it so you can share it privately on theAppExchange. After you register your app, you'll receive a URL that you can share with other users. Registered apps give you all the capabilities of published apps but don't expose the listing to the public.

Discussion

Once your package is uploaded and registered on the AppExchange, you can share the package URL with others. However, to make your application visible on the AppExchange public listing you must go through the publishing process. See the "AppExchange Packaging Guide" at na1.salesforce.com/help/doc/en/salesforce_appexchange_publish_guide.pdf or visit www.salesforce.com/appexchange/publishing.jsp for details.

- *Deciding Whether to Make a Package Managed or Unmanaged* on page 234
- *Registering a Namespace Prefix* on page 235
- *Tracking Package Users* on page 240
- "List of Locked Components" in the Salesforce online help
- "Publishing Apps on the AppExchange" at www.salesforce.com/appexchange/publishing.jsp
- "AppExchange Packaging Guide" at na1.salesforce.com/help/doc/en/ salesforce_appexchange_publish_guide.pdf

Upgrading a Released Package

Problem

You've published a managed package to the AppExchange and now you want to release a new version.

Solution

In the Developer Edition organization that hosts your managed package:

1. Click **Setup ➤ Exchange ➤ Shared Apps**, and click the name of your managed package.
2. Add or remove the package components that you want, and click **Upload to AppExchange**.
3. Follow the same steps as when you created the original package:

   a. Enter an incremental version number.

    Tip: You can refer to the version upload history at the bottom of the package detail page to decide on the version number you want to use for this package.

   b. Select Managed - Released or Managed - Beta.

    Tip: Salesforce strongly recommends that you go through a thorough beta test cycle to ensure that your package is functioning as your desire and you're comfortable no changes will need to be made to the package after it has been changed to Managed - Released.

   c. Add or alter the description, as necessary.

   d. Select the security settings.

   e. Click **Upload to AppExchange**.

After your package upload and registration is complete, you can alert all of your customers that there's a new version and direct them to the AppExchange to upgrade. If you have a managed package, you can monitor the progress of the upgrade in the License Management Application.

See Also

- *Posting a Package on the AppExchange* on page 242
- *Tracking Package Users* on page 240

Converting an Unmanaged Package into a Managed Package

Problem

You developed and posted an unmanaged package onto the AppExchange, but now you want it to be a managed package.

Solution

Prepare the package as a managed package in a Developer Edition organization, upload it to the AppExchange, and then contact your Partner Success Manager to update your listing:

1. If the package is based in a Developer Edition organization that already has another managed package, first register a new Developer Edition organization and install the unmanaged package from the AppExchange into that new organization.
2. If you've included app configuration instructions in an About tab that most installers would want to eventually remove, replace the extra tab with a custom s-control or Web page that you can link to with a custom link on the Home tab. This step is important because tabs can't be deleted from a managed package by installers—many Salesforce customers have a tab limit and don't want to install unnecessary tabs.
3. Register a namespace for the unmanaged package and set the License Management Organization (LMO) in the Developer Settings configuration page.
4. Upload the package to the AppExchange as a managed package.
5. Contact your Partner Success Manager so that you can replace your current unmanaged package listing with the managed package. To do so, log in to the AppExchange and click **Change Listing** in the Manage My Apps tab. Your Partner Success Manager can then make your AppExchange posting editable.

See Also

- "How to Convert to a Managed App," a presentation on the ADN at wiki.apexdevnet.com/images/c/c1/How_to_Convert_to_a_Managed_Package.ppt
- *Posting a Package on the AppExchange* on page 242
- *Registering a Namespace Prefix* on page 235

- *Tracking Package Users* on page 240

Chapter 13

Getting Started with Visualforce

At Dreamforce 2007, salesforce.com announced a whole new development paradigm for the Force.com platform: Visualforce.

Similar to the way Apex dramatically increases the power of developers to customize business logic, Visualforce dramatically increases the power of developers to customize the user interface. Whereas developers previously had to write s-controls or external Web pages from scratch in order to modify the Salesforce user interface, Visualforce now allows developers to use a simple, tag-based markup language to define custom pages and components.

With this markup language, each tag corresponds to a coarse or fine-grained component, such as a section of a page, a related list, or a field. The components can either be controlled by the same logic that's used in standard Salesforce pages, or developers can associate their own logic with a controller written in Apex. With this architecture, designers and developers can easily split up the work that goes with building a new application—designers can focus on the user interface, while developers can work on the business logic that drives the app.

This chapter includes basic recipes to help you get started. To find out more, visit the Apex Developer Network at www.salesforce.com/developer/.

 Note: As of September 2007, Visualforce is available as a Developer Preview only.

Enabling Visualforce in your Organization

Problem

You're excited to try out Visualforce, but you don't yet have it enabled in your Salesforce organization.

Solution

Sign up for the Visualforce Developer Preview program at www.salesforce.com/developer/. Currently only ADN members who have signed up for this program can use Visualforce.

See Also

- *Enabling Visualforce Developer Mode* on page 250
- *Creating Your First Visualforce Page* on page 251

Enabling Visualforce Developer Mode

Problem

Visualforce is enabled in your organization, but you don't have access to all of the development tools that are described elsewhere in this chapter.

Solution

Once Visualforce is enabled, users with the "Customize Application" user profile permission can enable Visualforce Developer Mode by editing their user record:

1. Click **Setup ➤ My Personal Information ➤ Personal Information**, and click **Edit**.
2. Select the `Developer Mode` checkbox, and then click **Save**.

Discussion

Enabling Developer Mode changes certain behaviors of your organization. Developer Mode provides you with:

- A special footer on any Visualforce page. The footer includes editors for the page itself and, if applicable, the associated Apex controller for the page.
- The ability to define new Visualforce pages on the fly, just by entering a particular URL. See *Creating Your First Visualforce Page* on page 251.
- More detailed messages for errors that occur on a Visualforce page.

See Also

- *Enabling Visualforce in your Organization* on page 250
- *Creating Your First Visualforce Page* on page 251

Creating Your First Visualforce Page

Problem

You're ready to create your first Visualforce page, but you don't know where to begin.

Solution

To create a new page:

1. With Developer Mode enabled, define a new page by entering a URL for the page in your browser's address bar as follows:

   ```
   https://<mySalesforceInstance>/apex/<myNewPageName>
   ```

   For example, if you want to create a page called "MyFirstPage" and your organization logs in to na3.salesforce.com, enter
   ```
   https://na3.salesforce.com/apex/MyFirstPage.
   ```

2. Because the page doesn't yet exist, you're directed to an intermediary page from which you can create your new page. Click **Create page** to create it on the fly.

    Note: If you don't have Visualforce Developer Mode enabled, you can also create a new page by clicking **Setup ➤ Build ➤ Pages**, and then clicking **New Page**.

   Visualforce pages can always be edited from this part of setup, but to see the results of your edits you have to navigate to the URL of your page. For that reason, most developers prefer to work with Developer Mode enabled so they can view and edit a page in a single window.

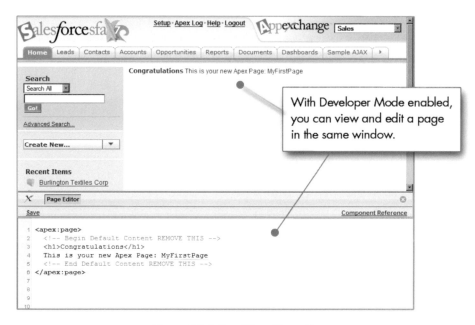

Figure 32: A New Visualforce Page

To edit your new page, click the **Page Editor** button that appears at the bottom of the browser. It expands the editor to show you the following code:

```
<apex:page>
    <!-- Begin Default Content REMOVE THIS -->
    <h1>Congratulations</h1>
    This is your new page: MyFirstPage
    <!-- End Default Content REMOVE THIS -->
</apex:page>
```

 Tip: You can resize the page editor by dragging it up or down with your mouse.

You can modify this page as much as you want—the only required tag for any page is the `<apex:page>` tag that begins and ends any page definition. For example, after entering the following code and clicking **Save** in the Page Editor, the page displays the text "Hello World!":

```
<apex:page>
    Hello World!
</apex:page>
```

Visualforce use the same expression language as formulas and s-controls—that is, anything inside {! } is evaluated as an expression. For example, you can display the current user's first name by adding the {!$User.FirstName} merge field to your page:

```
<apex:page>
    Hello {!$User.FirstName}!
</apex:page>
```

Visualforce pages can also be associated with a *controller*. Controllers provide a page with the data and business logic that make your application run. While you can define a custom controller for any Visualforce page with Apex, Salesforce includes standard controllers for every standard and custom object.

For example, to use the standard controller for accounts:

1. Add the standardController attribute to the <apex:page> tag, and assign it the name of the account object:

```
<apex:page standardController="Account">
    Hello {!$User.FirstName}!
</apex:page>
```

2. Click **Save** in the Page Editor.

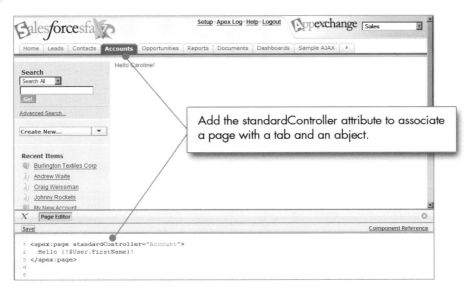

Figure 33: A Visualforce Page with a Standard Controller

After you save, the Accounts tab is now highlighted for this page, and the look-and-feel for the components on your page now match the Accounts tab. Additionally, the page is now associated with the Account object, and you can access fields on an account record by using expression syntax if you indicate the ID of the account in the URL for the page.

For example, to add an account's name to this page, use `{!account.name}` in the code:

```
<apex:page standardController="Account">
    Hello {!$User.FirstName}!
    <p>You belong to the {!account.name} account.</p>
</apex:page>
```

 Tip: Notice that we used the HTML paragraph tag (`<p>`) to place the second sentence on a new line. You can use any HTML that you might use in a regular HTML page in a Visualforce page.

Upon saving the page, the account name isn't yet displayed because you still must indicate the ID of an account record in the URL for the page. To do this:

1. Find the ID of an account by any means you wish. One easy way is to view the detail page of an account record, and copy the 15-character code at the end of the URL. For example, if you navigate to an account detail page with the following URL:

   ```
   https://na3.salesforce.com/001D000000HRgU6
   ```

   Then 001D000000HRgU6 is the ID for the account.

2. Back on your Visualforce page, add the account ID as a query string parameter to the URL in your browser's address bar. For example, if your page is located at:

   ```
   https://na3.salesforce.com/apex/MyFirstPage
   ```

   Add `?id=001D000000HRgU6` to the end of the URL:

   ```
   https://na3.salesforce.com/apex/MyFirstPage?id=001D000000HRgU6
   ```

Once an account ID is specified, the page displays the appropriate account name.

Figure 34: Accessing Account Data from a Visualforce Page

See Also

- *Enabling Visualforce in your Organization* on page 250
- *Enabling Visualforce Developer Mode* on page 250
- *Using the Visualforce Component Library* on page 255

Using the Visualforce Component Library

Problem

You want to add something more than text to a Visualforce page, but you don't know what's available, or how to do it.

Solution

Add components to your page based on what's available in the component library.

Discussion

Just as you can insert images or tables into an HTML document with the `<img>` or `<table>` tags, respectively, you can add user interface components to your Visualforce pages using tags that are defined in the component library.

For example, to add a component that looks like a section on a detail page, use the `<apex:pageBlock>` component tag:

```
<apex:page standardController="Account">
    <apex:pageBlock title="Hello {!$User.FirstName}!">
        You belong to the {!account.name} account.<br/>
        You're also a nice person.
    </apex:pageBlock>
</apex:page>
```

This code renders the following page:

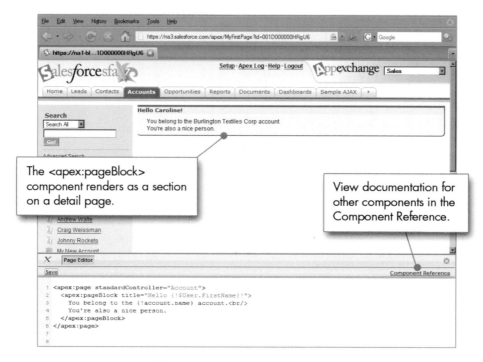

Figure 35: A <pageBlock> Element

Components also exist for other common Salesforce idioms, such as related lists, data tables, detail pages, and input fields. For example, to add the detail page for a particular record (including all related lists), add the `<apex:detail>` component tag with its one required attribute—the ID of the subject record:

```
<apex:page standardController="Account">
    <apex:pageBlock title="Hello {!$User.FirstName}!">
        You belong to the {!account.name} account.<br/>
        You're also a nice person.
    </apex:pageBlock>
    <apex:detail subject="{!account}"/>
</apex:page>
```

 Tip: If you want to add the detail page for a record without its associated related lists, set the `relatedList` parameter to false:

```
<apex:detail subject="{!account}" relatedList="false"/>
```

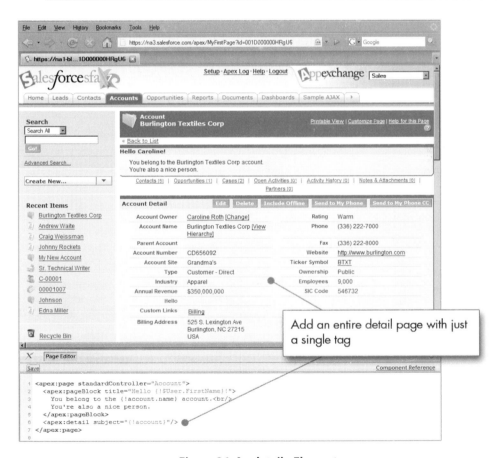

Figure 36: A <detail> Element

To browse the component library, click **Component Reference** in the Page Editor, or access it through the Salesforce online help. From this page you can drill down into any component to see the attributes that are available for each.

See Also

- *Creating Your First Visualforce Page* on page 251
- *Creating Your First Visualforce Controller* on page 258

Creating Your First Visualforce Controller

Problem

You want to write your own Visualforce page logic so you can capture the information you want on a page, and control how users navigate between pages in your application.

Solution

Define a custom *controller* for your page.

Discussion

A custom controller is simply an Apex class with a public `getName()` method that returns a string. For example, the following code is a valid controller class for a page that doesn't reference an object or field:

```
public class MyFirstController {

    public String getName() {
        return 'My First Custom Controller';
    }

}
```

After using your preferred Apex editor to create this controller class and save it, you can use it on a page by setting the `controller` attribute in the `<apex:page>` tag.

 Tip: If you use the page editor to set the `controller` attribute to an Apex class that doesn't yet exist, the page editor prompts you with an option to create the controller class on the fly.

For example, the following page uses the custom controller while displaying a greeting, and then prints the name of the controller itself:

```
<apex:page controller="MyFirstController">
    <apex:pageBlock title="Hello {!$User.FirstName}!">
        This is your new page for the {!name} custom controller. <br/>

    </apex:pageBlock>
</apex:page>
```

 Note: A Visualforce page can only reference one controller at a time. Consequently, you can't use the `standardController` attribute if you want to add a custom `controller` attribute to a page.

Notice in this example that you can use the `{!User.FirstName}` merge field in the page because the current user is a global object variable that's available no matter where you are in the application. Additionally, you can also use `{!name}` as a merge field to call the `getName()` method from the controller class.

As soon as you save a page with a valid custom controller, a second Controller editor is available alongside the Page Editor. This editor allows you to toggle back and forth between the tags that define your page's user interface and the Apex that defines the page's logic.

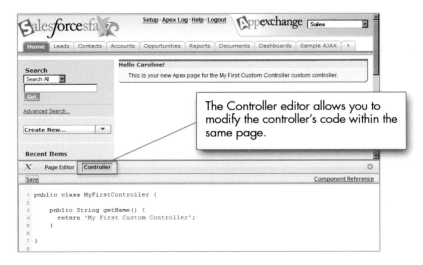

Figure 37: The Custom Controller Editor

If you want to reference data from a Salesforce object on your page, the controller also needs a `get<Object>()` method that returns the associated object. For example, the following controller could be used for the controller defined in *Creating Your First Visualforce Page* on page 251 because it includes a `getAccount()` method:

```
public class mySecondController {

    public Account getAccount() {
        return [select id, name from Account
                where id =
:System.currentPageReference().getParameters().get('id')];
    }

    public String getName() {
        return 'My Second Custom Controller';
    }
}
```

This `getAccount()` method uses an embedded SOQL query to return the account that matches an `id` parameter in the URL of the page. You can access this parameter value through the `System` global object variable using the `currentPageReference()` and `getParameters()` methods.

When using this custom controller with the page defined in *Creating Your First Visualforce Page* on page 251, the only difference in the display of the page is that the Accounts tab is not highlighted and the style of the page retains the green of the Home tab. To easily regain the Accounts tab styling while using the custom controller, add the `tabStyle` attribute to the `<apex:page>` tag. For example, with the `mySecondController` custom controller, this page displays exactly the same as the page defined in *Creating Your First Visualforce Page* on page 251:

```
<apex:page controller="mySecondController" tabStyle="Account">
    Hello {!$User.FirstName}!
    <p>You belong to the {!account.name} account.</p>
</apex:page>
```

See Also

- *Creating Your First Visualforce Page* on page 251
- *Using Query String Parameters in a Visualforce Page* on page 261
- *Building a Table of Data in a Visualforce Page* on page 263
- *Building a Form in a Visualforce Page* on page 265
- *Creating a Wizard with Visualforce Pages* on page 269

Using Query String Parameters in a Visualforce Page

Problem

You want to read and set query string parameters in a Visualforce page, either in a custom controller or in the page itself.

Solution

The way to read and set query string parameters depends on whether you access them from a custom controller or directly from a Visualforce page.

To read a query string parameter:

- If you're writing a custom controller, use the `System` global object variable and `currentPageReference()` and `getParameters()` methods to get query string parameters. For example, to get the value of the name query parameter in the following URL:

  ```
  https://na1.salesforce.com/001/e?name=value
  ```

  Use the following line in your custom controller:

  ```
  String value =
  System.currentPageReference().getParameters().get('name');
  ```

- If you're editing a page, use the `$PageContext` global variable in a merge field.

  For example, suppose you want to add the Open Activities related list to an account detail page, but instead of showing the account's activities, you want to show the activities of a specified contact. To specify the contact, the following page looks for a query string parameter for the contact's ID under the name `relatedId`:

  ```
  <apex:page standardController="Account">
      <apex:pageBlock title="Hello {!$User.FirstName}!">
          You belong to the {!account.name} account.<br/>
          You're also a nice person.
      </apex:pageBlock>
      <apex:detail subject="{!account}" relatedList="false"/>
      <apex:relatedList list="OpenActivities"

  subject="{!$CurrentPageReference.parameters.relatedId}"/>
  </apex:page>
  ```

For this related list to render in a saved page, valid account and contact IDs must be specified in the URL. For example, if `001D000000HRgU6` is the account ID and `003D000000OXDIx` is the contact ID, use this URL:

```
https://na3.salesforce.com/apex/MyFirstPage?id=001D000000HRgU6&
relatedId=003D000000OXDIx
```

To set a query string parameter:

- If you're writing a custom controller, use the `setParameters()` method with `System.currentPageReference()` to add a query parameter in a test method. For example:

```
String key = 'name';
String value = 'Caroline';
System.currentPageReference().setParameters().put(key, value);
```

 Note: The `setParameters()` method is only valid inside test methods.

- If you're editing a page, you can either construct a URL manually:

```
<apex:outputLink value="http://google.com/search?q={!account.name}">

    Search Google
</apex:outputLink>
```

Or you can use the `<apex:param>` tag as a child tag to write cleaner code:

```
<apex:outputLink value="http://google.com/search">
    Search Google
    <apex:param name="q" value="{!account.name}"/>
</apex:outputLink>
```

 Note: In addition to `<apex:outputLink>`, `<apex:param>` can be a child of other tags such as `<apex:include>` and `<apex:commandLink>`.

See Also

Building a Table of Data in a Visualforce Page

Problem

You want to display a set of records in a table in a Visualforce page.

Solution

Define a custom controller that returns the set of records you want to display, and then use the `<dataTable>` tag to display the results.

Discussion

To illustrate this example, let's first modify the sample controller that we defined in *Creating Your First Visualforce Controller* on page 258 so that it returns a list of associated contacts with an account record:

```
public class mySecondController {

    public Account getAccount() {
        return [select id, name,
                    (select id, firstname, lastname
                    from Contacts limit 5)
                from Account
                where id =
:System.currentPageReference().getParameters().get('id')];
    }

    public String getName() {
        return 'My Second Custom Controller';
    }
}
```

Now iterate over the resulting contacts with the `<dataTable>` tag. This tag allows us to define an iteration variable that we can use to access the fields on each contact:

```
<apex:page controller="mySecondController" tabStyle="Account">
    <apex:pageBlock title="Hello {!$User.FirstName}!">
        You belong to the {!account.name} account.
    </apex:pageBlock>
    <apex:pageBlock title="Contacts">
        <apex:dataTable value="{!account.Contacts}" var="contact"
                        cellPadding="4" border="1">
            <apex:column>{!contact.FirstName}</apex:column>
            <apex:column>{!contact.LastName}</apex:column>
        </apex:dataTable>
    </apex:pageBlock>
</apex:page>
```

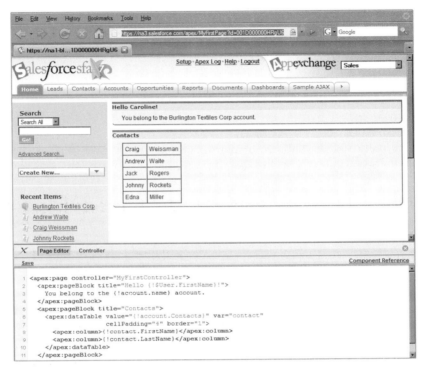

Figure 38: The <dataTable> Component

Notice that the <apex:dataTable> tag supports styling attributes like cellPadding and border. You can also style individual data elements with HTML tags. For example, the following <apex:dataTable> component makes the last name of each contact bold:

```
<apex:dataTable value="{!account.Contacts}" var="contact"
                cellPadding="4" border="1">
  <apex:column>{!contact.FirstName}</apex:column>
  <apex:column><b>{!contact.LastName}</b></apex:column>
</apex:dataTable>
```

See Also

- *Using Query String Parameters in a Visualforce Page* on page 261
- *Creating Your First Visualforce Controller* on page 258
- *Building a Form in a Visualforce Page* on page 265
- *Using AJAX in a Visualforce Page* on page 267
- *Creating a Wizard with Visualforce Pages* on page 269

Building a Form in a Visualforce Page

Problem

You want to create a Visualforce page that captures input from users.

Solution

Use the `<apex:form>` tag with one or more input components and a `<apex:commandLink>` or `<apex:commandButton>` tag to submit the form.

Discussion

To gather data for fields that are defined on a custom or standard object, use the `<apex:inputField>` tag. This tag renders the appropriate input widget based on the field's type. For example, if you use an `<apex:inputField>` tag to display a date field, a calendar widget displays on the form. If you use an `<apex:inputField>` tag to display a picklist field, a drop-down list displays instead.

For example, the following page allows users to edit and save the name of an account:

 Note: Remember, for this page to display account data, the ID of a valid account record must be specified as a query parameter in the URL for the page.

```
<apex:page standardController="Account">
    <apex:form>
        <apex:pageBlock title="Hello {!$User.FirstName}!">
            You belong to the {!account.name} account.<p/>
            Account Name: <apex:inputField
                                    value="{!account.name}"/><p/>
            <apex:commandButton action="{!save}"
                                value="Save New Account Name"/>
        </apex:pageBlock>
    </apex:form>
</apex:page>
```

Notice in the example that the `<apex:commandButton>` tag is associated with the 'save' action of the standard controller, which performs the same action as the **Save** button on the standard edit page. The `<apex:inputField>` tag is bound to the account name field by setting the value attribute with an expression containing familiar dot-notation.

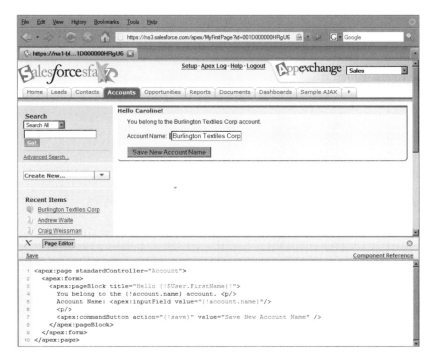

Figure 39: The <apex:form> Component with a Single Input Field

The <apex:inputField> tag can be used with either standard or custom controllers and enforces all security restrictions and other flags on the field, such as whether a value for the field is required, or whether it must be unique from the value on all other records of that type. Its only drawback is that if it's used to display variables in a custom controller that aren't bound to an object field, the variables might not display the way you want them to.

To gather data for these variables, use the apex:inputCheckbox, apex:inputHidden, apex:inputSecret, apex:inputText, or apex:inputTextarea tags instead. To learn more about these tags, browse the component library by clicking **Component Reference** in the Page Editor or accessing it through the Salesforce online help.

See Also

- *Using Query String Parameters in a Visualforce Page* on page 261
- *Building a Table of Data in a Visualforce Page* on page 263
- *Using AJAX in a Visualforce Page* on page 267
- *Creating a Wizard with Visualforce Pages* on page 269

Using AJAX in a Visualforce Page

Problem

You want to use AJAX in a Visualforce page so that only part of the page needs to be refreshed when a user clicks a button or link.

Solution

Use the `reRender` attribute on an `<apex:commandLink>` or `<apex:commandButton>` tag to identify the component that should be refreshed. When a user clicks the button or link, only the identified component and all of its child components are refreshed.

For example, the following page shows a list of contacts. When a user clicks the name of a contact, only the area below the list refreshes, showing the details for the contact:

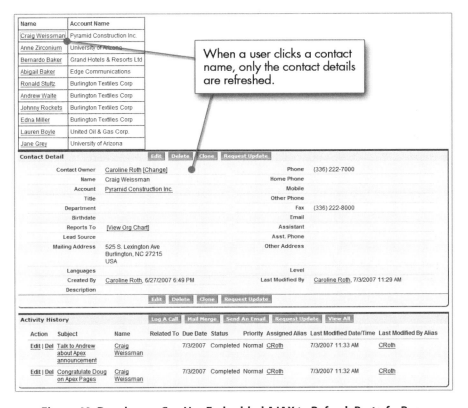

Figure 40: Developers Can Use Embedded AJAX to Refresh Part of a Page

This is the code used to display the page:

```
<apex:page controller="contactController" showHeader="true"
           tabStyle="Contact">
  <apex:form>
    <apex:dataTable value="{!contacts}" var="c"
                    cellpadding="4" border="1">
      <apex:column>
        <apex:facet name="header"><b>Name</b></apex:facet>
        <apex:commandLink reRender="detail">{!c.name}
          <apex:param name="id" value="{!c.id}"/>
        </apex:commandLink>
      </apex:column>
      <apex:column>
        <apex:facet name="header"><b>Account Name</b></apex:facet>
        {!c.account.name}
      </apex:column>
    </apex:dataTable>
    <apex:outputPanel id="detail">
      <apex:detail subject="{!contact}" title="false"
                   relatedList="false"/>
      <apex:relatedList list="ActivityHistories"
                        subject="{!contact}"/>
    </apex:outputPanel>
  </apex:form>
</apex:page>
```

Notice the following about the code for this page:

- Setting the reRender attribute of the <apex:commandLink> tag to 'detail' (the id value for the <apex:outputPanel> tag) means that only the output panel component is refreshed when a user clicks the name of a contact.
- The <apex:param> tag sets the id query parameter for each contact name link to the ID of the associated contact record.
- In the <apex:column> tags, an <apex:facet> tag is used to add the header row. Facets are special child components of some tags that can control the header, footer, or other special areas of the parent component. Even though the columns are in an iteration component (the data table), the facets only display once, in the header for each column.
- In the <apex:outputPanel> tag, the details for the currently-selected contact are displayed without the detail section title or complete set of related lists. However, we can add individual related lists with the <apex:relatedList> tag.

This is the Apex controller class for the page. It includes two methods: one to return a list of the ten most recently modified contacts and one to return a single contact record based on the id query parameter of the page URL:

```
public class contactController {

    // Return a list of the ten most recently modified contacts
    public List<Contact> getContacts() {
```

```
       return [SELECT Id, Name, Account.Name, Phone, Email
              FROM Contact
              ORDER BY LastModifiedDate DESC LIMIT 10];
   }

   // Get the 'id' query parameter from the URL of the page.
   // If it's not specified, return an empty contact.
   // Otherwise, issue a SOQL query to return the contact from the
   // database.
   public Contact getContact() {
      Id id = System.currentPageReference().getParameters().get('id');

      return id == null ? new Contact() : [SELECT Id, Name
                                           FROM Contact
                                           WHERE Id = :id];

   }

}
```

See Also

- *Using Query String Parameters in a Visualforce Page* on page 261
- *Building a Table of Data in a Visualforce Page* on page 263
- *Building a Form in a Visualforce Page* on page 265
- *Creating a Wizard with Visualforce Pages* on page 269

Creating a Wizard with Visualforce Pages

Problem

You want to create a three-step opportunity wizard that allows users to create an opportunity at the same time as a related contact, account, and contact role:

- The first step captures information related to the account and contact
- The second step captures information related to the opportunity
- The final step shows which records will be created and allows the user to save or cancel

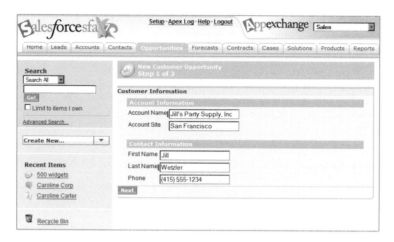

Figure 41: Step 1 of the New Customer Opportunity Wizard

Solution

Define three Visualforce pages for each of the three steps in the wizard, plus a single custom controller that sets up navigation between each of the pages and tracks the data that the user enters.

Discussion

The code for the three pages and the controller is included here; however, it's important to understand the best procedure for creating them because each of the three pages references the controller, and the controller references each of the three pages. In what appears to be a Catch-22 you can't create the controller without the pages, but the pages have to exist in order for you to refer to them in the controller.

Luckily, we can work our way out of this conundrum because we can define a page that's completely empty. Consequently, the best procedure for creating the wizard pages and controller is as follows:

1. Navigate to the URL for the first page, `https://<host>.salesforce.com/apex/opptyStep1`, and click **Create Page newOpptyStep1**.
2. Repeat the step above for the other pages in the wizard: `opptyStep2` and `opptyStep3`.

Now all three of the pages exist. Even though they are empty, they need to exist before we can create a controller that refers to them.

3. Create the `newOpportunityController` controller by adding it as an attribute to the `<apex:page>` tag on one of your pages (for example, `<apex:page controller="newOpportunityController">`, and clicking **Create Apex**

controller newOpportunityController. Paste in all of the controller code and click **Save**.

4. Now return to the editors for the three pages that you created and copy in their code. The wizard should now work as expected.

 Note: Although you can create an empty page, the reverse is not true—in order for a page to refer to a controller, the controller has to exist with all of its methods and properties.

The following Apex class is the controller for all three pages in the New Customer Opportunity wizard:

```
/*
 * This class is the controller behind the New Customer Opportunity
 * wizard. The new wizard is comprised of three pages, each of
 * which utilizes the same instance of this controller.
 */
public class newOpportunityController {

    // These four class variables maintain the state of the wizard.
    // When users enter data into the wizard, their input is stored
    // in these variables.
    Account account;
    Contact contact;
    Opportunity opportunity;
    OpportunityContactRole role;


    // The next four methods return one of each of the four class
    // variables. If this is the first time the method is called,
    // it creates an empty record for the variable.
    public Account getAccount() {
        if(account == null) account = new Account();
        return account;
    }

    public Contact getContact() {
        if(contact == null) contact = new Contact();
        return contact;
    }

    public Opportunity getOpportunity() {
        if(opportunity == null) opportunity = new Opportunity();
        return opportunity;
    }

    public OpportunityContactRole getRole() {
        if(role == null) role = new OpportunityContactRole();
        return role;
    }


    // The next three methods are used to control navigation through
```

```
    // the wizard. Each returns a reference to one of the three pages
    // in the wizard.
    public PageReference step1() {
        return Page.newOpptyStep1;
    }

    public PageReference step2() {
        return Page.newOpptyStep2;
    }

    public PageReference step3() {
        return Page.newOpptyStep3;
    }

    // This method performs the final save for all four objects, and
    // then navigates the user to the detail page for the new
    // opportunity.
    public PageReference save() {

        // Create the account. Before inserting, copy the contact's
        // phone number into the account phone number field.
        account.phone = contact.phone;
        insert account;

        // Create the contact. Before inserting, use the id field
        // that's created once the account is inserted to create
        // the relationship between the contact and the account.
        contact.accountId = account.id;
        insert contact;

        // Create the opportunity. Before inserting, create
        // another relationship with the account.
        opportunity.accountId = account.id;
        insert opportunity;

        // Create the junction contact role between the opportunity
        // and the contact.
        role.opportunityId = opportunity.id;
        role.contactId = contact.id;
        insert role;

        // Finally, send the user to the detail page for
        // the new opportunity.
        // Note that using '/' in the new PageReference object keeps
        // the user in the current instance of salesforce, rather than
        // redirecting him or her elsewhere.
        PageReference opptyPage = new PageReference('/' +
                                                    opportunity.id);
        opptyPage.setRedirect(true);

        return opptyPage;
    }

}
```

The following code defines the first page of the wizard (`newOpptyStep1`) in which data about the associated contact and account is gathered from the user (see *Figure 41: Step 1 of the New Customer Opportunity Wizard* on page 270):

```
<apex:page controller="newOpportunityController"
        tabStyle="Opportunity">
  <apex:sectionHeader title="New Customer Opportunity"
                     subtitle="Step 1 of 3"/>
  <apex:form>
    <apex:pageBlock title="Customer Information">

      <!-- This facet tag defines the "Next" button that appears
           in the footer of the pageBlock. It calls the step2()
           controller method, which returns a pageReference to
           the next step of the wizard. -->
      <apex:facet name="footer">
        <apex:commandButton action="{!step2}" value="Next"
                           styleClass="btn"/>
      </apex:facet>
      <apex:pageBlockSection title="Account Information">

        <!-- <apex:panelGrid> tags organize data in the same way as
             a table. It places all child elements in successive cells,

             in left-to-right, top-to-bottom order -->
        <!-- <apex:outputLabel> and <apex:inputField> tags can be bound

             together with the for and id attribute values,
             respectively. -->
        <apex:panelGrid columns="2">
          <apex:outputLabel value="Account Name" for="accountName"/>
          <apex:inputField id="accountName" value="{!account.name}"/>

          <apex:outputLabel value="Account Site" for="accountSite"/>
          <apex:inputField id="accountSite" value="{!account.site}"/>

        </apex:panelGrid>
      </apex:pageBlockSection>
      <apex:pageBlockSection title="Contact Information">
        <apex:panelGrid columns="2">
         <apex:outputLabel value="First Name" for="contactFirstName"/>

          <apex:inputField id="contactFirstName"
                          value="{!contact.firstName}"/>
          <apex:outputLabel value="Last Name" for="contactLastName"/>

          <apex:inputField id="contactLastName"
                          value="{!contact.lastName}"/>
          <apex:outputLabel value="Phone" for="contactPhone"/>
          <apex:inputField id="contactPhone"
                          value="{!contact.phone}"/>
        </apex:panelGrid>
      </apex:pageBlockSection>
    </apex:pageBlock>
```

```
    </apex:form>
</apex:page>
```

Notice the following about the code for the first page of the wizard:

- Some tags, including `<apex:pageBlock>`, can take an optional `<apex:facet>` child element that controls the header or footer of the component. The order in which the facet tag appears in the `<apex:pageBlock>` body doesn't matter because it includes a `name` attribute that identifies where the element should be placed. In this page of the wizard, the facet tag defines the **Next** button that appears in the footer of the `pageBlock` area.

- An `<apex:commandButton>` tag represents a user control that executes a method in the controller class. In this page of the wizard, the **Next** button calls the `step2()` method in the controller, which returns a `PageReference` to the next step of the wizard. Command buttons must appear in a form, because the form component itself is responsible for refreshing the page display based on the new `pageReference`.

```
<apex:facet name="footer">
  <apex:commandButton action="{!step2}" value="Next"
                      styleClass="btn"/>
</apex:facet>
```

- An `<apex:panelGrid>` tag organizes a set of data for display. Similar to a table, it simply takes a number of columns and then places all child elements in successive cells, in left-to-right, top-to-bottom order. For example, in the Account Information area of this page, the "Account Name" label is in the first cell, the input field for `Account Name` is in the second cell, the "Account Site" label is in the third cell, and the input field for `Account Site` is in the fourth.

```
<apex:panelGrid columns="2">
  <apex:outputLabel value="Account Name" for="accountName"/>
  <apex:inputField id="accountName" value="{!account.name}"/>
  <apex:outputLabel value="Account Site" for="accountSite"/>
  <apex:inputField id="accountSite" value="{!account.site}"/>
</apex:panelGrid>
```

- The `value` attribute on the first `<apex:inputField>` tag in the preceding code excerpt assigns the user's input to the name field of the account record that's returned by the `getAccount()` method in the controller.

- The `<apex:outputLabel>` and `<apex:inputField>` tags can be bound together when the `id` attribute value on `<apex:inputField>` tag matches the `for` attribute value on `<apex:outputLabel>`. Binding these tags together improves the user experience because it provides special behavior in the Web page. For example, clicking on the label puts the cursor in the associated input field. Likewise, if the input is a checkbox, it toggles the checkmark.

The following code defines the second page of the wizard (`newOpptyStep2`) in which data about the opportunity is gathered from the user:

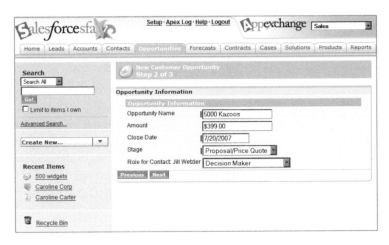

Figure 42: Step 2 of the New Customer Opportunity Wizard

```
<apex:page controller="newOpportunityController"
           tabStyle="Opportunity">
  <apex:sectionHeader title="New Customer Opportunity"
                      subtitle="Step 2 of 3"/>
  <apex:form>
    <apex:pageBlock title="Opportunity Information">
      <apex:facet name="footer">
        <apex:outputPanel>
          <apex:commandButton action="{!step1}" value="Previous"
                              styleClass="btn"/>
          <apex:commandButton action="{!step3}" value="Next"
                              styleClass="btn"/>
        </apex:outputPanel>
      </apex:facet>
      <apex:pageBlockSection title="Opportunity Information">
        <apex:panelGrid columns="2">
          <apex:outputLabel value="Opportunity Name"
                            for="opportunityName"/>
          <apex:inputField id="opportunityName"
                           value="{!opportunity.name}"/>
          <apex:outputLabel value="Amount" for="opportunityAmount"/>
          <apex:inputField id="opportunityAmount"
                           value="{!opportunity.amount}"/>
          <apex:outputLabel value="Close Date"
                            for="opportunityCloseDate"/>
          <apex:inputField id="opportunityCloseDate"
                           value="{!opportunity.closeDate}"/>
        <apex:outputLabel value="Stage" for="opportunityStageName"/>

          <apex:inputField id="opportunityStageName"
                           value="{!opportunity.stageName}"/>
          <apex:outputLabel value="Role for Contact:
                                   {!contact.firstName}
                                   {!contact.lastName}"
                            for="contactRole"/>
```

```
            <apex:inputField id="contactRole" value="{!role.role}"/>
         </apex:panelGrid>
      </apex:pageBlockSection>
   </apex:pageBlock>
</apex:form>
</apex:page>
```

Notice the following about the code for the second page of the wizard:

• Because this page displays two buttons in the `pageBlock` footer, they're wrapped in an `<apex:outputPanel>` tag. This tag needs to be used because `<apex:facet>` expects only one child component.

> **Note:** You also must use an `<apex:panelGroup>` tag within an `<apex:panelGrid>` if you want to place more than one component into a single cell of the grid.

• Although the code for placing the `Close Date`, `Stage`, and `Role for Contact` fields on the form is the same as the other fields, the `<apex:inputField>` tag examines the data type of each field to determine how to display it. For example, clicking in the `Close Date` text box brings up a calendar from which users can select the date.

The third block of code defines the third page of the wizard (`newOpptyStep3`) in which all inputted data is displayed, and the user can decide to save or cancel the operation:

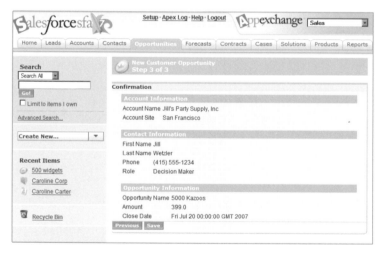

Figure 43: Step 3 of the New Customer Opportunity Wizard

```
<apex:page controller="newOpportunityController"
           tabStyle="Opportunity">
  <apex:sectionHeader title="New Customer Opportunity"
                      subtitle="Step 3 of 3"/>
  <apex:form>
```

```
    <apex:pageBlock title="Confirmation">
      <apex:facet name="footer">
        <apex:outputPanel>
          <apex:commandButton action="{!step2}" value="Previous"
                              styleClass="btn"/>
          <apex:commandButton action="{!save}" value="Save"
                              styleClass="btn"/>
        </apex:outputPanel>
      </apex:facet>
      <apex:pageBlockSection title="Account Information">
        <apex:panelGrid columns="2">
          <apex:outputText value="Account Name"/>
          <apex:outputText value="{!account.name}"/>
          <apex:outputText value="Account Site"/>
          <apex:outputText value="{!account.site}"/>
        </apex:panelGrid>
      </apex:pageBlockSection>
      <apex:pageBlockSection title="Contact Information">
        <apex:panelGrid columns="2">
          <apex:outputText value="First Name"/>
          <apex:outputText value="{!contact.firstName}"/>
          <apex:outputText value="Last Name"/>
          <apex:outputText value="{!contact.lastName}"/>
          <apex:outputText value="Phone"/>
          <apex:outputText value="{!contact.phone}"/>
          <apex:outputText value="Role"/>
          <apex:outputText value="{!role.role}"/>
        </apex:panelGrid>
      </apex:pageBlockSection>
      <apex:pageBlockSection title="Opportunity Information">
        <apex:panelGrid columns="2">
          <apex:outputText value="Opportunity Name"/>
          <apex:outputText value="{!opportunity.name}"/>
          <apex:outputText value="Amount"/>
          <apex:outputText value="{!opportunity.amount}"/>
          <apex:outputText value="Close Date"/>
          <apex:outputText value="{!opportunity.closeDate}"/>
        </apex:panelGrid>
      </apex:pageBlockSection>
    </apex:pageBlock>
  </apex:form>
</apex:page>
```

Notice that the third page of the wizard simply writes text to the page with
`<apex:outputText>` tags.

See Also

*   *Using Query String Parameters in a Visualforce Page* on page 261
*   *Building a Table of Data in a Visualforce Page* on page 263
*   *Building a Form in a Visualforce Page* on page 265
*   *Using AJAX in a Visualforce Page* on page 267

Glossary

AJAX Toolkit

A JavaScript wrapper around the API that allows you to execute any API call and access any object you have permission to view from within JavaScript code.

AJAX Tools

An AppExchange app that includes a collection of Web-based utilities for developers working with the AJAX Toolkit, s-controls, or Apex.

Anonymous block, Apex

An Apex script that does not get stored in the metadata, but that can be compiled and executed through the use of the `ExecuteAnonymousResult()` API call, or the equivalent in the AJAX toolkit.

Force.com

A platform for building on-demand applications from salesforce.com. Force.com combines a powerful user interface, operating system, and database to allow you to customize and deploy on-demand applications for your entire enterprise.

Force.com Builder

The point-and-click tools that allow you to build app components declaratively, through the Salesforce administrative setup menu.

Apex

A procedural scripting language that allows developers to execute flow and transaction control statements on the Force.com platform server in conjunction with calls to the API. Using syntax that looks like Java and acts like database stored procedures, Apex allows developers to add business logic to most system events, including button clicks, related record updates, and custom s-control display.

Apex Ant Tool

A toolkit that allows you to write an Apache Ant build script for migrating Apex between two Salesforce organizations.

Apex log

A debug console that displays the debug log for any Apex in your organization that executes as the result of a trigger while the console is open. The debug console also includes a text area at the bottom of the window that allows you to enter and execute anonymous statements.

Apex WSDL

A WSDL for developers who want to run or compile Apex scripts in another environment or build a new Apex IDE.

Apex Developer Network (ADN)

The website at www.salesforce.com/developer/ that provides a full range of resources for platform developers, including sample code, toolkits, an online developer community, and the test environments necessary for building apps.

App

A collection of components such as tabs, reports, dashboards, and custom s-controls that address a specific business need. Short for "application."

AppExchange app menu

A menu that enables users to switch between customizable applications (or "apps") with a single click. The AppExchange app menu displays at the top of every page in the Salesforce user interface.

AppExchange directory

A Web directory where hundreds of AppExchange apps are available to Salesforce customers to review, demo, comment upon, and/or install. Developers can submit their apps for listing on the AppExchange if they wish to share them with the community.

AppExchange package

A collection of application components that are posted as a unit on the AppExchange. See also *Managed package* on page 284.

Application programming interface (API)

The interface that a computer system, library, or application provides in order to allow other computer programs to request services from it and exchange data between them.

Approval process

An automated process your organization can use to approve records on the platform. An approval process specifies the steps necessary for a record to be approved and who must approve it at each step. Approval processes also specify the actions to take when a record is approved, rejected, or first submitted for approval.

Auto number

A custom field type that automatically adds a unique sequential number to each record.

Cascading style sheets

Files that contain all of the information relevant to color, font, borders, and images that are displayed in a user interface.

Child relationship

A relationship that has been defined on an SObject that references a selected SObject as the "one" side of a one-to-many relationship. For example, if you expand the Child Relationships node under the Account object, contacts, opportunities, and tasks are included in this list.

Class, Apex

A template or blueprint from which Apex objects are created. Classes consist of other classes, user-defined methods, variables, exception types, and static initialization code. In most cases, Apex classes are modeled on their counterparts in Java and can be quickly understood by those who are familiar with them.

Client app

An app that runs outside the Salesforce user interface and uses only the API—typically running on a desktop or mobile device. These apps treat the platform as a data source, using the development model of whatever tool and platform for which they are designed. See also *Composite app* on page 281 and *Native app* on page 285.

Component library, Visualforce page

The list of tags and attributes that can be used in a Visualforce page.

Composite app

An app that combines native platform functionality with one or more external Web services, such as Yahoo! Maps. Composite apps allow for more flexibility and integration with other services, but may require running and managing external code. See also *Client app* on page 281 and *Native app* on page 285.

Controller, Visualforce page

An Apex class that provides a Visualforce page with the data and business logic it needs to run. Visualforce pages can use the standard controllers that come by default with every standard or custom object, or they can define custom controllers.

Controlling field

Any standard or custom picklist or checkbox field whose values control the available values in one or more corresponding dependent fields. See also *Dependent field* on page 282.

Custom field

Fields that can be added to customize an object for your organization's needs.

Custom link

A custom URL defined by an administrator to integrate your data with external websites and back-office systems.

Custom object

An entity that you build to store information that's unique to your app. See also *Object* on page 285 and *Standard object* on page 289.

Dashboard

A graphical representation of data from up to 20 summary or matrix reports arranged in a two- or three-column layout. Every user can select a favorite dashboard to display on his or her Home tab.

Database

An organized collection of information. The underlying architecture of the platform includes a database where your data is stored.

Database table

A list of information, presented with rows and columns, about the person, thing, or concept you want to track. See also *Object* on page 285.

Date literal

A keyword in a SOQL or SOSL query that represents a relative range of time such as *last month* or *next year*.

Dependent field

Any custom picklist or multi-select picklist field that displays available values based on the value selected in its corresponding controlling field. See also *Controlling field* on page 281.

Developer Edition

A free Salesforce edition that allows you to get hands-on experience with all aspects of the platform in an environment designed for development. Developer Edition accounts are available on the Apex Developer Network website at www.salesforce.com/developer/.

DML statement

An Apex statement that inserts, updates, or deletes records from the Force.com platform database.

Email template

A built-in feature that enables you to create form emails that communicate a standard message, such as a welcome letter to new employees or an acknowledgement that a customer service request has been received.

Enterprise Edition

A Salesforce edition designed to meet the needs of larger, more complex businesses. In addition to all of the functionality available in Professional Edition, Enterprise Edition organizations get advanced customization and administration tools that can support large-scale deployments.

Enterprise WSDL

A strongly-typed WSDL for customers who want to build an integration with their Salesforce organization only, or for partners who are using tools like Tibco or webMethods to build integrations that require strong typecasting. The downside of the Enterprise WSDL is that it only works with the schema of a single Salesforce organization because it's bound to all of the unique objects and fields that exist in that organization's data model. See also *Partner WSDL* on page 286.

Entity relationship diagram (ERD)

A data modeling tool that helps you organize your data into entities (or objects, as they are called in the Force.com platform) and define the relationships between them.

Field

A part of an object that holds a specific piece of information, such as a text or currency value.

Field dependency

A filter that allows you to change the contents of a picklist based on the value of another field.

Field-level security

Settings that determine whether fields are hidden, visible, read only, or editable for users based on their profiles.

Flex Toolkit for Force.com

An Adobe® Flex™ library that allows you to access Salesforce data from within a Flex 2 application.

Force.com Explorer

A lightweight, Windows-based tool that lets you browse the schema within your organization, edit data values, and build and test SOQL and SOSL queries.

Force.com Toolkit for Eclipse

An Eclipse plug-in that allows developers to manage, author, and debug s-controls and Apex classes and triggers in the Eclipse development environment.

Force.com Web Services API

An application programming interface that defines a Web service that provides direct access to all data stored in Salesforce from virtually any programming language and platform. See also *Application programming interface (API)* on page 280.

Foreign key

A field whose value is the same as the primary key of another table. You can think of a foreign key as a copy of a primary key from another table. A relationship is made between two tables by matching the values of the foreign key in one table with the values of the primary key in another. See also *Primary key* on page 286.

Formula field

A type of custom field that automatically calculates its value based on the values of merge fields, expressions, or other values.

Governor limits

Apex execution limits that prevent developers who write inefficient code from monopolizing the resources of other Salesforce users.

Group

A set of users that can contain individual users, other groups, or the users in a role. Groups can be used to help define sharing access to data.

Group Edition

A Salesforce edition designed for small businesses and workgroups with a limited number of users. Group Edition offers access to accounts, contacts, opportunities, leads, cases, dashboards, and reports.

Home tab

The starting page from which users can view a dashboard, choose sidebar shortcuts and options, view current tasks and activities, or select each of the major tabs.

HTML s-control

An s-control that contains the actual HTML that should be rendered on a page. When saved this way, the HTML is ultimately hosted on a platform server, but is executed in an end-user's browser. See also *S-Control* on page 288.

HTTP debugger

An application that can be used to identify and inspect SOAP requests that are sent from the AJAX Toolkit. They behave as proxy servers running on your local machine and allow you to inspect and author individual requests.

ID

A unique 15- or 18-character alphanumeric string that identifies a single record in Salesforce.

Inline s-control

An s-control that displays within a record detail page or dashboard, rather than on its own page.

Instance, Salesforce

A server that hosts an organization's Salesforce data (for example, na1.salesforce.com, na2.salesforce.com, and so on). The platform runs on multiple instances, but data for any single organization is always consolidated on a single instance. As long as you use the URL that is returned from the API's `login()` call, you should never need to know the actual instance that hosts an organization's data.

Integration user

A Salesforce user defined solely for client apps or integrations.

Junction object

A custom object that enables a many-to-many relationship between two other objects.

Layout

See *Page layout* on page 286.

License Management Application (LMA)

A free AppExchange app that allows you to track sales leads and accounts for every user who downloads a managed package of yours from the AppExchange. See also *License Management Organization (LMO)* on page 284.

License Management Organization (LMO)

The organization in which you've installed the License Management Application (LMA). See also *Managed package* on page 284.

Lookup relationship

A relationship between two objects that allows you to associate records with each other. On one side of the relationship, a lookup field allows users to click a lookup icon and select another record from a list. On the associated record, you can then display a related list to show all of the records that have been linked to it.

Managed package

A collection of application components that are posted as a unit on the AppExchange, and that are associated with a namespace and a License Management Organization. A package must be managed for it to be published publicly on the AppExchange, and for it to support upgrades. See also *AppExchange package* on page 280.

Manual sharing

Record-level access rule that allows record owners to give read and edit permissions to other users who might not have access to the record any other way. See also *Record-level security* on page 287.

Merge field

A field you can place in an email template, custom link, s-control, or formula to incorporate values from a record. For example, `Dear {!Contact.FirstName}`, uses a contact merge field to obtain the value of a contact record's `First Name` field to address an email recipient by his or her first name.

Metadata-driven development

An app development model that allows apps to be defined as declarative "blueprints," with no code required. Apps built on the platform—their data models, objects, forms, workflows, and more—are defined by metadata.

Metadata WSDL

A WSDL for users who want to use the API metadata calls.

Multitenancy

An application model where all users and apps share a single, common infrastructure and code base.

MVC (Model-View-Controller)

A design paradigm that deconstructs applications into components that represent data (the model), ways of displaying that data in a user interface (the view), and ways of manipulating that data with business logic (the controller).

Namespace

A one- to 15-character alphanumeric identifier that distinguishes your package and its contents from packages of other developers on the AppExchange, similar to a domain name. Salesforce automatically prepends your namespace prefix, followed by two underscores ("__"), to all unique component names in your Salesforce organization.

Native app

A type of app that is built exclusively via metadata configuration and without coding. Native apps run entirely on the platform without need for external services or infrastructure. See also *Client app* on page 281 and *Composite app* on page 281

Object

In Force.com terms, an object is similar to a database table—a list of information, presented with rows and columns, about the person, thing, or concept you want to track. Each object automatically has built-in features like a user interface, a security and sharing model, workflow processes, and much more.

Object-level security

Settings that allow an administrator to hide whole tabs and objects from a user, so that they don't even know that type of data exists. On the platform, you set object-level access rules with object permissions on user profiles. See also *Field-level security* on page 282 and *Record-level security* on page 287.

onClick JavaScript

JavaScript code that executes when a button or link is clicked.

One-to-many relationship

A relationship in which a single object is related to many other objects. For example, each Candidate may have one or more related Job Applications.

Organization-wide defaults

Settings that allow you to specify the baseline level of data access that a user has in your organization. For example, you can make it so that any user can see any record of a particular object that's enabled in their user profile, but that they'll need extra permissions to actually edit one.

Outbound message

A SOAP message from Salesforce to an external Web service. You can send outbound messages from a workflow rule or Apex.

Package

See *AppExchange package* on page 280

Page layout

The organization of fields, custom links, related lists, and other components on a record detail or edit page. Use page layouts primarily for organizing pages for your users, rather than for security.

Partner WSDL

A loosely-typed WSDL for customers, partners, and ISVs who want to build an integration or an AppExchange app that can work across multiple Salesforce organizations. With this WSDL, the developer is responsible for marshaling data in the correct object representation, which typically involves editing the XML. However, you're also freed from being dependent on any particular data model or Salesforce organization. See also *Enterprise WSDL* on page 282.

Personal Edition

A free Salesforce edition designed for an individual sales representative or other single user. Personal Edition provides access to key contact management features such as accounts, contacts, and synchronization with Outlook. It also provides sales representatives with critical sales tools such as opportunities.

Picklist

A selection list of options available for specific fields, for example, the `Country` field for a Candidate object. Users can choose a single value from a list of options rather than make an entry directly in the field.

Picklist values

The selections displayed in drop-down lists for particular fields. Some values come predefined, and other values can be changed or defined by an administrator.

Platform Edition

A Salesforce edition based on either Enterprise Edition or Unlimited Edition that does not include any of the standard Salesforce CRM apps, such as Sales or Service & Support.

Primary key

A relational database concept. Each table in a relational database has a field in which the data value uniquely identifies the record. This field is called the primary key. The relationship is made between two tables by matching the values of the foreign key in one table with the values of the primary key in another. See also *Foreign key* on page 283.

Production organization

A Salesforce organization that has live users accessing data.

Professional Edition

A Salesforce edition designed for businesses who need full-featured CRM functionality. Professional Edition includes straightforward and easy-to-use customization, integration, and administration tools to facilitate any small- to mid-sized deployment.

Profile

A component of the platform that defines a user's permission to perform different functions. The platform includes a set of standard profiles with every organization, and administrators can also define custom profiles to satisfy business needs.

Query locator

A parameter returned from the `query()` or `queryMore()` API call that specifies the index of the last result record that was returned.

Query string parameter

A name-value pair that's included in a URL, typically after a '?' character. For example:

`http://na1.salesforce.com/001/e?`**`name=value`**

Queue

A collection of records that don't have an owner. Users who have access to a queue can examine every record that's in it and claim ownership of the records they want.

Quirks mode

A browser implementation that supports legacy Web pages that rely on Web browsers' incomplete or incorrect implementations of HTML and CSS to display properly. Browsers revert to quirks mode if you forget to set the `DOCTYPE` properly at the top of a Web page, or if you don't use well-formed HTML. See also *Standards mode* on page 289.

Record

A single instance of an object. For example, Software Engineer is a single Position object record.

Record-level security

A method of controlling data in which we can allow particular users to view and edit an object, but then restrict the individual object records that they're allowed to see. See also *Organization-wide defaults* on page 286, *Role hierarchy* on page 287, *Sharing rules* on page 288, and *Manual sharing* on page 284.

Related list

A section of a record or other detail page that lists items related to that record.

Relationship

A connection between two objects in which matching values in a specified field in both objects are used to link related data. For example, if one object stores data about companies and another object stores data about people, a relationship allows you to find out which people work at the company.

Role hierarchy

A record-level security setting that defines different levels of users such that users at higher levels can view and edit information owned by or shared with users beneath them in the role hierarchy, regardless of the organization-wide sharing model settings. See also *Record-level security* on page 287.

Running user

The user whose security settings determine what data is displayed in a dashboard. Because only one running user is specified per dashboard, everyone who can access the dashboard sees the same data, regardless of their personal security settings.

S-Control

A component that allows you to embed custom HTML and JavaScript into Salesforce detail pages, custom links, Web tabs, or custom buttons. For example, you can define a custom s-control containing JavaScript and address merge fields to display a map of a contact's address. See also *HTML s-control* on page 283, *URL s-control* on page 290, and *Snippet* on page 288.

Sandbox organization

A nearly identical copy of a Salesforce production organization. You can create multiple sandboxes in separate environments for a variety of purposes, such as testing and training, without compromising the data and applications in your production environment.

Salesforce SOA (Service-Oriented Architecture)

A powerful capability of Apex that allows you to make calls to external Web services from within Apex code.

Search layout

The organization of fields included in search results, lookup dialogs, and the recent items lists on tab home pages.

Session ID

An authentication token that's returned when a user successfully logs in to Salesforce. The Session ID prevents a user from having to log in again every time he or she wants to perform another action in Salesforce.

Session timeout

The amount of time a single session ID remains valid before expiring. While a session is always valid for a user while he or she is working in the Web interface, sessions instantiated via the API expire after the duration of the session timeout, regardless of how many transactions are still taking place.

Sharing model

A security model that defines the default organization-wide access levels that users have to each other's information.

Sharing rules

Rules that allow an administrator to specify that all information created by users within a given group or role is automatically shared to the members of another group or role. Sharing rules also allow administrators to make automatic exceptions to org-wide defaults for particular groups of users.

Snippet

A type of s-control that's designed to be included in other s-controls. Similar to a helper method that is used by other methods in a piece of code, a snippet allows you to maintain a single copy of HTML or JavaScript that you can reuse in multiple s-controls. See also *S-Control* on page 288.

SOAP (Simple Object Access Protocol)

A protocol that defines a uniform way of passing XML-encoded data.

SOQL (Salesforce Object Query Language)

A query language that allows you to construct simple but powerful query strings and to specify the criteria that should be used to select the data from the database.

SoqlXplorer

A lightweight, OS-X-based tool that lets you graphically browse the schema within your organization, and build and test SOQL queries.

SOSL (Salesforce Object Search Language)

A query language that allows you to perform text-based searches using the API.

Standard object

A built-in object included with the Force.com platform. You can also build custom objects to store information that's unique to your app. See also *Custom object* on page 281 and *Object* on page 285.

Standards mode

A browser implementation that respects all parts of the HTML and CSS language specifications. To use standards mode, you must set the DOCTYPE properly at the top of a Web page. See also *Quirks mode* on page 287.

Successforce Ideas

A forum where salesforce.com customers can suggest new product concepts, promote favorite enhancements, interact with product managers and other customers, and preview what salesforce.com is planning to deliver in future releases. Visit Successforce Ideas at ideas.salesforce.com.

Tab

An interface item that allows you to navigate around an app. A tab serves as the starting point for viewing, editing, and entering information for a particular object. When you click a tab at the top of the page, the corresponding tab home page for that object appears.

Test method

An Apex class method that verifies whether a particular piece of code is working properly. Test methods take no arguments, commit no data to the database, and can be executed by the runTests() system method either via the command line or in an Apex IDE, such as Eclipse with the Force.com Toolkit for Eclipse.

Time-dependent workflow action

A workflow action that occurs before or after a certain amount of time has elapsed. Time-dependent workflow actions can fire tasks, field updates, outbound messages, and email alerts while the condition of a workflow rule remains true.

Time trigger

A setting that defines when time-dependent workflow actions should fire.

Trigger

A piece of Apex that executes before or after records of a particular type are inserted, updated, or deleted from the database. Every trigger runs with a set of context variables that provide access to the records that caused the trigger to fire, and all triggers run in bulk mode—that is, they process several records at once, rather than just one record at a time.

Trigger context variables

Default variables that provide access to information about the trigger and the records that caused it to fire.

Unit test

See *Test method* on page 289

Unlimited Edition

A Salesforce edition designed to extend customer success through the entire enterprise. Unlimited Edition includes all Enterprise Edition functionality, plus Apex, Force.com Sandbox, Force.com Mobile, premium support, and additional storage.

Unmanaged package

An AppExchange package that cannot be upgraded or controlled by its developer. Unmanaged packages allow you to take any app components and move them "as is" to the AppExchange without going through a lengthy publishing process. They're ideal for moving components between organizations for a one-time transfer.

URL (Uniform Resource Locator)

The global address of a website, document, or other resource on the Internet. For example, http://www.salesforce.com.

URL s-control

An S-Control that contains an external URL that hosts the HTML that should be rendered on a page. When saved this way, the HTML is hosted and run by an external website. URL s-controls are also called Web controls. See also *S-Control* on page 288.

Validation rule

A rule that prevents a record from being saved if it does not meet the standards that are specified.

Visualforce

A simple, tag-based markup language that allows developers to easily define custom pages and components for apps built on the platform. Each tag corresponds to a coarse or fine-grained component, such as a section of a page, a related list, or a field. The components can either be controlled by the same logic that's used in standard Salesforce pages, or developers can associate their own logic with a controller written in Apex.

Web control

See *URL s-control* on page 290.

Web service

A mechanism by which two applications can easily exchange data over the Internet, even if they run on different platforms, are written in different languages, or are geographically remote from each other.

WebService method

An Apex class method or variable that can be used by external systems, such as an s-control or mash-up with a third-party application. Web service methods must be defined in a global class.

Web tab

A custom tab that allows your users to use external websites from within the application.

Wizard

Any tool with a user interface that leads a user through a complex task in multiple steps.

Workflow action

An email alert, field update, outbound message, or task that fires when the conditions of a workflow rule are met.

Workflow email alert

A workflow action that sends an email when a workflow rule is triggered. Unlike workflow tasks, which can only be assigned to application users, workflow alerts can be sent to any user or contact, as long as they have a valid email address.

Workflow field update

A workflow action that changes the value of a particular field on a record when a workflow rule is triggered.

Workflow outbound message

A workflow action that sends data to an external Web service, such as another on-demand application. Outbound messages are used primarily with composite apps.

Workflow queue

A list of workflow actions that are scheduled to fire based on workflow rules that have one or more time-dependent workflow actions.

Workflow rule

A "container" for a set of workflow instructions that includes the criteria for when the workflow should be activated, as well as the particular tasks, alerts, and field updates that should take place when the criteria for that rule are met.

Workflow task

A workflow action that assigns a task to an application user when a workflow rule is triggered.

Wrapper class

A class that abstracts common API functions such as logging in, managing sessions, and querying and batching records. A wrapper class makes your integration more straightforward to develop and maintain, keeps the logic necessary to make API calls in one place, and affords easy reuse across all components that require API access.

WSDL (Web Services Description Language)

An XML file that describes the format of messages you send and receive from a Web service. It's the language that your development environment's SOAP client uses to communicate with external services like Salesforce.

About the Authors

Caroline Roth is a Senior Technical Writer at salesforce.com, focused on platform features such as Apex and Visualforce. Her previous books with salesforce.com include *Creating On-Demand Applications: An Introduction to the Force.com Platform*. Caroline is a member of the 1% Time Council for the salesforce.com Foundation, and has a degree in Symbolic Systems with a focus on Human-Computer Interaction from Stanford University.

Michael Polcari is a Member of the Technical Staff at salesforce.com, focused on platform features for the Financial Services vertical. Mike was one of the first Apex developers, and is an emeritus member of the salesforce.com Foundation steering committee. Mike has a degree in Computer Science from Cornell University.

Ron Hess is a Developer Evangelist for salesforce.com, focusing on developer and partner success and education. Prior to joining salesforce.com, Ron worked as a business analyst and CRM program manager for a salesforce.com customer. He is the author of the open source Salesforce Excel Connector and has been developing with Web services since 2001. Ron has a degree in Computer Information Systems from California State University, Chico.

Andrew Waite is a Senior Product Manager for Apex and Visualforce at salesforce.com. During his more than four years with salesforce.com, Andrew has also worked as a Member of the Technical Staff and as a Principal Consultant for the Professional Services organization. Andrew has a degree in Management from Purdue University.

Greg Campbell is a Senior Product Manager for AppExchange Packaging at salesforce.com. Prior to joining salesforce.com, Greg was a certified salesforce.com partner and developed applications on the Force.com platform for over four years. Greg has a degree in Mechanical Engineering from the University of California at Santa Barbara.

Blake Markham is a Senior Consultant and Technology Program Manager at salesforce.com. He has been designing and developing applications for the Force.com platform since 2004. Blake has a degree in Computer Science with a focus in Computer Graphics from the Georgia Institute of Technology.

Index

Index

D

E

F